RICKI HERBERT
A NEW FIRE

RICKI HERBERT
A NEW FIRE

RICKI HERBERT WITH RUSSELL GRAY

HarperSports
An imprint of HarperCollins*Publishers*

National Library of New Zealand Cataloguing-in-Publication Data
Herbert, Ricki.
Ricki Herbert : a new fire / Ricki Herbert with Russell Gray.
ISBN 978-1-86950-746-6
1. Herbert, Ricki. 2. Soccer players—New Zealand—Biography.
I. Gray, Russell, 1943- II. Title.
796.334092—dc 22

First published 2009
Harper*Sports*
An imprint of HarperCollins*Publishers (New Zealand) Limited*
P.O. Box 1, Shortland Street, Auckland 1140

Copyright © Ricki Herbert and Russell Gray 2009

Ricki Herbert and Russell Gray assert the moral right
to be identified as the authors of this work.

All rights reserved. No part of this publication may be reproduced,
stored in a retrieval system or transmitted in any form or by any
means, electronic, mechanical, photocopying, recording or otherwise,
without the prior written permission of the publishers.

ISBN: 978 1 86950 746 6

Cover design by Gra Murdoch at Aqualuna Design
Front cover photograph by Darren Staples/Reuters/Picture Media
Back cover photograph by *The Dominion Post*
Typesetting by Springfield West

Printed by Griffin Press, Australia

70gsm Classic used by HarperCollins*Publishers* is a natural, recyclable product
made from wood grown in sustainable forests. The manufacturing processes
conform to the environmental regulations in the country of origin, Finland.

Dedication

This book is dedicated to Raewyn, Sacha, Kale, Clive, Shirley, Deborah, and my in-laws, Valerie and the late Leo Smith. Without their tremendous support, none of what I have achieved would have been possible.

— RH

CONTENTS

Forewords

Acknowledgements

1	Football, football, football	17
2	Starting out	29
3	Youngsters make their mark	40
4	One for all and all for one	50
5	On the world stage	73
6	Living the dream	85
7	From wolves to horses	99
8	Learning the coaching ropes	110
9	Back with the All Whites	126
10	The devil's advocate	139
11	Salvage job at the Knights	145
12	The Phoenix rises	154
13	Recruitment starts	175
14	The Kiwi contingent	200
15	Kick-off	228
16	Looking ahead	258
17	The man who gave the Phoenix wings	264
18	A true football man	270

FOREWORD
by Tommy Docherty

The first time I set eyes on Ricki Herbert was while New Zealand were playing Australia in 1983, and there was something about Ricki that made him stand out. I wasn't surprised to find out that he had made such an important contribution to New Zealand's World Cup campaign, and once I heard he was considering a professional career in Australia I wanted him at Sydney Olympic, the club I was managing at the time. It was a decision I didn't regret for one moment.

From the day he joined us in Sydney, he was a model professional, both on and off the field. The thing I admired most about him was his dedication. To Ricki, football wasn't just a job, it was a vocation, and after a lifetime in the game I can tell you there aren't many like that about. He was never motivated by money — he played football because he loved the game.

When I left Australia and became manager of Wolverhampton Wanderers, I had no hesitation in asking him to join me there. During the time he played for me, we talked a lot and a mutual respect developed between us, which is why we still keep in touch over two decades later.

The more we talked, the more obvious it became that he wanted to be involved in football for the rest of his life, so I wasn't surprised to hear he had gone on to coach New Zealand as well as managing his country's only professional club.

There is nothing 'safe' about being a manager or coach, as I can testify. Over the years I've had 17 houses — it would have been easier to buy a caravan at the outset — but I'm sure Ricki will handle anything that is thrown at him.

It has been a privilege to work with, and become a friend of, Ricki Herbert and I wish him well for the future. With the love he has for football, he deserves to succeed.

TOMMY DOCHERTY
Manchester
February 2009

FOREWORD
by John Adshead

Ricki Herbert was one of the few New Zealand players from my era who went on to play professional football in England, which was testament to him being a very good athlete and a player who learnt quickly.

We had some very talented young players during the campaign that culminated in the All Whites reaching the 1982 World Cup finals.

While Wynton Rufer got most of the headlines because he scored goals, you need quality players like Ricki Herbert at the back as well, and Ricki also scored one or two important goals himself on the way to Spain!

I wasn't surprised that Ricki went on to earn a living in football, firstly as a player and later as a coach, because he was always studious and professional in everything he did.

Taking over at a new club, as Ricki did at Wellington Phoenix, is a testing time for any coach. It takes time to build a team from scratch, and what he has learnt in the first two years will stand him in good stead for the club's third season.

I wish him luck in his endeavours at the Phoenix, and hope that this book is a success.

JOHN ADSHEAD
Mt Maunganui
March 2009

ACKNOWLEDGEMENTS

Having watched Ricki Herbert's football career develop from his national-league debut for Mount Wellington as a teenager through to him becoming head coach of Wellington Phoenix, I was delighted to be asked to co-author this book with him.

As a journalist, I was privileged to be part of the amazing World Cup campaign that Ricki and his All Whites team-mates embarked on in 1981, and as proud as anyone in the country when they finally achieved their goal of taking their place alongside the world's best in Spain.

Little did I know then, or as I watched Ricki retire from playing and take up coaching, that he would be instrumental in giving me a new lease of life five years after I had left daily journalism and taken to the golf course.

When Ricki asked me to become kit man — or gear steward, as the Aussies call it — for the Phoenix, I didn't have to think twice. Since then, I have had a ball, looking after a great bunch of players at New Zealand's only professional football club. It also gave me an opportunity to try and put into words what Ricki has meant to football and what the game has meant to Ricki. Putting the manuscript together has brought back fond memories for us both.

To Ricki and Raewyn, along with the Phoenix players and staff, including Wellington Phoenix photographer John Serepisos, thank you for your co-operation, and to my wife, Barbara, thanks for your support and for the loan of your office, yet again.

RUSSELL GRAY
Wainuiomata
March 2009

ACKNOWLEDGEMENTS

For three decades I have been fortunate enough to live my dream in football, and I am indebted to the many people who have helped, encouraged and inspired me along the way.

No-one has been more supportive and understanding than my family. For as long as I can recall, Mum and Dad, along with my elder sister, Deborah, have encouraged me to follow my dreams, and continue to do so to this day.

When Raewyn entered my life, she quickly became my soul mate; someone I could share the good times with, and turn to when things weren't going as well as I would have liked. Raewyn has been my rock. When things were at their darkest, as we all battled to come to terms with getting a new football club up and running, it was Raewyn who kept my sanity intact.

Raewyn's mum, Valerie, and her late father, Leo, also happily became part of our support team, even though I whisked their daughter to the other side of the world within a couple of days of our wedding.

It hasn't all been plain sailing, especially for Raewyn and our twins, Sacha and Kale, who have had to support each other during my absences. None of what I have achieved would have been possible without their understanding and patience, and I thank them from the bottom of my heart.

I would also like to thank Terry Serepisos for providing me, along with the New Zealand public, the opportunity to be involved in professional football.

This book wouldn't have been possible without the help of Russell Gray, whom I first met 28 years ago when he was working as a journalist covering the All Whites' World Cup campaign.

Russell is now gear steward for the Wellington Phoenix; and for me one of the most memorable training sessions we have had was the one at Westpac Stadium when, while the players were doing their warm-up, I asked Russell if he would be interested in writing this book with me.

We have both enjoyed the time spent reminiscing while putting the book together, and hope that you, the reader, enjoy it just as much.

RICKI HERBERT
Wellington
April 2009

FOOTBALL, FOOTBALL, FOOTBALL

In the annals of New Zealand football, 1961 could hardly be described as a vintage year, with two international matches played against an England XI resulting in a 8–0 beating at Wellington's Basin Reserve and, five days later, a 1–6 loss at the Auckland Showgrounds.

There was one bright spot for Kiwi football that year, however — though no-one could have guessed it at the time — with the birth of Ricki Lloyd Herbert in the south Auckland suburb of Papatoetoe on 10 April, eight weeks before that Basin Reserve mauling.

Every parent hopes their child will make something of him- or herself in one sphere or another, but sport-loving Clive and Shirley Herbert, who already had a two-year-old daughter they'd christened Deborah, could not, even in their wildest dreams, have envisaged the impact their new son would have in the world's biggest and most popular sport.

Over three action-packed decades, Ricki Herbert has played a leading role in New Zealand football: reaching the 1982 World Cup finals; playing professionally for famous English club Wolverhampton Wanderers; going on to coach the All Whites; and, perhaps most importantly for the game's future in the country, helping to preserve professional football in New Zealand by being instrumental in the inception of the Wellington Phoenix.

Such exciting adventures were a long way off when Ricki set off for his first day at Papatoetoe Central Primary School, where the classrooms backed onto a vast expanse of greenery known as the Recreation Ground.

That first day probably wasn't as daunting for young Ricki as it was for some of the other new boys. The route was familiar, as was the patch of grass behind the school, because he had recently joined the Papatoetoe Soccer Club, which trained there. He became even more at ease with the ground over the next few years, as the school football teams played there also.

The fact that Ricki joined the Papatoetoe club wasn't surprising. It was generally accepted that if you were born in Papatoetoe, it was only natural you should play for the club, especially as it had one of the biggest and most successful junior sections in the Auckland region.

Along with Manurewa and Papakura, Papatoetoe — which boasted around 40 teams — was one of the 'big three' junior clubs in south Auckland. Manukau City had its moments and was tough to beat, but when the honours were handed out at season end one of the 'big three' inevitably topped the standings.

Papatoetoe was Ricki's footballing home for the next 12 years, until Mount Wellington, New Zealand's top club, came calling.

On the school front there was also consistency, with the young

Herbert going on to Papatoetoe Intermediate and then Papatoetoe High School, a path he believes helped make his school days as enjoyable as anyone could hope for, thanks to having the same friends around him all the way through.

Happy as his school days were, the minute school was over for the day, Ricki was off like a shot to kick a ball around with his mates. Even at such a tender age, football was Ricki's passion, and it had been that way from the moment he'd joined the Papatoetoe club.

While the majority of his peers were dreaming of becoming All Blacks, Ricki's sights were firmly set on a professional football career. Rugby never entered the equation, apart from throwing a ball around and having a few light-hearted kicks at goal at the rugby club on the other side of the Recreation Ground.

For a start, the lads he mixed with weren't into rugby either, although there did come a time when Ricki turned to rugby to get himself out of a tight situation. It was during his high-school days, when he had joined Mount Wellington and was already playing in the club's national-league team.

'The teacher running the soccer First XI decided he wanted me in the team and said I had to play for the school rather than Mount Wellington. It was the first and only time I came across a club–school clash, and I didn't like it.

'Here I was with the opportunity to play in a senior national competition and this guy was insisting I play for his team instead because I was obliged to represent the school. I thought that was ludicrous, so set about finding a way around the problem. The answer turned out to be simple: register to play rugby for the school instead! Fortunately for me, the person running the Second or Third XV, I can't remember which, could see how ridiculous the situation was and said he would help me. I signed up for his team, which meant I was meeting my obligations of playing sport for the school. It worked out well: I would be with the rugby team on Saturday morning, kicking a few goals or playing out on the wing, and then off to the real football in the afternoon.'

Sport was important in the Herbert household, and it was soon obvious that young Ricki had inherited his mum's and dad's sporting genes.

Clive was one of the country's leading cyclists, winning New Zealand titles on road and track before going on to ride professionally in Australia, and later managing the New Zealand cycling team at the Mexico Olympics.

Shirley Herbert didn't need a bike to go fast. She was quick enough on two feet, following in her champion-runner father's footsteps and becoming Auckland's 100-yards sprint champion. Not a bad effort for someone disqualified after each of the three races she won on her first visit to the Onehunga Athletics Club as a 13-year-old at a children's day meeting. The problem that day was that young Shirley didn't know she had to stay in her designated lane on the track. She quickly learnt and never looked back.

Given his parents' background in cycling and athletics, it would perhaps have been natural for Ricki to head in a similar sporting direction, but it was never likely to happen.

'As a kid I spent hours at Papatoetoe Velodrome, and many of the country's top riders would come around home and be on the rollers in the basement. I had a little bike when I was small, but looking back I don't think there was ever any chance of me going into the sport seriously, because I honestly don't remember having the passion or desire for it.

'It was a different matter when it came to football. For as long as I can remember, all I ever really wanted was to become a footballer. In that regard I was fortunate that, besides being so involved with cycling, Dad had played football and loved it as much as I did. Throughout my days at Papatoetoe, Dad coached the majority of the teams I was in. When John Houghton asked me to go over to Mount Wellington, Dad moved as well, and coached the club's under-19 side. That's the type of support I had from my parents and, looking back, you realize just how important that was. I've always been very close to Mum and Dad, and the bond between Dad and myself became even stronger because of the time we spent together through football.

'When I was growing up there wasn't much football on television, unlike today, and one of the highlights of the week for Dad and me was Sunday lunchtime and *Match of the Day* with Brian Moore. While we watched the old black-and-white television, I would tell Dad that's what I wanted to do when I got older and where I wanted to be playing. I loved that hour every Sunday, and, even when I began playing national league for Mount Wellington, watching the programme was still a ritual. The players would have lunch, then watch *Match of the Day* before we played. Every football-loving kid in New Zealand would adopt an English team to support. Chelsea was the team I followed, and I couldn't get enough football magazines to read.

'I suppose you could say my head was in the clouds as far as football went. As a 10- and 11-year-old, I would send letters to English clubs asking for a trial. I wouldn't get a reply, but that didn't matter. It was the excitement of writing the letter, being able to dream about what might happen, rather than actually getting a reply.'

Life was pretty simple for kids like Ricki growing up in the 1960s, with television in its infancy and the idea of computers about as far-fetched as the possibility of a man walking on the moon. Home was 5 Richards Avenue, a safe Papatoetoe cul-de-sac that Shirley Herbert remembers always being full of laughing youngsters.

'There were a dozen kids in the street. They all played together, and when it came to birthdays everyone went to the others' party.

It made for a lovely atmosphere. Debbie and Ricki were naturally happy, good kids. While Ricki was into football, Debbie loved ballet and did very well at it.

'We supported them and followed them everywhere they played or danced. A lot of parents don't do that these days, for various reasons, and I think that makes a difference in the way their children grow up. Even when he was older, Ricki would look for us in the crowd at games. He might not be able to pick us out, but he always knew we were there.

'Having an interest in things as healthy as sport and dancing can only be good. I remember Ricki starting out in football as a four-year-old. His socks were up over his knees, and at times he was probably digging in the mud with his fingers when he should have been chasing the ball. That didn't matter, because he was happy doing something he loved.'

Most of the time it was up to kids to make their own fun, and all that was needed for football was a set of goalposts and a ball. Even goalposts weren't absolutely necessary; a couple of jumpers thrown on the ground provided just as good a target. What better way to spend your spare time?

For Ricki and his mates, it was football, football and more football. Day in, day out, they would kick a ball around. The big days came at weekends when they would play for Papatoetoe. Even that wasn't always enough to satisfy their appetites, however, and once the match was over they would dash off for informal games amongst themselves.

Two of Ricki's best mates in those days were Gary Neilson and Mark Ollerenshaw. They would stay at each other's houses and, according to Ricki, it was perfect. Gary's home was a farm, and during school holidays the days were passed playing football or riding trail bikes. Mark lived next to a park, where jumpers on the ground became makeshift goals and away they would go. Life isn't as simple these days, with more and more distractions for youngsters, and sport is more regimented than it was when Ricki was starting out.

'With most sports, things are now based around planned training sessions and coaching. Of course, while we were growing up we had formal training sessions, but that wasn't enough. We couldn't get enough of the game, so would then go off and play amongst ourselves. We simply played football all the time. I understand times have changed and the educational side of the game is now seen as more important — I'm not saying it wasn't important then, but there wasn't the same emphasis as today.'

While football was always to the forefront so far as Ricki and his mates were concerned, Ricki ran at the Otahuhu Athletics Club from time to time, and turned his hand to softball during summer. He played first base, which meant he was involved in all the action, suiting him down to the ground, and he was good enough to go to the national softball tournament in Dunedin with the Auckland under-16 team.

'The other game I was always keen on but never played a lot of was golf. I still love it, but only get to play very rarely simply because of a lack of time. Another of my good friends, Steve Berryman, lived in Omana Road and his house backed on to the fairway of the 12th hole at The Grange. Steve and his brother Jeffrey did some casual greenkeeping duties at the club, and whenever I stayed over at their place I would help them.

'We would be up at five in the morning, getting the dew off the greens with a hose pipe, as well as searching the bushes for golf balls. I loved those mornings. The three of us would play quite a bit socially and really enjoyed it, but in the end we always gravitated back to our first love, which was football.'

One of the biggest plusses of being involved in a team sport for young Ricki was the amount of social activity it generated. 'There always seemed to be a birthday party on the go, or you would be sleeping over at a team-mate's place. Looking back, I think every young person I knew was involved in sport, as were their families. Dad coached every team I played for until I was 14, and Mark Ollerenshaw's dad, Val, was the manager. Dad and Val became great friends, which meant the two families socialized a lot.

'We had a very good team, and it has always been a fact, in junior and senior football, that good teams attract good players. That was the case with us, and we regularly won our competitions.

'Today you hear people lamenting how hard it is to get kids involved in sport, and I wonder if perhaps the attitude of parents has something to do with that. Maybe they can't be bothered making an effort to give the type of support I enjoyed right from the start from my family.

'You hear people saying they don't go to watch Team Wellington play at Newtown Park because they can't get a car park. When I went to Newmarket Park with Dad, there would be thousands at the game and you had to park a long way from the ground. That certainly didn't put people off going — if anything, it added to the atmosphere with hundreds of people walking through the streets to the ground just before kick-off, talking football, with their sons alongside kicking a ball.

'Can't get a car park? Do they think Man United fans go to Old Trafford and park right outside? They probably get a train or bus from the city centre, never mind driving right up to the ground. Sometimes I think New Zealanders are spoilt in that regard — if they can't have the chairman's car park in front of the ground, they'll stay at home.'

The Newmarket Park Ricki speaks of so fondly became his second home while growing up. Unlike today, when clubs have their 'home' grounds and their own agendas, Newmarket Park was a facility shared by the Auckland football community, and every winter weekend big games would be played there. Every weekend Ricki couldn't wait to get down to what even today he describes as a very special place.

'On Sundays, national-league games would be played at the Park, but Sunday also meant washing the car or mowing the lawns. I would be kicking a ball around and hurrying Dad along, pestering him about how long it would be before we could set off for the ground.

'Once we got there, I would join my mates behind the goal, kicking a ball around in five-a-side games and chasing the national-league game's ball when it came past the goal.

'The biggest thing for us was that all New Zealand's best players would be playing there, and you were almost close enough to touch them. I loved seeing players such as Alf Stamp, Brian Hardman and Roy Drinkwater plying their skills. There would be between 5,000 and 10,000 people on the concrete terraces, and it was fantastic seeing the top teams play each other. Trans Tours United would come up from Christchurch to play Mount Wellington, Blockhouse Bay or North Shore, and you got to see the likes of Steve Sumner, Bobby Almond, Brian Turner, Keith Nelson and Ron Armstrong in action.

'Those players were our heroes, and if anyone had tried to tell me that I'd not only end up playing with and against them, but that I'd be in the New Zealand team with them at a World Cup final a few years later, I would have laughed at them.

'At that time I would have given anything just to play on Newmarket Park, and I remember vividly the day in 1977 when that dream became a reality, and I played there for Mount Wellington. It is hard to explain the feeling you get on first walking out onto a pitch where you have watched your heroes play. It became even better when I got to play there for the New Zealand under-19 side against Australia in 1979, even though we lost 2–1, with Shane Rufer getting our only goal.'

In 1979, subsidence problems caused the closure of Newmarket Park, an event Ricki remembers well. 'It was a sad day for Auckland and for New Zealand football.'

Looking back on high school, Ricki says he was an 'OK'

student, good enough to leave with School Certificate in three subjects and pretty successful in keeping himself out of trouble. Only once did he find himself bending over in the office of the headmaster, Hugh Richards, for a caning, and he swears the incident in question wasn't of his own making.

'I was sitting in class minding my own business when one of my "mates" whacked me on the head with a book. It gave me such a start, I just turned around and thumped him. Unfortunately for me, that was the only part of the incident the teacher saw. I remember going to Dad's work and sheepishly telling him what had happened and how unlucky I had been!

'I did at times get offside with the teacher who took our accounting class. Some of us would chat amongst ourselves. I might say to the lad next to me that I fancied number seven in the last race at the trots on Friday night. What did he reckon? It was nothing serious, but the lady teacher felt I was being a bit disruptive. She told me to sit at the back of the class and read. She didn't care what I read as long as I didn't disturb the rest of the class, so I happily sat quietly at the back of the class reading the *Best Bets* or a football book. It didn't do me any harm, because accounting was one of the subjects I got School Cert in.

'I'm not trying to make out that I was an angel in high school. I would be telling lies if I said I didn't have a drink now and again. Everybody did. It was kind of cool to have a couple of beers, but we would never dream of getting our hands on three dozen and getting hammered. That just didn't happen in the circles I mixed with, and, to be honest, I don't believe it was very prevalent amongst kids overall at that time. Maybe I was also lucky with my choice of friends, because we were never involved in serious things such as motor accidents.

'I used to drive a Blue Morris J3 van — it had been one of my dad's work vehicles, and was passed on to me when he upgraded. Today it would be looked down upon as a piece of rubbish, but it got me around and only once gave me problems, and those were of my own making.

'While I knew how to ride a motorbike, I had never really had the chance, so when Debbie was going out with my mate Gerard George's brother — who happened to have a nice bike — I couldn't resist offering to swap him the van for his bike one night. He agreed, so he and Debbie went off in the van while Gerard and I went down the motorway to the Paradice ice-skating rink feeling oh-so-cool on the bike.

'We had a great time on the ice, but when we came out . . . disaster. Could we get the bike to start? No chance. We tried everything. I couldn't contact Debbie and her boyfriend, and time was ticking away. Mum and Dad were always pretty good about how late we could stay out, but there was a time limit and I was over it. Not only that, but they didn't know I was riding a bike or that I had lent out the van. I had a trifecta I didn't want!

'It led to a two-week driving ban from Dad, and during that time I had to walk to football and softball training, which took 45 minutes to an hour each way. Inconvenient that might have been, but there was no way it would keep me away, because football was everything — training just as much as the games. The one time Dad stopped me playing because I had been late for training, after going to my friend Nigel Harbrow's house on the other side of the Recreation Ground, I was devastated. It taught me a timely lesson and it didn't happen again.

'Overall, I think I was a normal kid who had good mates, went to a lot of parties and had a few beers, but I like to think I have never let my parents down by getting into trouble with the police or taking drugs. Like any kid, I had my moments, but they were few, and I believe much of that came down to my involvement in sport, and that, through football in particular, I had friends who thought the same way about things. When you enjoy each other's company and love sport the way we did, then it tends to keep you on the right path. There were fewer distractions when

I was growing up than those confronting today's kids. It was all about making your own fun rather than becoming isolated by spending too much time in front of a computer, television or PlayStation. It might sound strange to congratulate someone for simply doing the right thing, but I admire those young people today who are strong enough to ignore the wrong kind of peer pressure so many succumb to.

'A stable home environment is also vital in shaping a youngster's future, as are the values they grow up with. Mum and Dad were always fantastically supportive of Debbie and myself in whatever we did. They also set values.

'If we were going somewhere — perhaps to something connected to the transformer company Dad owned — we were expected to dress appropriately. I can honestly say we didn't go anywhere looking scruffy. It obviously made an impression on me, because I am no different now when it comes to making sure I'm correctly dressed for the occasion. I don't hesitate to ring Phoenix owner, Terry Serepisos, to check out the dress code if I'm accompanying him to a function I'm not sure about. That's just my nature and it goes back to my parents' influence.'

Given the time they have spent together through football, Ricki and his father have a very close relationship that is now almost as much like brothers as father and son.

Ricki was also very close to his sister, Debbie, during their formative years and they still are close. It helped that he got to know her husband, Paul Mertens, early in the piece thanks to Paul playing in one of the teams Clive coached at Papatoetoe.

'When Paul and Debbie began going out, he was around our house a lot. We would go out for a few bevvies, and still do when we get the chance. Today, Debbie and Paul's children (Ben, Samantha and Jacob) are as close to my two (Sacha and Kale) as Debbie and I were.'

STARTING OUT

There is no doubt that New Zealand's thrilling campaign to win a place in the 1982 World Cup finals in Spain was kick-started in 1980 at Mount Wellington's Bill McKinley Park. That night, in front of a capacity crowd of around 7,000, John Adshead's new-look All Whites gave regular World Cup finalists Mexico a 4–0 beating that left New Zealand football fans as shell-shocked as the bemused Mexicans.

The foundations for that surprise result, and the wonderful months that followed, had been laid 10 years earlier when the New Zealand Football Association launched its national league. For more than a decade the possibility of a national-club competition had been bandied about, before all the talking and planning finally came to fruition in 1970.

The top three finishers in the 1969 Northern League — Mount Wellington, Eastern Suburbs and Blockhouse Bay — were joined by Central League qualifiers Western Suburbs, Stop

Out, Gisborne City and Hungaria, as well as the newly formed Christchurch United team from the South Island.

At last, New Zealand's top footballers had the opportunity to play against each other on a regular basis in a truly national competition. Within months, it was obvious that the new competition was raising playing, coaching and refereeing standards markedly, and that in turn led to a more competitive national team.

First-year honours went to Blockhouse Bay, on goal difference from Eastern Suburbs, with Christchurch United two points back in third place, three ahead of Mount Wellington.

Eastern Suburbs won the 1971 competition ahead of Mount Wellington, while the following year Mount Wellington flexed its muscles for the first time to take the championship. Mount Wellington went on to be crowned champions five times over the next 10 years as well as finishing runner-up three times, and, along with Christchurch United, were dominating the competition.

By 1977, former player John Houghton, who had been forced into early retirement after sustaining a serious knee injury while playing for New Zealand against Australia at Newmarket Park, was coaching Mount Wellington. Right from the start, Houghton was an ambitious, aggressive coach who wanted his team to play the ball to feet at every opportunity, and he made sure that training sessions emulated what he wanted on match day.

It was into this environment that a young Ricki Herbert took his first steps towards a glittering domestic, international and professional career. 'I liked the look of Ricki from the start, and he trained with us for a couple of seasons as a 15- and 16-year-old,' Houghton remembers. 'You could see straight away that he was a top-class athlete, and never seemed out of place in the surroundings he had come into.

'Most of our training involved one-touch 7-v-7 games. It ensured players developed a good first touch, because they were always looking to see whom they should pass it on to. We would play man to man, and if your man got away and scored, then you did 10 press-ups. That made them concentrate!

'At the start I didn't want to embarrass Ricki among all those top players, and I made sure I partnered him with players who would mentor him and help develop his skills. While there was nothing formal, you could say that Ricki did a two-year apprenticeship and then I introduced him gradually into the team.

'Young lads like Ricki and Billy de Graaf would clean the other players' boots as part of the learning process. I saw nothing wrong with that, because it teaches discipline.'

Looking back on his time cleaning boots, Ricki, like Houghton, also sees nothing wrong with what some would consider a menial task. 'I remember them throwing the boots to me for cleaning,' he says. 'I don't know what they expected my reaction to be, but I didn't hesitate. I picked the boots up and cleaned them. If cleaning boots was good enough for young professionals in England, why should it be above someone like me trying to make his way in the game?

'I knew how hard it was going to be to break into a team with so many quality players in it, and I had no illusions as to where I stood in the pecking order. I don't know whether they expected me to do it without a murmur, but to this day I believe it was one of the best things I ever did. I think it showed them that I wasn't too big for my boots, pardon the pun, and that I knew my place. That didn't mean I wasn't after one of their places in the starting XI — I definitely was — but I believe from that moment most of them thought, *This guy's OK, not a cocky young bugger.*

'It is a bit different nowadays. A young player joining a club might have clauses in his contract requiring him to perform certain duties similar to boys going into an apprenticeship in other trades. There are two ways of looking at the way clubs treat young players. I don't think it does any harm to expect them to do some tasks. In fact, during my first year as coach at the Phoenix, the three young players on our roster did have certain responsibilities, but there was nothing demeaning, and the tasks they performed were related to training. Things such as putting up the goal nets and looking after the players' training water bottles.

'I had no problem with that, but, even so, I changed it going into our second season, because I didn't want them to feel separated from the rest of the squad. After all, they were fighting for a place in the starting team along with much more experienced players. The change didn't stop the youngsters doing things off their own bat, because that's the type of lads they are, and I think the senior pros respect them for it just as the Mount Wellington players did with me when I didn't object to cleaning their boots.'

The Mount Wellington line-up in the mid-1970s was like a who's who of New Zealand football, with virtually every player an international.

With Sandy Davie in goal behind a defence made up of players such as Glenn Dods, Tony Sibley, Stu Carruthers and Ron Armstrong, the Mount had a solid foundation upon which those further forward, such as Brian Turner, Clive Campbell, Keith Nelson, Warren Fleet and Bill McClure, could build.

For a teenager like Ricki, who was determined to forge a career as a professional footballer, joining a club that was winning everything was a fantastic opportunity. If hard work as well as talent was needed to break into the star-studded line-up, then it was right up his street. He loved training, and to be doing it amongst such a talented bunch of players made it even sweeter.

As one of the 'glamour' clubs of the national league, there was a perception around much of the country that Mount Wellington must have been paying the players very well to keep such a star-studded bunch happy.

According to Ricki, that wasn't the case. The club had a signing-on pay structure in place that put players on different levels, from youngsters like him through to experienced players and established internationals. His signing-on fee was $50. That doesn't sound much, but back then, to a young kid who was being paid for doing something he loved, it was very attractive.

'It didn't take me long to realize that money wasn't the reason players were so happy at Mount Wellington. The club really looked after them, making sure they travelled well and stayed in decent hotels when they needed to be away from home. When players are treated well, they feel comfortable in their surroundings. It helped create a terrific atmosphere in the dressing room, and at times you would feel you were amongst family rather than playing for a national-league football club.

'Those early days in a well-run club made an impression on me. When I began coaching at Central United later in my career, I deliberately set out to replicate what the Mount had been doing, by making sure a good structure was in place and that the players were looked after on and off the pitch. If you want to attract quality players without stretching the club financially, that is what you have to do, and I like to think I was successful in that regard.'

Looking back on those early days in senior football Ricki acknowledges that, for a kid like him, being able to join a club that was winning trophies, and then break into a team full of internationals, was beyond his wildest dreams. In his debut season, 1977, he managed to chalk up 12 games before becoming a regular in the starting line-up the following year. As soon as he made the first team, Ricki promptly found his feet and felt comfortable in the surroundings, despite being very much the baby of the side.

'I quickly found out that the Mount Wellington players looked after each other. I'm not suggesting anyone held my hand because I was the new kid on the scene. There was simply an acceptance that if John Houghton had picked you to start then you were good enough. The other players knew you had proved yourself in training, so there were no thoughts like: *We'll be playing with 10 men today, because we've got to look after the new kid.* Rather, the attitude was that here was a good young player who had earned his place in the side, so that would be good for the team.

'Having such quality players around me undoubtedly made it so much easier to settle in and try to show people that I was well worth my place. What more could a young centre-back ask for than to slot into a defence that had Sandy Davie in goal, Tony Sibley at right back, Ron Armstrong at left back, and Stu Carruthers alongside him in the centre? Sandy had a wealth of experience and was a great organizer. If you got caught out and the ball went past, you sort of knew that Sandy would be there sweeping up behind to get you out of trouble. Communication among our defenders was outstanding, and we tried not to over-complicate things. You knew your role, your strengths and weaknesses, and just got on with it.

'Off the field the players were a great social bunch, but once they got on the training pitch they were footballers first and foremost. Everything was well-organized, and that transmitted itself onto the pitch come match day.

'There was a real belief within the team that comes from having quality players who were used to winning things. Even when we weren't playing as well as we could, everyone sensed that sooner or later in the game we would score.'

Former New Zealand international and Mount Wellington stalwart Dave Taylor had been at the club five years when Ricki made his debut, and he remembers the youngster's arrival well.

'Ricki had the right attitude from day one, and had a mature approach despite his age. Yes, he was treated like an apprentice, which is virtually unheard of these days, but he took it all in his stride. He would listen to the coach and senior players, and I sometimes think that is a lost art now with young players believing they are better than they are, with nothing to learn. Those who listen are the ones who make something of themselves, and Ricki's record in football bears that out.'

Ricki and Dave got on well from the start, and their friendship developed further when Ricki's future wife, Raewyn, worked alongside Dave's wife, Penny, at a local hairdresser's, culminating in Dave being best man at Ricki's wedding.

Dave confirms Ricki's theory that the togetherness of the team, both on and off the pitch, had a massive bearing on the club's success during the 1970s and early 1980s.

'The bond between the players was so strong that if you were unable to train through injury you felt you were letting the boys down. We socialized a lot off the field as well, which further built up that feeling. There seemed to be a social function to go to virtually every weekend, and it was just like training: everyone turned up.

'Sure the lads enjoyed a few beers — and perhaps Ricki's 21st birthday party epitomized how we managed to combine socializing and playing. The party was on Saturday night, and we were still going strong at two o'clock on Sunday morning. Later that day we were playing Gisborne, which was always a grudge match, and we beat them four or five nil!

'When the ties between players are so strong, they last. I play socially these days, and players from that era such as Keith Nelson, Ronnie Armstrong and John Leijh are also in the team. So was Warren Fleet, until he needed a knee reconstruction. We have a few young 'uns in the team to do the running, and it's a good excuse for a few beers after the game on a Sunday afternoon.'

In Ricki's second season with Mount Wellington, when he had become a first-team regular, they were pipped for the national-league title by Christchurch United on goal difference after both teams finished on 32 points from their 22 games.

The following season, in what was now a 12-team competition, positions were reversed, with Mount Wellington distancing the other 11 teams and finishing 14 points in front of their second-placed great southern rivals. That season, Mount Wellington won all 11 of their home matches and nine of their away games, losing only twice. One of those losing games was to Nelson, with none other than Ricki Herbert in their team.

At the end of the previous season, Ricki had thought long and hard before telling John Houghton that he was moving to Nelson United. His reason for leaving? To sample professional football through a three-month stint at top-flight English club Middlesbrough, to be organized by Nelson United coach Doug Moore, who was coaching the New Zealand under-19 team alongside Barrie Truman.

Ricki had played under Moore for the under-19s against Australia at Newmarket Park, and the coach had made it plain that he would like Ricki in the Nelson team alongside some other promising young players. To entice Ricki south, Moore also dangled the carrot of time with Middlesbrough, where he had a good contact.

While Ricki's heart was with Mount Wellington and the players he had become close to, the dream of professional football was still strong enough to persuade him to take a chance and move away from home for the first time in his life. It was a brave decision when you consider that, as well as leaving his family, he was leaving the best team in the country.

When Ricki had joined Mount Wellington, the club had

received a bonus through Clive Herbert also changing allegiance from Papatoetoe. Herbert Senior carried on coaching with the Mount, before becoming chairman of the club and doing what John Houghton describes as 'a marvellous job'.

Now Clive and Ricki were in the family car heading south to Nelson, where Clive Herbert deposited his son at the home of Natalie and Winston Williamson, who ran Nelson Travel and were big football fans.

'Leaving Mount Wellington was a very difficult decision, but I couldn't pass up the chance to follow my dream. Leaving the family was also tough, but the Williamsons helped me settle. As it turned out, Nelson had a decent young side that, if it had stayed together, could have turned into a very useful team. Players such as Ken Cresswell, Keith Mackay, Peter Simonsen, Roger Fitzgerald, John Slotemaker, and John Enoka had got them into the Chatham Cup final the previous season, where they lost 1–0 to Manurewa.

'I really enjoyed my season there, especially when we beat Mount Wellington 3–0 at Rutherford Park! That was in the era when local linesmen were used and would be in the bar after the game having a beer. I'm not suggesting anyone cheated, but there was always a bit of banter from the big city clubs that things seemed to go the home team's way in places like Nelson, Gisborne and Napier. I know that for sure, because I said the same things when I travelled with Mount Wellington!'

The closer Ricki came to leaving for England and Middlesbrough, the more excited he was at the thought of working alongside professional footballers on a day-to-day basis, even though he knew it was only going to be for three months.

'When Doug was organizing the trip, there was never any suggestion that the visit might result in me getting a contract to play for Middlesbrough. At no time did that come into the conversation. Sure, in the back of my mind there was the thought that hey, if I impress the manager, John Neal, and the coaching staff at Middlesbrough enough they might take me on. I wouldn't have been human had I not had a few thoughts in that direction, but overall I was realistic and took the venture for what it was: a chance to gain some professional experience.

'Sometimes when you look forward to something as much as I did that trip, the real thing can become an anticlimax — but not this time, in fact far from it. It was everything I expected it to be. I played a few games for the reserves and the younger teams, but it was just great to soak up the atmosphere that surrounds a top English football club. It's hard to explain to people outside England just what football means over there. People live and breathe football, and every kid who has kicked a ball in earnest dreams of being involved. It's a fact of life that most of those kids never get even close to playing professionally, so to be able to go to the other side of the world and be accepted into a club was unbelievable for me.

'Craig Johnston, who was probably Australia's best-known footballer at the time, was at the club and, with us coming from the same part of the world, it was perhaps natural that we should end up talking quite a bit. Craig was really supportive.

'I loved training every day and, even though I was coming out of part-time football where most clubs just trained Tuesday and Thursday nights, it wasn't a shock to me. At Mount Wellington we often trained Saturday mornings as well as two nights during the week. We would play on the Sunday, and on Monday I would be out running on my own. I had no real idea why I was doing it apart from the benefit to me psychologically that I was training. I would also do work on my own on Wednesday.

'As I've got more involved with sports science — especially in the Wellington Phoenix's second season, when we were joined by top English fitness trainer Eddie Baranowski — I have come to realize that "more" isn't always better, and that pushing yourself too hard can be bad physiologically. At that time, however, I just wanted to be constantly training, running and playing. The fact

I had been training with older players also stood me in good stead when I found myself at Middlesbrough among players my own age.

'What did strike me was the quantity of the young players, not to mention their quality. Back home we might have one or two with pretty special skills, but over there everyone could perform, otherwise they wouldn't be at a professional club. Obviously some were better than others, but overall the level was high and even the lowest denominator was good.

'I stayed in digs with a local newspaper reporter who had some kind of connection with the club. When I got time off I played a bit of golf or went to the movies, but I didn't really want to be away from the club. I had only a short time there, and wanted to be in what was a strange, exciting place every moment possible.

'For a young New Zealander, going into such an environment can be a real culture shock. Nothing at home can really prepare you for the emotion that surrounds football in England and Europe, where talented players are identified at a very young age and nurtured by clubs from then on. That's why the Phoenix is so important to New Zealand football. It gives young Kiwis something to aim for, somewhere to experience the life of a professional and to provide a stepping stone to the rest of the footballing world. Even going to watch first-team games at Middlesbrough, and the way we were treated at the ground on match day, made me feel like a little professional. It might have been only three months, but what a magic three months for a football-mad kid.'

YOUNGSTERS MAKE THEIR MARK

Regulars to Mount Wellington's Bill McKinley Park had never witnessed anything like the scenes that confronted them in 1980, on a cool, clear August night.

Crowds of between 2,000 and 3,000 had become the norm over the past decade, as Mount Wellington established itself as one of the country's top clubs; but that night, almost 7,000 people packed the homely little stadium to capacity to watch New Zealand host highly-ranked perennial World Cup qualifiers Mexico.

Such a turnout was probably due to the fact that New Zealand football fans rarely had the chance to see world-class players in the flesh. Indeed, the last time New Zealand had even played a home international was 14 months earlier, when they beat Australia for the first time in 25 years, 1–0, at Auckland's Newmarket Park.

Those who began streaming through the turnstiles almost two hours before kick-off surely could have had no inkling of the major upset they were about to witness, but there was a feeling of anticipation amongst them that was hard to explain. It would have been more understandable had they been resigned to a heavy loss. After all, since that night 14 months earlier the national team had undergone a world tour that, despite some promising performances, was being remembered for six successive losses in Britain, culminating in a humiliating 8–1 hammering at the hands of Scottish club Dundee.

Worse still was a disastrous internal series during May, in which the national team drew 1–1 with a Southern Region side in Christchurch and lost 1–2 to a makeshift Central Region selection in Wellington.

One cause for optimism was the new blood that manager John Adshead and his recently acquired assistant Kevin Fallon had introduced into their squad. The squad still contained established players, such as Dave Bright, Ron Armstrong, Duncan Ormond, Steve Sumner and Brian Turner, but Fallon's influence was noticeable with the inclusion of John Hill, Keith Mackay and Grant Turner from his high-flying Gisborne City club. Another making his international debut that night was Mount Wellington's 18-year-old central defender, Ricki Herbert.

Given the results in Britain and the internal series, there would have been a few footballers around the country thinking they might be in with a chance of selection, but Ricki hadn't really given such a possibility much thought. 'To be honest, I hadn't taken much notice of what was happening with the New Zealand team while it was overseas. I definitely didn't think that if they kept losing I might have a chance, because I didn't even know I was in the running. There had been no suggestion from anyone that I was even being considered for the national team.

'Looking back, I guess because I was part of a Mount Wellington team that was going so well, I was probably in with a chance, but my only concern at that time was playing well for my club. When I was picked for the squad it really did come out of the blue so far as I was concerned. Being chosen was a great thrill, and I was determined to enjoy every moment of the experience even though I had no high expectations of being in the team.

'I'm sure that when the squad was originally picked, the best I could have hoped for was a place on the bench, but as it happened Glen Adam fractured his cheekbone in a national-league game the day before the squad assembled, and that opened the door for me. Glen became one of my best mates and we often roomed together during the World Cup campaign, but it was his misfortune that gave me the chance to show that I was up to the challenge of international football.'

Going into such an environment for the first time can be a daunting experience, even for an established player, never mind a teenager, but Ricki took it in his stride. It undoubtedly helped that he had been playing regularly for Mount Wellington alongside players such as Brian Turner and Ron Armstrong, and that could have been one of the reasons Adshead put Ricki and Brian Turner together as roommates, something Ricki remembers fondly.

'Brian used to eat chocolate and drink Coca-Cola like you would never believe. I can remember the night before the Mexico game, the table in our unit being full of chocolate and big bottles of coke. I thought that if it was OK for Brian Turner to drink and eat this stuff, then it must be all right! At that time sports science was virtually unheard of in football, certainly in New Zealand, and I thought Brian must know what he was doing. Perhaps it helped him sleep or whatever, so I tucked in and helped him eat and drink it all.

'I think it's a credit to Brian and myself that we have evolved over the years and adapted to what is required to be a successful coach today. Some people can't accept change and adopt the attitude that if it was good enough for them, then it's good enough for players today. I'm not one of them.'

While not overawed, Ricki was aware of his place in the scheme of things and he was determined to make an impression while making sure he didn't rock the boat.

'You just got on with the job and did what you were told to do. That was the way it was. Nothing was ever challenged by young guys like me. I'm not saying senior players challenged the management either, but for a raw teenager going into a national squad it definitely wasn't an option. We only had time for a couple of training sessions before the Mexico game, and so far as the new young guys were concerned it was a case of: "Jump? How high? Run? How far?" Whatever it was, you just did it.'

Ricki knew little about John Adshead and Kevin Fallon. He had never worked under Adshead, but had played against Fallon and was aware of his reputation for working his players hard.

'That didn't worry me, because I loved training and at times trained for the sake of training. As the All Whites' campaign progressed, we would be sent a training programme to follow for the next three weeks, probably written by Kevin Fallon. It would be so many 5-kilometre runs a week, so many of this and so many of that. I would do everything required in the programme and then add more.

'I was so dedicated to what I was doing, and so desperate to succeed in football, that I felt I had to do more than was asked of me. Now when I have the Phoenix fitness trainer Ed Baranowski telling me to pull a player from a regular training session because he's been pushing himself too hard, I think back to those days and shudder.

'At the time, however, what I was doing worked for me. Those around me when I went into camp with the All Whites, both management and players, knew I was fit and quick and prepared to back myself against other players in those areas. I guess at times such an attitude was part of the reason I got in the team ahead of others.'

Over the years, some players who worked under Fallon during the World Cup campaign have criticized his methods, but Ricki isn't one of them. 'Kevin had some fantastic strengths. As a young player you knew 100 per cent where you stood with him from the start. I think it was accepted among the players that those who worked hard physiologically were looked upon more favourably by Kevin. At the end of the day where you stood in that area was a reflection on where you stood so far as getting your foot in the door or not was concerned.

'If you were a good athlete, could run, and were quick, you had an advantage. You only had to look at the new All Whites who had come out of Gisborne: they were all good athletes. When we were all tested, they were always near the top. I took that on board and kept working as hard as I could.'

It didn't take long for even one as young as Ricki to spot the differences between Adshead and Fallon, who at times throughout the World Cup campaign were referred to as 'the odd couple' by sections of the New Zealand media. It is easy to see where that tag came from. Even those in the media who had previously had little to do with New Zealand football before the campaign took off quickly realized a different approach was needed for each of the coaches. While Adshead was almost always available and open to reporters — to a degree that media from outside New Zealand found amazing — Fallon often presented a brooding presence that could be intimidating to those who didn't know him. Even media personnel who had a good relationship with Fallon would often weigh up his mood before making an approach.

'The Mexico game was the first time I had worked with John, and it didn't take long to realize what a good man-manager he was. He would sit down with you, and when the conversation was over you would be feeling pretty good about yourself and how things were going in camp — even if you had gone in feeling unhappy about things!

'Everyone in the squad knew from day one that they could knock on John's door at any time and he would be receptive and helpful. You wouldn't think about doing that with Kevin, because his forte was on the training field, not chatting to players about how they were feeling. I don't know John's reasons for bringing him in as a coach, but it was only natural that Kevin, being a top-class defender himself, should work almost exclusively with defenders, and that formula was tremendously successful.

'I could count on one hand the number of training sessions during that whole World Cup campaign where I worked with John. Many a time we defenders would look up the other end of the pitch and see Steve Wooddin and his fellow attackers doing a nice light bit of shooting practice, while we were almost on our knees after countless one-on-ones, knowing that more were coming. The sweat would be pouring out of us while the strikers would have their shirts off and the sunscreen on.

'Kevin worked day in, day out, with the back four; he worked with individual players, spent hours on one-on-one defending, and looked after all the fitness work. Throughout the campaign, no-one was more supportive of, and passionate towards, the players than Kevin. He wanted them to succeed, and that approach played a large part in what was achieved. People can be critical of Kevin in hindsight, but no-one can deny how passionate he was. Of course there were lots of times where you would go: "Bloody hell, again? The hill? Another 10?" But you would just shut up and get on with what he was asking of you. Fortunately, I had the ability to do the hard yards because of the work I had put in ever since I began kicking a ball. Some within the squad struggled physically, while others were capable of doing it but didn't. That's life.

'I didn't know if Kevin had any input into team selection, because that is something the players weren't really aware of — certainly not young raw ones like myself — but John always announced the team. People have since told me that Kevin did have some say in selection, and if that is the case I am pleased, because I quickly became aware when taking up coaching how important input from those working with you can be. A coach needs to be challenged. You don't want those around you saying yes all the time, because no coach, not even someone as successful as Sir Alex Ferguson, gets it right all the time.

'That's where Brian Turner has been so useful to me with the All Whites. He challenges me if he thinks it's necessary, and that's fine so long as it's constructive. Brian will question why I am playing certain players if he doesn't think I have made the right choice. He did that when I brought Shane Smeltz into the New Zealand team. I listened to what Brian was saying but stuck to my guns, because I always knew Shane would establish himself in international football. I got that one right, but that isn't always the case.'

Footballers today, even in New Zealand, are disappointed if the hotels they stay in aren't five-star, but when the All Whites went into camp to prepare for the game against Mexico, five-star was far from the case. 'Home' then was the Alexandra Park Motel. Those who stayed there early in the campaign remember it fondly, but it was far from the upmarket establishments now commonplace for most sportsmen. Indeed, seven of the squad squeezed into a house on the grounds while the rest shared rooms in the motel complex.

It was in one of those rooms that Ricki slept restlessly the night before making his international debut. 'It wasn't that I was intimidated about playing at that level against a team that regularly made the World Cup finals and was high up on the world rankings. Rather, it was more the anticipation and the fact I was venturing into the unknown. To be honest, there was also a little fear. What if I make a mistake that costs the team? I was just an 18-year-old kid who didn't want to let anyone down.'

The history books show that Ricki didn't let anyone down that night, and neither did his team-mates, some of whom would have felt the same apprehension he did while willing sleep to come.

From the first whistle the All Whites threw themselves into the game, and within three minutes Ricki's, and his fellow newcomers', nerves had been settled, thanks to Brian Turner thumping home a penalty to give them the lead. Steve Wooddin made it 2–0 after 25 minutes, and, when Turner added a third before half-time, the capacity crowd were both yelling their lungs out and shaking their heads in disbelief.

The second half was just as exciting, and, when Grant Turner marked his debut with the fourth goal, the icing was on the cake.

Those privileged enough to be invited into the All Whites' cramped McKinley Park dressing room at the final whistle will never forget what they saw and heard. Steam from the showers made it difficult to see more than a few yards, but the shouting and laughing was there for all to hear. One or two players sat exhausted on the red benches that ran around the room, while others chatted excitedly amongst themselves.

John Adshead was his usual bubbly self as he talked animatedly with those of the media who'd made it inside. Kevin Fallon, resplendent in his new grey suit, leaned against the wall looking as though he couldn't believe what he had just witnessed, and he wasn't alone. Most of the 7,000 who had paid to get in felt the same way.

How did such a massive upset happen? All these years later, Ricki shakes his head as he thinks back to that night. 'What happened that night was beyond my wildest dreams, and I'm sure it was the same for the other players. John and Kevin were probably just as ecstatic as we were, because they were making their debut as a coaching partnership. How did it come about after such a poor run of results? If you knew the recipe that made it happen, it would make great reading.

'It was similar to when I went to the Knights years later as coach and managed to turn things around. People asked me how I managed to transform the team. I couldn't explain why it had happened, because there is no recipe. There are some processes you can follow that make people get into a different space, and I just think we were all in the right space at the right time.

'I also think there were similarities between what John and Kevin were doing and what I did many years later when I took over the All Whites coaching position. For my first game as New Zealand coach in 2005 against Australia at Fulham's Craven Cottage, I made nine changes to the side that played in the All Whites' previous game. Many were forced on me by injuries and the unavailability of senior players, and I thought: *What the hell, let the young players show what they can do.* When I look back at some of those who played that night — the likes of Tony Lochhead, Shane Smeltz, David Mulligan, Adrian Webster, and Brett Fisher — their attitude appeared to be that I had shown faith in them, so they went out to show me in return that they were worth it.

'They did prove it as well, because we only lost 0–1 to an 86th-minute goal. Would it have been different had players such as Ryan Nelsen, Simon Elliott, Ivan Vicelich and Chris Killen been on the field? Who knows? What I do know is that no-one could have given me more that night than those who did play. I think there was the same response from the guys given their chance that night against Mexico.

'In both cases, all of a sudden the landscape changed with a younger group of players coming through. By younger, I don't mean just age-wise. It is also an experience thing. The All Whites team I began with was full of new faces, so much so that two players had more caps between them than the rest of the side put together. But right from the start I felt I was on the right track, and that's probably how John felt when the new combination of players he put together for the Mexico game produced such a result.

'You also have to be brave enough to stay with what you believe in, and that's what John and Kevin did, even though it wasn't all plain sailing. The following month we went to Canada for two games, losing 0–3 in Vancouver and 0–4 at Edmonton. We didn't play well. Putting my coach's hat on, perhaps I can now understand what happened. You get a result like we did over Mexico, and then you can have a dip. The important thing is to get things back on track as quickly as possible.'

ONE FOR ALL AND ALL FOR ONE

New Zealand's sporting landscape was undergoing an early climate change in 1981 as the ramifications of the controversial South African rugby tour hit home with the public. For years, rugby had had things all its own way on the sporting front. Win or lose — and the latter was almost a collector's item — the All Blacks were the country's favourite sons. Come the arrival in New Zealand of the Springboks from apartheid-torn South Africa and things began to change.

The most rabid All Black supporters on the whole couldn't have cared less about what was happening on the African continent, so long as New Zealand could continue its fierce rugby rivalry with the Springboks. Now, however, those rugby fans found themselves up against opponents just as determined and competitive as the All Blacks and Springboks were on the field.

Led by an organization calling itself Halt All Racist Tours, those who despised apartheid set about disrupting the Springboks' visit with a passion that spilled into confrontation throughout New Zealand. The country was divided over the tour, even within families, and the New Zealand Rugby Union found itself vilified by protesters and newspaper leader-writers alike.

As opposition to the tour mounted and clashes between police and protesters escalated, the country became desperate for something to fill the void left by rugby being toppled from its pedestal as New Zealand's most popular sport. It just so happened that New Zealand was about to embark on a campaign that would hopefully end with the All Whites qualifying for the 1982 World Cup soccer finals in Spain.

To describe such an outcome as improbable was an understatement, given the All Whites' record on the world stage. Sure, there had been a 1–0 win over Australia in June 1979, and a totally unexpected 4–0 success over regular World Cup qualifiers Mexico 14 months later. Between those successes, however, had been several disappointing results.

Apart from New Zealand Football Association chairman Charlie Dempsey, who was spearheading the campaign, and the coach he had appointed, John Adshead, few gave the All Whites a chance of reaching their goal. The All Whites were undaunted by the scepticism. While anti-apartheid protesters were dropping flour bombs from a light aircraft on the All Blacks and Springboks during the final rugby test, the All Whites were preparing to drop a few bombs themselves on the world football stage.

Twenty countries were to take part in the Asia/Oceania qualifying zone, and 18 of those were to be disappointed with only two spots at the finals in Spain up for grabs. New Zealand started out in the Oceania group, along with Australia, Fiji, Taiwan and Indonesia. Despite the 1979 loss to the All Whites, Australia was seen as the warm favourite to advance to the next stage, where the Oceania winner would be up against the top qualifiers from the three Asian groups.

As New Zealand had recently been beaten by Fiji, many pundits were picking the Indonesians — who had a reputation for being hard to beat on their own patch — as the team most likely to challenge the Aussies, who had spent up large in preparing the Socceroos.

On Anzac Day, 25 April 1981, the All Whites began what was to become the longest, most travelled campaign by any team in World Cup history against Australia. They had come together only eight days earlier. Not early enough time in many people's eyes, but training camps cost something the NZFA was desperately short of — money.

It was a lack of finance that had, in the past, forced New Zealand to play World Cup qualifying matches as a tournament rather than home and away, as was the norm elsewhere in the world. Dempsey had been determined not to go down that road this time, and, despite knowing it would mean finding hard-to-come-by financial support, he was successful.

Looking back, Ricki feels that that decision was as important as any made during the whole campaign. 'It meant New Zealanders had something to be involved in over a long period of time, as opposed to a two-week-long tournament that probably wouldn't get the media coverage it deserved. That meant the public became part of the campaign as the games progressed.

'The fact that the format meant we had to cover a lot of miles didn't really bother us, because we are an OK nation when it comes to travelling. As the campaign gathered momentum, I believe it gave us an advantage. There was nothing better than coming together for away games in places like Kuwait or Saudi Arabia, something that was just fantastic as far as we were concerned. We looked forward to going to those places. We had a good travelling squad and no-one was fazed by the distances. I don't think it was the same for the opposition. Coming to New Zealand took them out of their comfort zone, whereas it's in our nature to deal with things like long distances and living out of suitcases in hotels. You couldn't wait to get back into camp to meet up with the other lads again and get on another plane. It was an adventure and everyone loved it.'

It was a good job that the All Whites enjoyed the travel, because at one point they had to play four games in 13 days. 'You wouldn't do that now, but back then there wasn't a lot of sports-science information to draw on. We were measured as athletes, but nothing like today's players are. Four games in such a short time didn't bother us, but it helped that we were on a good run of results. Had the campaign not started as well as it did, it could have been very different. Would the squad have been as united had a few points been dropped early on and the campaign begun to dwindle? I don't think so. Being successful makes the difficult things — such as plane delays, poor food, and hotels perhaps not up to expectation — much easier to cope with and, because you cope with them together, it builds character within the team.'

When the All Whites and Socceroos faced off at Auckland's Mount Smart stadium on a warm, sunny April afternoon, the great rivals produced a pulsating encounter that set the stage for what was to come in the months ahead.

Three times New Zealand fell behind in the first half, only for goals by Grant Turner and Steve Wooddin to keep them in the hunt at half-time. All Australia's goals came about due to the inability of the All Whites' defence to deal with high balls hoisted into their penalty area at set pieces. In the dressing room at half-time, the players were furious with themselves, and the coaches were just as unhappy at what they saw as a lack of discipline.

It was a different story in the second spell as the All Whites took control, with the Aussies seemingly happy to try to hold on to their one-goal advantage. Despite New Zealand pressing relentlessly, it wasn't until the 80th minute that the equalizer arrived, courtesy of a Steve Sumner header from a John Hill cross.

'The defence was Kevin Fallon's responsibility, and he didn't take conceding three goals from set pieces lightly. The refreshing thing was — and I'm sure Kevin appreciated it — that there was a response to things that, collectively, everyone knew we could have done better. To get ourselves back into the match and take a point from it was really positive, especially after giving those goals away.

'Our goalkeeper Richard Wilson copped a bit of flak from that first half, but I didn't agree with his critics. Perhaps we just didn't give him the room he needed, because Richard was always very commanding in the penalty area, and, once we gave him the bit of space he needed to come and collect the ball, he showed how good he was. Australia had some tall players such as Eddie Krncevic, who got two of their goals, while in our back four of John Hill, Bobby Almond, Glenn Dods and myself, I was the only one over six foot.'

Fallon appreciated the spirit his players showed and how the team pulled itself together, telling the *Sunday Times*: 'We'll beat them in Sydney. They looked a very ordinary side and our lads have got more guts than they have.'

How true that comment turned out to be.

There was no such pressure on Wilson in the second game, when Fiji was beaten 4–0 in Ba. A Brian Turner hat-trick and a goal from Duncan Cole had the All Whites in control throughout, and maximum points put New Zealand top of the group, a position they held to the end of the stage. Beating Fiji was important, because it put points on the board and meant that, if the All Whites kept on getting results, the other teams would always be chasing them. That's a good position to be in.

The players were in a good frame of mind as they headed out of Fiji for Hawaii, where they would have a couple of days' break before heading to Taipei for the next game against Taiwan.

Arriving in Honolulu at 7 a.m. and finding their hotel rooms would not be ready for several hours, the tired Kiwis treated the locals to a bizarre sight as they headed for Waikiki Beach in their new grey travel suits, paddling in the surf while carrying their dress shoes.

It was one of those moments that might have upset highly paid professionals from other nations, but for the down-to-earth Kiwis it was a case of 'hey, it happened, let's make the most of it and have a laugh'.

They weren't laughing, however, when they saw the playing surface at Taipei Stadium. Adshead described it as atrocious, but again the All Whites took it all in their stride, although they couldn't find a way through a packed defence and had to settle for a scoreless draw against a team they had beaten 6–0 on both of their previous meetings four years earlier. Ricki did get the ball in the net with a powerful header, but the goal was disallowed, with the referee ruling that Steve Sumner had strayed offside.

Four days later, the New Zealanders were in action again, this time against Indonesia in Jakarta in front of a partisan 95,000 crowd at Senayan Stadium. The All Whites looked nervous in the opening minutes, and had an early reprieve when Bambang Nurdiansyah hit the crossbar with an overhead volley.

Was playing in front of such a huge, partisan crowd the reason for the cautious start? 'I've been asked so many times about playing in front of big, hostile crowds, and to be honest you don't really sense it. That was a huge stadium with a moat in front of the terraces to stop pitch invasions, but once you are out in the middle you just have a clear focus on what is happening around you on the field. The main reason I remember that game is that it was stopped for a while because the crowd started a fire high up in the stand and some were throwing rocks onto the pitch. That does tend to get your attention!'

Brian Turner settled New Zealand's nerves with a glancing header from a Steve Wooddin cross in the 18th minute, and the two points were sewn up in the 77th minute when Grant Turner beat the Indonesian offside trap by racing on to a long clearance from Richard Wilson and nodding past the onrushing Indonesian goalkeeper.

Between those two strikes, there were times when the New Zealand defence was under extreme pressure, but it held firm even when the All Whites were tiring in the humid conditions. Afterwards Fallon, never one to hand out praise lightly, described it as the most outstanding performance he had seen from a New Zealand team. 'The pressure was right on those lads; they showed tremendous courage in daunting circumstances. I was so proud of them.'

Reminiscing over those words from hard-man Fallon, Ricki can understand where he was coming from. 'Now that I'm a manager, I can fully appreciate how Kevin felt. You are in an environment that is challenging, absolutely daunting. Your team is playing really well, has got its nose in front but can't nail the game down with a second goal. The heat and humidity is sapping your energy and they are really coming at you. You still have the ball a lot but your backs are against the wall. You get that vital second goal, and when the final whistle goes you've won 2–0.

'The relief is hard to explain, and I can understand where Kevin was coming from. It was a very difficult away game. When we played them at home later we caned them 5–0, but by then they were out of contention and, as I alluded to earlier, they were one of the teams that didn't travel well.'

Ricki might not have been concerned about the 95,000 inside the stadium, but the rock-throwers made him take notice and there were a few more surprises outside the ground. Riot police were needed to get the New Zealand team bus away from the stadium as thousands of Indonesians vented their fury at their own team for losing to a country they had been expected to beat.

Even that didn't worry Ricki too much. 'I've only ever once been in a situation where I feared for my safety. It was against Chinese Taipei some years later and a shocking tackle off the ball took me out. My ankle went up like a balloon immediately, and

I was taken off to have it strapped up. You could tell the game was going to explode, and when Grant Turner was taken out he reacted. All of a sudden it was all on. I thought, *What am I going to do? I can't run!* The only thing for it was to jump on Glen Adam's back. Glen ran across the track with me hanging on like a jockey, while the other players were having a running battle on the touchline even though the game was over. We managed to get under the tunnel to the dressing room before the lights were turned off. After a while, we thought it was safe to venture out.

'Our manager, Alan Jones, and Allan Boath were the first out, and as they headed for the bus that was probably 20 metres away, people came at them from both sides. I was right behind them and the only question in my mind was: *do I follow them or go back?* With my injured ankle it was an easy decision; I went back. They made it safely onto the bus, but the rest of us waited until the situation was brought under control. Then I was carried to the bus, again on someone's back!'

From the outset, John Adshead was adamant that six points from the first four games would keep the All Whites on track to win the group, and that was what they had in the bank on leaving Jakarta for Australia. In contrast, the Australians, playing only their second game in the group, had one point. They knew nothing less than a win would keep them in contact with their trans-Tasman rivals.

The New Zealand players knew they had a perfect opportunity to derail the Aussies' World Cup hopes by taking maximum points from the Sydney Cricket Ground encounter, and they were in the mood to do just that.

'We were in a great frame of mind,' Ricki recalls. 'We knew from our first meeting with them that we were the better team, especially since we had tightened our defence and hadn't conceded a goal in the three games we'd played since. If we needed any more motivation, we got it on reading what one of Australia's leading soccer writers thought about us. Tommy Anderson said we were nothing better than the sewage flowing beneath the Sydney Harbour Bridge. By then there was a huge bond within the squad, and something like that made us even more determined to succeed. Another thing we felt was that for once against Australia we were in the driving seat. Most times in the past it had been the other way around, and New Zealand teams had had to battle to get close to them.

'The abiding memory from the game for me was Grant Turner's goal that put us 2–0 up with just minutes to go. I swear to this day that Grant's header from the edge of the box was one of the best goals I've ever seen in football. Not just from a New Zealander . . . from anyone anywhere in the world. For someone to have the technique to put the ball with pace and power into the area of the goal he did was phenomenal. If that goal had been scored today, it would be shown again and again on television. That's how good it was. It came at a perfect time as well. There were only a few minutes to go when that goal went in, and it killed the Aussies. We had got our noses in front early through a Steve Wooddin goal, and then showed we were a good team in our own right.

'Grant had his critics because of his aggressive, hard-running style, but he also had plenty of admirers. There were times when he was perhaps misunderstood, but those who played alongside him always knew he would be there when they needed him, and at the end of the day he frightened those bloody Australians to death.'

There was a moment later in the campaign, however, when Turner's hard-man image was in danger of going out the window. It came late in the game against Saudi Arabia at Mount Smart. The All Whites were trailing 1–2 when Turner clashed heads with a Saudi defender and lay, seemingly concussed, by the side of the goal as Ricki powered a header into the net for the desperately needed equalizer.

A few hours later, Turner had discharged himself from hospital and was having a beer in the bar at the Vacation Hotel, much to John Adshead's dismay. In the book he co-authored with Fallon, *New Zealand's World Cup — The Inside Story*, Adshead wrote:

> The injury could well have been a cop-out. It happens with players. The team's losing and they think 'I'll get out of this, it's not my fault' and off they go.

Reminded of the incident, Ricki smiled. 'I can see him now, lying by the goalpost. The ball hits the net and the crowd roars. At that moment I'm sure I saw Grant's eyes open for a fraction of a second. One thing I do know is that with Grant friendship is a lasting thing. We remained friends once the World Cup was over, and today, 26 years later, I usually get a message from Grant before Phoenix games wishing us luck.'

The 2–0 win made Kiwis back home realize that perhaps this New Zealand football team really did have something special and could, against all expectations, actually go all the way to the World Cup finals.

'We showed that day that we were a good side, and then went on to prove it by qualifying for Spain. New Zealand had beaten Australia in the past, but it had always seemed to be a one-off thing and the success had never been built on. By taking three out of four points from two games against Australia and going on to perform just as well in the second phase, this team showed it wasn't a flash in the pan.'

While Ricki rightly lauds Turner's fantastic strike, he also played a big part in the success over Australia. The *Sunday News* reported the next morning:

> [Australia's] much-vaunted danger men, Eddie Krncevic and Peter Sharne, didn't fire a shot against a New Zealand defence which was locked tighter than a bank vault. If New Zealand had a special hero it was 19-year-old Mount

Wellington centre-back Ricki Herbert. He was given the job of cancelling out Krncevic, the lanky striker who found the back of the net twice at Mount Smart, and did it so well that the Australian was subbed off without ever getting a clear shot at goal.

After Sydney, it was a case of New Zealand making sure there were no slip-ups in the three remaining home games against Indonesia, Chinese Taipei and Fiji. Not only did the All Whites take maximum points from the three matches, they did it without conceding a goal, taking their record to an amazing seven World Cup matches without conceding.

After beating Indonesia 5–0 and Chinese Taipei 2–0, they finished with a flourish by hammering Fiji 13–0 at Mount Smart, with skipper Steve Sumner scoring six times from midfield. The winning margin was a record in World Cup matches and equalled the highest winning score in international football outside the World Cup. The previous World Cup record had been held by West Germany, who beat Cyprus 12–0 in 1969; while in international matches Spain had beaten Bulgaria 13–0 in 1933, and West Germany had defeated Finland by the same score in 1940. New Zealand's World Cup record stood for many years but is now held by Australia, who beat American Samoa 31–0 in 2002 with Archie Thompson scoring 13 goals.

The first part of the campaign had taken four months, during which eight games had been played, with six won and two drawn, and 31 goals scored and three conceded.

The sceptics were getting fewer, the country was starting to get behind the team, and the players loved every moment. 'When we arrived back from Sydney, Auckland Airport was packed with people welcoming us, and the Vacation Hotel, where we were staying, became the place to be after home games. The bar was always packed, and while people were there because we were successful, I also think it had a lot to do with the squad being full of down-to-earth lads. I can't imagine many of the teams fighting for places at the World Cup finals mixing as we did with the fans after games. They were sharing the moment with us, and we were happy that they wanted to.'

What the New Zealand public most wanted, however, was for the All Whites to show that their deeds so far weren't a fluke. They wanted their new heroes to be competitive in what was going to be a much tougher, more demanding environment.

Standing in the All Whites' path to Spain were China, Kuwait and Saudi Arabia. New Zealand had to finish first or second to make the finals — easy enough on paper, but not so in practice. The All Whites had already played more games than those they were now up against, as the other three groups had each been played in a tournament format. Saudi Arabia hosted its group in Riyadh and played four games, Kuwait's three games were played on home soil, while China played five matches in Hong Kong.

When representatives of the four countries met to finalize arrangements for the play-offs, it soon became apparent that Saudi Arabia and Kuwait weren't too keen on travelling, and both pushed for a tournament to be hosted in Riyadh. To that end, Saudi's negotiators said that they would pay the other three teams' expenses to and from and during the tournament, as well as offering other incentives. Such an offer must have been tempting for Adshead and Dempsey, who attended the meeting on cash-strapped New Zealand's behalf, but there was never any chance of them accepting. They even declined the lavish gifts they and the other countries' representatives had thrust upon them before negotiations began.

Dempsey and Adshead stuck to their guns and would accept nothing less than home-and-away fixtures as FIFA regulations decreed, unless agreement could be reached by all participants. China supported New Zealand's stand and, as with the first round of games, Dempsey won the day — at a price. The cost of the play-off games, with training camps, player payments and travel bills, was estimated at $500,000 — money the NZFA didn't have.

'We'll get the money. We've got to, it's as simple as that,' Dempsey told *The Times*. 'We are trying to prune costs but it won't be at the players' expense. The days of players making sacrifices to represent their country are gone.'

The All Whites arrived back at camp to prepare for the first game in Beijing in a confident mood after their exploits during the first stage and eager to get back into action.

'For myself and the other younger players, the thought of going into the unknown was exciting. Some of the older lads had played in Asia, but for us it was a new experience. The fact we had done so well in the first stage had given us confidence, and there was this feeling that we were edging closer to the World Cup finals all the time.

'While there was probably a little uncertainty, there definitely wasn't any fear factor within the squad. To be honest, there hadn't been from the start. Once we got through those first difficult 45 minutes against Australia — a lot of which was our own doing — there was a positive outlook. The fact that we had gone more than 675 minutes without conceding a goal gave us the feeling that we were always going to be difficult to beat.

'That side of the game became almost as important as winning. We started to think, *OK, we've gone 700 minutes without conceding, let's make it 790*. There were times when teams had chances to score and we rode our luck a little bit, but that defensive record was something we had become very proud of, and I don't just mean defenders. Everyone played a part in keeping those clean sheets. There was plenty of depth in the squad, and you had to be on your game if you wanted to stay in the starting XI.'

That proud defensive record came under severe threat when the group got underway in Beijing. The All Whites had their share of possession and chances in the first half, but the second spell was more difficult as the Chinese poured forward, desperate for the goal which would give them an important home win and two points. Once again, however, the New Zealand defence was equal to everything thrown at it, and the Kiwis went home satisfied they'd got a point on the board from their first game.

The return match at Mount Smart Stadium 10 days later was just as tight. Neither team could break the deadlock until right on half-time, when Ricki Herbert brought the 27,000-strong crowd to its feet with a magnificent headed goal.

New cap Bill McClure, in for a suspended Steve Wooddin, took a corner on the left. He flighted it perfectly onto the head of Brian Turner, lurking at the near post, and the striker nodded it across goal for Ricki to rise above the defence and power the ball into the net. Looking back, Ricki says that if the game was played today he might not have even been in position to score that winning goal.

'In modern football, teams often tend not to send defenders forward for set pieces right on half-time. Rather, they try to lock things down and go into the break at 0–0. For whatever reason, no-one called me back when I went up for the corner. Ten days earlier in Beijing I had gone forward for a corner, almost on half-time, and when we got back to the dressing room was told that we shouldn't be sending people forward so close to the break, as we had almost been caught out by a counter-attack. I probably got a bit carried away with the game being at home and the big crowd roaring us on. Thankfully no-one called me back.

'The near-post flick-on was something we had worked on in training. It was a lovely delivery by Bill, a deft touch by Brian, and it was there for me to finish it off. It was a pretty good feeling. So was the fact that we had taken three points out of four off a team that was expected to be one of the main contenders in the group.'

Thai referee Vijit Getkaen took an obvious dislike to the physical nature of the All Whites' play. Adshead was diplomatic in his comments after the game, saying his players would have to learn to live with such decisions, but Dempsey said they were considering asking FIFA to substitute European officials in place of Asians.

That didn't happen, but how Dempsey must have wished he had gone through with the request, given what happened seven days later when Kuwait came to Auckland and snatched a controversial 2–1 win.

At the centre of the controversy was Indonesian referee Hardjowasito Sudarso, whose rulings during the second half, when Kuwait trailed 0–1 to a Steve Wooddin goal, incensed the parochial home crowd and led to scenes never before seen at a New Zealand sporting event. As Sudarso left the pitch under police escort, he was pelted with cans, had punches thrown at him, and beer sprayed in his face. An hour later Sudarso and his two Thai linesmen were still locked in their dressing room. It had taken that long for police to clear an angry crowd from the door.

What had enraged the crowd and made it a sad day for New Zealand football were two penalty decisions that went against the All Whites. Richard Wilson brilliantly saved the first, awarded when the ball hit Steve Sumner on the elbow as he tried to get out of the way.

Eleven minutes later Sudarso pointed to the penalty spot again when the ball hit defender John Hill on the shoulder as he turned his back on the ball. Before the kick could be taken, a young man ran onto the field and hurled a beer can at Sudarso, who, fortunately for everyone concerned, ducked and evaded the missile. Sudarso immediately threatened to call the game off, and it took 10 minutes of discussion between the referee, Charlie Dempsey and the police before he agreed to continue, with police posted around the touchline.

This time Faisal Al-Dekheel made no mistake with the spot kick, and from that point the All Whites couldn't find the rhythm they had played with in the first 45 minutes. It was no surprise when Jassem Yacoub won the game with a diving header four minutes from time.

The decisions were hard to stomach, and Ricki has no doubts that they threw the All Whites off their stride. 'It certainly caught us off-guard. We had been through a lot together and nothing had got to us before that day, but we were deflated after what happened in those minutes. You don't mind losing a football match, but to have it taken off you in such a manner really hurt.

'There was no intent by either Steve or John to handle the ball. They simply couldn't get out of the way, and I don't believe 99 per cent of referees would ever have given those decisions. Everyone has an opinion on what happened, but at the end of the day the fact is that Sudarso never refereed an international again.

'In hindsight, what happened that day probably took us to another level psychologically. It was like, "OK, guys, the only ones who are going to get us through this is ourselves. We can't rely on referees or anyone else. We have to do the job."

'As for the lad who threw the can, I suppose I had mixed emotions. Most of us thought *Good on you, mate,* because that's how we all felt. It isn't something you want to see in sport, but in a way it was representative of how everyone in the crowd felt. He saw something he felt wasn't right and reacted as he did.'

There was a six-week break before the last home game against Saudi Arabia, and the time lapse could have been the reason for what was undoubtedly the All Whites' worst performance of the whole campaign.

Even ever-reliable goalkeeper Richard Wilson had an off day, with one of Saudi Arabia's two goals going through his hands and legs. In the end Ricki came to the rescue with a trademark header after Steve Sumner had flicked on Duncan Cole's long throw three minutes from the end. The goal gave New Zealand a 2–2 draw, but left them with a mountain to climb with away games against Kuwait and Saudi Arabia to come. 'We played well below our best in that one, but the one thing that sticks in my mind is that we still kept doing what we had been doing throughout. Set pieces were one of our biggest strengths and, even as the minutes ticked away, we didn't change anything. We just kept going, and in the end Duncan's long throw gave us an opportunity for an equalizer and thankfully I was able to take it.'

Thanks to taking only three points from a maximum six available in home games, the All Whites needed to win their final two games to make it to Spain.

Kuwait had already qualified when the Kiwis arrived for their penultimate game. They had proved themselves the best team in the group, showing just what a difficult task New Zealand faced if they were going to take the maximum points needed from the last two games.

Sport can be full of the cruellest luck imaginable, and that night in Kuwait's Al-Qadsia Stadium the All Whites struck the worst of it.

They had arrived in Kuwait hellbent on putting the record straight after the refereeing inadequacies that had given Kuwait an ill-deserved 2–1 win in Auckland. It appeared they were going to do just that when they were 2–1 up and little more than 30 seconds away from the win they wanted to keep their World Cup hopes alive.

Then tragedy — something this team had become accustomed to — struck. Kuwait was awarded a corner that was vehemently contested by goalkeeper Richard Wilson, who insisted he had stopped the ball crossing the line.

From the right wing, the ball floated to the far post, was headed back across goal, and Sami Al Hashash got up above the Kiwi defenders to nod in the equalizing goal. The All Whites couldn't believe it. After the disappointing effort against Saudi Arabia, they had turned in a superb performance, coming from a goal down to lead the group winners until that final, cruel blow.

'I have never felt more disappointed than at that moment. Here we were playing Kuwait away from home, and to do what we had done, only to have it snatched away from us at the death . . . We were shattered. I don't think I've ever seen a team as shattered as we were that night. It was hard to get off the canvas, because you felt you had been hit with a sucker punch. We felt down and out, absolutely down and out.'

At least the point left New Zealand with a slim chance of getting to Spain: to force a play-off with China, they had to beat Saudi Arabia by five goals in Riyadh on AstroTurf, a surface totally foreign to them.

Everyone connected with the squad made the right noises leading into the game. 'There's always a chance.' 'It's possible to win by five away from home.' 'Why not, strange things happen?' In reality, even the players and coaching staff really didn't believe they could pull it off. Kevin Fallon said after the game that he felt terrible because he didn't have the faith to believe it could happen.

That the All Whites found themselves 5–0 up before half-time (two each to Brian Turner and Wynton Rufer, with one to Wooddin) only added to the bemusement of the players and thousands watching on television back home. One more goal in the second half and there would be no need for a play-off: superior goal difference to China would take them through. On the other side of the coin, one Saudi Arabian goal and China would be off to Spain.

There were no second-half goals. Incredibly, at the final whistle Adshead had to persuade his team that they had something to celebrate. 'For a minute or two in the dressing room afterwards they were angry with themselves for not going on and scoring again,' Adshead said. 'But I soon put the whole thing into perspective for them. Before the game we were dead and buried. Nobody gave us a show. We pulled it out of the bag, and here they were blaming themselves for not scoring again.'

For Ricki, the key to what was a stunning achievement was the drive from within the team, not that he thought there was any real chance of beating Saudi by five away from home. 'I don't think anyone could put their hand on their heart and say we were going to get that result. I certainly couldn't. Sure, we took the approach that that was the situation we faced and that we would give it a go. But to say we honestly thought it would happen? No way.

'In this case, I don't think what happened had anything to do with the coaching staff. There had always been this drive within the team — and what did we have to lose? We had started off on this journey with no-one (if they are totally honest) ever thinking New Zealand would be playing at the World Cup finals in Malaga and Seville. The one thing in our favour was the team culture that had developed along the way. When we were faced with the challenge of winning by five in Saudi the attitude was: *What have we got to lose? Let's go for it*. We'd had a few challenges along the way and come through them.

'Then you have the situation we faced at half-time. It was hard to keep our emotions in check. Five up, score one more goal and we qualify. Concede a goal and we are out. Psychologically, that is tough to get your head around. We did have several chances to score in that second half. I remember hitting the crossbar with a header. It just wasn't meant to be on the night.

'Now we had another game to play — China at a neutral venue. Winning that was more realistic than winning 5–0 in Riyadh. The application, the dedication, the passion for the All Whites jersey, the commitments people made to that campaign were all amazing. Marriages broke up; jobs were lost. We were living on the smell of an oily rag, paid $50 a day. OK, I was a young guy and $300 if we were in for a week wasn't bad, but it was tough for the married guys.

'It became that nothing was more important than the team, which was something I had never experienced. I honestly believe it was that belief in each other and the collective that got us through that night in Riyadh.'

As the team flew back to Auckland, Christmas was only a couple of days away, but Charlie Dempsey had no time for shopping as he began negotiating where the play-off with China would take place. China's first choice was Tokyo, but Dempsey was having none of that. Their next preferences were Kuala Lumpur, Singapore or Hong Kong. Dempsey countered with Sydney or Melbourne, venues totally unacceptable to China. Dempsey even proposed Spain with the game to be played in Madrid three days before the World Cup finals draw, pointing out that the whole world would be watching to see whether New Zealand or China would take up the 24th and final place in the competition.

Eventually, FIFA decided Singapore would host the game in its 60,000-capacity National Stadium on 10 January, which meant no Christmas for the players either.

'I remember us spending a night in a hotel in Bahrain after the win over Saudi, and we were sitting round the swimming pool having a quiet beer when we realized it would be training rather than eating and drinking over Christmas. No-one worried about that. We had been through so much, what did it matter if we missed Christmas? Instead of beer and turkey, we were out running, making sure we did whatever Kevin Fallon's programme said we should be doing, and why not? It had worked so far.'

Throughout the campaign it seemed that nothing would ever go smoothly — something always seemed to crop up to cause problems and Singapore was no exception.

FIFA regulations state that no team may practise on the match surface on the day of the game, but must be allowed one training session before the match. When the All Whites arrived in Singapore at 7 p.m. local time on the Friday, Adshead was told that he wouldn't be able to train on the ground the following day as he had requested, because of a religious festival being held there, and it was suggested that training should take place immediately. Adshead refused, pointing out that the team had been travelling for hours and the players had already left for their hotel.

Dempsey and Adshead were determined not to give in, and Adshead went so far as to threaten that New Zealand would refuse to play on the Sunday as scheduled. Realistically, he knew there was no chance of getting away with that, but he had FIFA and local officials worried enough to accede to his request for the All Whites to walk on the playing surface Sunday morning in their boots. That was normally strictly forbidden, but so relieved were officials that the game — for which 60,000 tickets had been sold — was going ahead on schedule, they offered no argument.

On the Saturday, New Zealand trained on a field adjacent to the stadium. To describe the surface as substandard would be an understatement, and Adshead's fear that it could cause an injury was borne out when defender Bobby Almond went over on an ankle. Physiotherapist Doug Edwards immediately diagnosed a bad sprain and suggested that such an injury would normally rule out a player for around 10 days. That would have meant breaking up the central defensive partnership of Almond and Ricki Herbert. Many observers felt that much of the All Whites' success had been built on the foundation of that pairing, and Adshead was desperate to keep it intact. Bobby Almond was adamant that he would be able to play with the help of an injection. Adshead wasn't so sure, but decided to take a gamble that paid off handsomely as Almond lasted the full 90 minutes.

It was a night that New Zealanders — the few who were in Singapore's National Stadium and the hundreds of thousands watching on television — will never forget. Steve Wooddin gave the All Whites a 25th-minute lead, Wynton Rufer made it 2–0 two minutes into the second half with a goal of stunning quality from 27 metres, then the Kiwis withstood a final Chinese barrage after they pulled a goal back with 14 minutes left to play. Wave after wave of Chinese attacks swept towards Richard Wilson's goal, but the All Whites' defence held. When Brazilian referee Romualdo Arppi Filho put the whistle to his lips for the final time, the most amazing qualification campaign in World Cup history was over and New Zealand was in the finals.

Ricki finds it hard to describe that night. Even today when he watches a video of the game, the hairs on his neck stand up.

'Those last few minutes felt like hours. The game seemed to go on forever. The Chinese were coming at us time and again. The referee was giving them free kicks just outside the penalty area, and when they did score he had given them an indirect free kick *inside* the penalty area! We were tentative going into tackles, because you didn't want to give up any more free kicks. The grass was tough and long. We were cramping up, and all the time willing the minutes away.

'When we won, it was almost surreal. At a moment like that you tend to drift into a vacuum of emotion. Guys were on the ground crying, while others hugged each other. I remember one thing. For the first time in the whole campaign I didn't give a stuff about what time I got back to the hotel. I think Glen Adam and myself got back at seven or eight in the morning. Time was irrelevant. I remember we got a rickshaw home, and the guy who was supposed to be pulling sat in it, and we were doing the "driving" down Orchard Road. Talk about drunk in charge of a rickshaw. It was an unbelievable feeling. We had a few beers on the plane home as well, and what a welcome we got at Auckland Airport.

'Someone gave me a ride into town where I met my best mate, Dave Taylor. We called into a couple of bars on the way up Queen Street to meet our wives and out we went for the night. It was an amazing time in my life. I don't know the right words to describe it — all I know is that it was bloody fantastic.

'Of course it was hard work a lot of the time. I can't speak for the rest of the guys, but I can honestly say that from the start to the finish my application to the campaign was impeccable. Sure you had a few beers with your team-mates, but I stuck to doing whatever was asked of us throughout. Perhaps the most pleasing thing for me was that in books the coaches wrote about that era they said that whenever I came into camp I looked like an athlete. I had done the hard yards. That is what got me into the team and kept me there.'

Brian Turner, one of the mainstays of the campaign, and a two-goal hero in the fantastic win over Saudi Arabia, missed the China trip because of suspension. Watching the game on television at his home in the Auckland suburb of Sandringham, Turner found the tension too much to bear when China pulled a goal back and then went in search of an equalizer. He spent the closing stages of the game walking the streets of Sandringham, checking his watch every few seconds trying to gauge when the match would be over. As he opened the front gate to his house, the door opened and his wife, Liz, shouted, 'You made it!'

'I burst into tears,' Turner reminisced 26 years later, his eyes moistening again. 'I sat down and sobbed my heart out.'

That was how much being part of that team meant to the players.

ON THE WORLD STAGE

The pinnacle of any footballer's career is representing their country at the World Cup finals, but even some of the world's most talented players never get that chance.

The mercurial George Best, ranked by many as the equal of Pele, missed out on strutting his stuff there, but the dream was about to come true for 21-year-old Ricki Herbert as New Zealand headed for Spain and the 1982 finals.

The reality of what a bunch of Kiwis had achieved began to hit home as Ricki and his All Whites team-mates waited to find out which teams they would be playing against. 'It took a little time for what had happened to sink in. After starting out on this campaign all those months ago, here we were with New Zealand's name in the hat alongside most of the world's top nations.

'We were all hoping that when New Zealand's name came out it would be in a group with some of the really big names — and, wow, did we get our wish because they didn't come any bigger than Brazil. Not only that, but this was arguably the best Brazilian team ever put together, even though they didn't go on to win the tournament, after being upset by Italy.

'The other two countries drawn in our group were Scotland and Russia, with Scotland's presence particularly special for the five or six players in our squad with British connections. Even the born-and-bred Kiwis in the squad were well aware of the big names in the Scottish team — such as Kenny Dalglish, Graeme Souness, Joe Jordan, Gordon Strachan, and Steve Archibald — after watching them on *Match of the Day* every week.

'I think there was a bit of interest around the world in New Zealand as well. We were the last team to qualify for the finals, and had been through the longest qualifying campaign in the tournament's history. While the likes of Brazil and Italy were always going to be the focal point for the media, I think we also captured a bit of worldwide attention as well because we were different.

'Television New Zealand invited BBC commentators Alan Parry, Barry Davies and Tony Gubba, who would all be working at the World Cup finals, to do the commentating in our second stage of qualifying. While commentators are supposed to be impartial with their calls, it was obvious they wanted us to do well. I think that was because we didn't put obstacles in their way, as some of the "top" countries tended to do. Rather, we embraced them and helped them do their job. The relationship that developed between them and the squad was special, and I think they were delighted when we qualified. In the end they almost became fans of the All Whites!

'There was also a strong relationship between everyone in the group — players and management alike — and the Television New Zealand people who covered the games from the start of the campaign. That was important in helping get the public behind us. The way John Adshead co-operated with the media, and Television New Zealand in particular, was a good ploy. At times John even allowed cameras into the dressing room. It was something that could have backfired on him, but the team kept winning and everyone was happy. For the first time New Zealand footballers had profiles, and even today the names of those who took part in the campaign are recognized and respected throughout the country.'

It speaks volumes for the profile a young Ricki Herbert developed during this period that the two major books written about the campaign — *New Zealand's World Cup: The Inside Story* by John Adshead and Kevin Fallon with Armin Lindenberg, and *New Zealand Soccer: The Impossible Dream* by Ian Garner and Ian Walter — both feature Ricki's photograph on the cover. One shows him celebrating the vital winning goal against China, while the other shows Ricki competing with Brazil midfielder Socrates. 'It was nice to be recognized like that, and I've often wondered if I figured on those covers because I was a young Kiwi kid who grew up in south Auckland and went on to play in a World Cup. Perhaps if they had featured someone who was born in Scotland it might not have had the same message for people. What happened to me showed that dreams do come true.'

There was an added bonus for Ricki with an invitation to spend almost three months at English club Southampton as part of his preparations for the finals. While it wasn't the first time he had been to an English professional club, the circumstances were different this time. When Doug Moore had arranged for him to spend time at Middlesbrough, Ricki was a raw youngster just starting out in the game. Now he was a fully-fledged international who was going to play in the World Cup finals, something most of the Southampton squad couldn't put on their CV. Kevin Keegan was one who could, and Alan Ball had a World Cup winners' medal after England's success in the 1966 finals. The rest would have loved to be going where Ricki was headed.

'I remember my first day there. I was so excited to be in that sort of environment. I trained with the first team, including Kevin Keegan. I was into everything, trying to impress. I ended up being called into the manager's office and told that he would decide what training I would do. It was just pure emotion on my part: I wanted to absorb everything that was going on around me.

'I played in a mid-week game at The Dell against Gothenburg, in a team that included Kevin Keegan, Mick Channon, Alan Ball, Ivan Golac and David Armstrong. We drew 3–3 and I felt I did OK. When I got the chance to go to Southampton, the possibility of getting a professional contract was in the back of my mind and, looking back, I think I did have a shot at it. Why would they have played me in the game against Gothenburg if that wasn't the case?

'Apparently Mick Channon told the manager he should consider signing me. It didn't happen, and they signed Mark Wright, who went on to play for Liverpool and England, to play in the centre of their defence. Whether it had come down to a choice between Mark Wright and myself I'll never know, but the signs are that it did.

'That's the way football is. Sometimes you're in the right place at the right time; sometimes things just don't work out as you hope. There are thousands of stories like that in the game, but for a young Kiwi trying to make his way in the game, it was an exciting adventure, even if it didn't have a happy ending.

'It also left me with some lovely memories, one of which came rushing back when I heard that Alan Ball had died. On my last night in Southampton, Alan picked me up in his red Mercedes from the private hotel I was staying in and took me to a nightclub. To me it was fantastic that a person of Alan's standing should take the trouble to do that, and before we parted he put his arm around me and wished me luck for the rest of my career. Years later when I took over as coach of the All Whites and we were preparing for a series against Malaysia, Alan came down for a speaking engagement. As soon as he saw me, he came up and gave me a big hug — that he should do that when I hadn't seen him for years gave me a very special feeling.'

Back in the All Whites' fold after his Southampton adventure, Ricki soon settled in to what had become a familiar environment. There was a comfortable feeling not only among the players, but also between management and players, even though Kevin Fallon could be a hard taskmaster when necessary.

As the finals drew closer, there was more and more competition for places in the starting line-up. Good as it had been for those who had been regular starters during the qualifying campaign, the only thought now was to keep their spot when the curtain went up on the biggest show in the footballing world.

It was during those times that accessibility to the management team of Adshead and Fallon became incredibly important for the players who needed feedback on how they were performing in the eyes of the coaches. While Adshead was the outlet for most of the squad, Ricki's conversations were invariably with Fallon.

'Working with Kevin your performances in training needed to be impeccable, otherwise you could find yourself on the end of a tongue-lashing, but I always found him balanced and any conversation you had with him was straight-up. With Kev there was no bullshit. Now 25 or so years older, you look back and know there were times when you might have questioned things, but at the end of the day it worked for me and the coaching partnership worked for the team overall.

'I still regard myself as being really fortunate to go into a campaign that was so successful. Before I got in the side, the national team had gone through a period where they lost six successive games on a tour of Britain and had been beaten by both Fiji and Tahiti. I didn't know what it felt like to go through that kind of experience.'

His Southampton experience meant Ricki missed the early part of the All Whites' final World Cup build-up, but he played a part in a five-match series against a League of Ireland side, and a three-game series with English first-division side Watford.

Finally, what had been a four-month build-up was over, and the big moment had come. It's hard to describe the atmosphere in the Vacation Hotel bar that June afternoon as players, management and the media contingent that was to accompany the team to Spain sat around waiting to set off for the airport. There was a camaraderie between the three groups that, sadly, no longer happens for a variety of reasons. But at the time, they were all about to set off together on an experience none of them, if they are totally honest, had really expected to become a reality.

While the countries that New Zealand would be playing against — and, indeed, all the other 23 taking part — enjoyed the support of a big back-room staff that meant they wanted for nothing, the All Whites were backed up by a small, hardworking, loyal group.

Along with the coaching duo of Adshead and Fallon, the All Whites' management group was made up of physiotherapist Doug Edwards, doctor Ellis Grieve, masseur Dutchy de Ridder, and kit-man extraordinaire Arthur Egan, a tireless worker for players and management throughout the long campaign. Egan knew exactly how his players liked their tea made, and would wake them in their hotel room each morning with a freshly made cuppa.

Then there was Dawn Hair, a solo mother with three teenagers. When the All Whites were in camp in Auckland, Dawn acted as a surrogate mum to all 22 players, making sure they wanted for nothing. She would arrive at the team hotel by 10.30 a.m.

and leave around 4 p.m. with sacks of dirty washing. Next day it would be back washed and neatly pressed.

The day before the team flew out to Spain, defender Bobby Almond was chatting casually to Adshead. 'It's such a pity that Dawn can't come with us after all she's done,' Almond said. The comment struck a chord with Adshead, who immediately set about making sure she would be rewarded for all her hard work on the team's behalf. With the support of the whole squad, Adshead raised enough money to pay for her return travel to Spain. When Aunty Dawn — as the players knew her — arrived at Auckland Airport to see the boys off, she got the shock of her life as Adshead handed over her plane tickets. It was an emotional moment as a crying Aunty Dawn thanked everyone for making her own dream come true, but it typified what the All Whites were all about. The whole campaign might have been done on a shoestring, but it had been done from the heart.

When the squad eventually took off from Mangere, they were in the Economy section of the aircraft. On leaving New York for Madrid, however, everyone — including the media contingent — had been upgraded to Business Class on the TWA jumbo thanks to Charlie Dempsey, who organized the upgrade with the help of travel agent Bill Mabey.

Perhaps chairman Dempsey was prompted by the gentle chiding he had received on the first leg when he came down from First Class to chat. 'My backside might be on that First-Class seat, but my heart's back here with the lads,' he said without a flicker of a smile.

The players didn't mind him travelling 'up front'. As a self-made millionaire, he was probably paying for it himself anyway, but they knew that, without his faith and drive when it came to raising the necessary finance for the campaign, they wouldn't be sitting in the plane at all.

'We didn't mind where we were seated. It was different in those days, and we could enjoy a beer on the plane. No-one cared if they were sitting in 66F — that was just us. Back then you could lie on the floor if you wanted to stretch out, and the drinks trolley was back there anyway. Not that we minded being upgraded to Business Class: because it wasn't the way we usually travelled, it was special for us.'

When the party finally landed in Malaga after stops at Tahiti, Los Angeles, New York and Madrid, they couldn't believe what greeted them. 'The security was amazing. There were police with guns all over the airport, and as we drove up the coast to our hotel near Marbella the players couldn't believe how many armed police were along the route. There were also police on motorbikes either side of our massive bus, and police cars front and back.

'At every intersection and on each bridge we passed under, they were there with their guns at the ready. It was just the same when we arrived at our hotel, and it was something we got used to as the days passed.

'We got exactly the same security as every other team. The only difference between our bus and the Italian bus was that ours had the New Zealand flag on the side. To FIFA, we were just as important as Brazil or Spain. That made us feel good.'

The hotel was a far cry from the humble Alexandra Park Motel where the adventure began, and even the Vacation Hotel, which had become the players' second home, paled dramatically compared to the Hotel Don Carlos, nestled in secluded grounds well off the Malaga–Marbella highway. While the All Whites had stayed in some nice places during their travels over the past 15 months, they were impressed with their new surroundings. Parkland, woods, tennis courts, swimming pool, private beach . . . you name it, the Hotel Don Carlos had it.

'It was a fabulous hotel in a fantastic setting, but we were there to work and Fallon made sure there was no slacking. While other guests were sleeping off the excesses of the previous night, we were out at seven every morning on a 3- to 5-kilometre run. When we got back, there would be 100 abdominal exercises to complete.

Hard work had got us this far, and there was no reason to change things. In the modern day a lot of things are challenged; we just did what was required of us and got the rewards.'

Everything was rosy so far as Ricki was concerned, but that was about to change as the first game against Scotland drew closer. After playing in every qualifying game, and scoring goals at vital times, Ricki was considered by most — and certainly the media — as a certain starter in that opening game. Then one or two whispers started to circulate that Sam Malcolmson, born and brought up in Scotland, was going to get the nod.

When Adshead read out the team following a training session at the local Marbella club, Herbert's name was missing. Goalkeeper Richard Wilson and midfielder Duncan Cole, both of whom had also played in all 15 qualifiers, were also left out. The names of full-back Glenn Dods and striker Brian Turner — regulars in the starting line-up until that point — and Grant Turner, who sustained a tournament-ending ankle injury in training, were others missing.

All three Scottish-born players in the squad — Adrian Elrick, Sam Malcolmson and Allan Boath — were in the starting team. While Elrick had been a regular throughout, the same couldn't be said about Malcolmson and Boath.

'I was shocked and hurt when that team was named. It was the biggest disappointment I've ever had in football, and I didn't see it coming. I remember going to the back of the bus and bawling my eyes out while Steve Sumner sat with me telling me to hang in there. I couldn't say anything to Steve. I was too emotional.

'Once that initial hurt passed, there were two ways I could deal with what had happened. One, I could accept it and move on; or I could throw my toys out of the cot. I chose the first. I was determined that when my chance came again, I would take it; and that everything I did would be spot-on. I got my chance when I went on as a substitute in the Scotland game, and I took it. From that point on, I never looked back.

'I'm sure a lot of people thought Sam Malcolmson had got the nod ahead of me so he could play against his "old" country, and when people mentioned that possibility to me I couldn't disagree. Some people said he got in ahead of me because they thought Joe Jordan, who was big and physical, was going to play. If that was the case, why didn't Malcolmson play against Australia when Eddie Krncevic, also big and physical, was playing upfront? Considering Krncevic scored two goals in the 3–3 home draw, why wasn't Malcolmson picked for the away game? I played, Eddie hardly got a touch of the ball and was subbed off. Move it on a couple of games, and against Brazil I was marking a 6-foot 4-inch guy. Why wasn't Malcolmson in then? People can think about those things and make up their own minds about the reasons for him being chosen ahead of me for the Scotland game.'

It took the All Whites time to settle down at Malaga's La Rosaleda Stadium in their first game at a World Cup finals, and with just over half an hour gone they found themselves 0–3 down after being tormented by Scotland's livewire right-winger Gordon Strachan.

There was more confidence amongst the New Zealanders in the second half, and, 10 minutes in, Steve Sumner bundled the ball over the line, despite the best efforts of goalkeeper Alan Rough. The All Whites had their first goal in the finals.

Ten minutes later, however, the unthinkable happened. The All Whites scored again, making it 3–2. Was a massive upset on the cards? Sadly, the answer was no. Scotland scored twice from set pieces to win 5–2, but the two goals New Zealand scored against them put the Scots out of the tournament on goal difference and let Russia go through.

Ricki got on the field as a replacement for an injured Bobby Almond, and played in the All Whites' next two games. Next up for the All Whites were the Russians and, while the Soviet Union won 3–0, it was New Zealand's best performance at the tournament. 'Russia were a really good, tough, well-organized team with the amazingly quick Blokhin up front, but we earned a bit of respect due to the way we played, and we had a couple of really good scoring chances. Only a really good save by their keeper Dasaev stopped Kenny Cresswell getting on the score sheet.'

Then it was time for the All Whites' grand finale against tournament favourites and perennial World Cup winners Brazil, before a packed stadium in Seville. 'The best thing for me about the Brazil game was that, even though they had already qualified for the next stage, they paid us the respect of playing their strongest team against us.

'My preparation was the same as for any other game — apart from meeting Pele in the dressing room — but lining up for the national anthems and looking along at some of the world's best players was a bit special.

'Once the whistle goes it is just another game, but there was something a little different about this one. I can still see and hear it now. Whenever the music from the Brazilian fans in the stand got faster, the game got faster. The tempo of the game was being dictated by the music. It was quite amazing.

'They played total football. Junior would suddenly appear on the right wing, even though he was playing left-back. The movement of the players was amazing, and their techniques . . . well, they were the best in the world. It was a real test of our discipline to keep our shape against players such as Zico, Socrates, Eder, Cerezzo, Junior, Falcao and Serginho. OK, they beat us 4–0, but then they beat Scotland 4–1.'

When the final whistle blew, New Zealand's great football adventure was over. 'Things did feel a little bit flat when it finished. For some of the guys, it was the end of their careers; others were heading off for a holiday. We had been together for so long and been through so much, it was hard to imagine that we wouldn't ever be together again. I remember going into the dressing room and getting changed without any fuss.

'Then it was time to be with Raewyn and do some travelling. After all the time we had been apart over the last 15 months or so, it was neat to be together. I took her to England to meet the people I had stayed with in Southampton, and then we went around Europe . . . France, Switzerland, Italy. It didn't take us long to realize how expensive hotels were in Europe, so we bought a tent! The first time we used it was at a camping ground in a little place called Piano, overlooking Sorrento.

'There we were putting the tent up and people were looking at all the World Cup gear I had lying around. Word soon spread that there was a guy staying in a tent who had played in the World Cup. They must have found that really strange when you consider how Italians revere their national team players. Each night we would climb into a horse and cart and go into Sorrento to a beer-and-pizza place we had found. The guy who owned it knew I had played in the tournament and really looked after us.

'We had a fantastic time, and even watched Italy win their semi-final which made for a great atmosphere. Being with Raewyn and enjoying Europe so much meant that there was no time to look back. As I said, it was a bit flat at the final whistle, but then I was on a high again, this time for a very different reason.

'What an adventure, though. I wouldn't have missed it for the world.'

LIVING THE DREAM

After the highs of the World Cup finals, and the dramatic way New Zealand earned its place in football's showpiece, it was a case of 'back to reality' for the players once the final whistle blew on their game against Brazil.

For some, it was a return to New Zealand's national league; others would continue to ply their trade in the Australian National Soccer League (NSL); one or two would retire from the international scene and gradually fade out of senior football all together.

For Ricki, however, there was still much to aim for. Fantastic as being part of the All Whites' adventure had been, his dream of playing football professionally was still just that . . . a dream. He'd had a small taste of what it would be like to play the game for a living, though, during the World Cup campaign when the squad had spent weeks together in training camps and travelling to games.

The biggest problem standing in the way of his goal was the fact that New Zealand had no professional football, and wasn't likely to have in the foreseeable future. Australia's NSL was a professional competition, and during training camps he had talked to Richard Wilson, Glenn Dods and Duncan Cole, who at that time were playing across the Tasman. Whether it was a stepping stone to where he really wanted to be — playing professionally in England — remained to be seen, but if the chance came along, Ricki was determined to grab it with both hands and give it his best shot.

The first approach he had came from Canberra, where Duncan Cole was playing. Ricki had no hesitation in crossing the Tasman and taking up an offer to trial with the club. They offered him a contract, but that same night he got a call from his father, Clive, back in Auckland, to say that Tommy Docherty, manager of glamour club Sydney Olympic, had been on the telephone and was keen to sign him.

'I had to tell Canberra I needed time to weigh up what I wanted to do, and needed to go back to New Zealand and talk to my family. I talked to Sydney before going home and they tried to convince me to sign then and there, but I really did need to weigh everything up before making a decision. A few days later, one of the Sydney officials, Jim Pettin-Ellis, flew to Auckland and I signed the contract there.

'I believe Tommy Docherty, who was well-known worldwide, had watched one of our games against Australia and decided then that he wanted to sign me for Olympic. It wasn't England, but it was professional football, and for me that was all that mattered. I had no idea whether it would lead to anything else, but I was going to be doing something I really loved for a living.

'I got on really well with Tommy Docherty, who often would pick me up and drive me to training. Tommy was the type of person who could crack a joke but also be a strict disciplinarian when he needed to. We had some lovely conversations, and I remember fondly the encouragement and direction he gave me in those early days, words that would help shape me as a player and person for years to come. He was not only my football manager; he was my mentor and friend.

'I found him to be an incredible man and so genuine. I never got tired of listening to him talk football. His knowledge of the game was second to none, which wasn't surprising considering he had played for Celtic, Preston North End, Arsenal and Chelsea, as well as representing Scotland. He was also a fine tactician; again not surprising, when he'd managed 14 clubs throughout the world, including Chelsea, Aston Villa, FC Porto and Manchester United. He'd also managed Scotland's national team.

'Some good managers are poor coaches. Some coaches aren't articulate enough to get their views across, but Tommy Docherty had it all. His managerial skills were excellent, and his man-management skills set him apart from most others. As you can see, I thought the world of Tommy, and to this day I have kept in frequent contact with him and still hold him in the highest esteem.

'I had a one-year contract with Olympic and enjoyed my time there. At the end of the contract, I went back to New Zealand to play in the national league with Auckland club University Cowan. Tommy Docherty also left Olympic at the end of that season. He told me he was going back to England, and that if he ended up in management again over there he would want to sign me. I wonder how many players have heard that sort of thing over the years? My immediate thought was, *Wow, how good would that be?* But at the same time you don't want to get too carried away, because it can lead to disappointment.'

Ricki got back to doing what he did best: playing football for University Cowan and New Zealand. Then, almost a year after

Tommy Docherty had returned to England, Ricki got a call from Scotsman Tom McNab, himself an icon in New Zealand and a friend of Docherty, saying the now-manager of Wolverhampton Wanderers wanted him to get in touch with a view to joining the club.

'The call came out of the blue, and even today I can't find the words to describe the elation I felt when Tom McNab broke the news to me. I was on such a high that a dream I'd had for so long was about to become a reality. From as far back as five years old, I'd had set my heart on becoming a professional footballer in England. The burning desire and passion inside me just wouldn't go away. I'd think about it during the day, and dream about it when I slept. In my dreams I could see myself playing; I could hear the roar of the crowd when I scored a goal. Then I would wake up feeling exhausted and realize it was a dream. As I got older, the desire to play overseas remained strong. With New Zealand being a rugby-mad country, I'm sure most people thought I was strange having such a passion for what they referred to as "that round-ball game".'

The dream looked to become a reality very quickly, with Wolves forwarding a preliminary contract to his parents' house by facsimile within days. It is an evening Ricki remembers vividly.

'As I opened the door, there was Dad with a big smile on his face. The first thing I did was ask him what was going on, because it wasn't every day that Dad would meet me with a grin from ear to ear. I looked over at Mum, who was sitting at the kitchen table looking at a sheet of paper. Then it hit me: the contract I had always dreamed about was finally here. I'd made it!

'I took off on a run around the house. I was shouting "I made it! I made it!" at the top of my lungs. The rest of the night was spent on the telephone telling everyone I could think of what had happened. It wasn't something that happened every day. In fact, in those days New Zealand footballers plying their trade overseas was a rarity. Wynton Rufer, a team-mate in Spain, was the only player I could think of who was playing professionally in Europe at that time.'

Just prior to getting McNab's telephone call, Ricki had heard that two weeks later he would be going with the New Zealand team on a four-week, six-match tour of Britain. This gave him the opportunity to meet Docherty and Wolves' chief scout Sammy Chapman prior to the first game in Newcastle, and sign a formal contract.

In many ways it was fitting that Ricki finally sealed a professional contract while on New Zealand duty. 'While playing professionally was always my dream, playing for the All Whites was another love of my life. To play for your country is always an honour, and something that had been close to my heart from the first time I pulled on a New Zealand shirt. I had been away with the national side many times, but signing that contract in Newcastle made this particular trip extra special.'

The All Whites' whistle-stop tour took them from one end of the British Isles to the other. After the opening game in the northeast against Newcastle United, which was lost 0–3, it was down to Berkshire in the south of England, where the All Whites beat Reading 2–1. Then it was up to Scotland for a 0–5 beating at the hands of Glasgow Rangers; back to the English midlands and a 1–4 loss to Leicester City; further south to Portsmouth, where they lost 2–3; and finally back to Nottingham in the midlands, where an England B team edged the game 2–0.

After the All Whites' match against England B in Nottingham, Ricki paid a flying visit to Wolves' Molineux ground to meet up with Docherty and finalize arrangements for his return.

If that made for a busy schedule, off the football pitch life was about to get positively hectic for Ricki. Once the Wolves contract was confirmed, Ricki and his girlfriend of five years, Raewyn Smith, decided they would get married before heading off to England together. The wedding was set down for 24 November 1984, at the Edgar Faber Chapel in Auckland's Roskill Masonic

Village, 11 days after the All Whites' final tour match in Nottingham. With Ricki in Britain, organizing the wedding fell on Raewyn's shoulders and she was thankful for the help the Smith and Herbert families provided.

'Weddings aren't the easiest things to arrange, and the added stress of moving to England straight afterwards, and not knowing what we would face there, meant things got a little bit much for both of us at times. I had so much on my mind. I was thinking about the wedding and what Raewyn was going through, trying to concentrate on playing for the All Whites, and still coming to terms with the thrill of signing a professional contract. I was only 23 and starting to feel a bit stressed with it all. Imagine how Raewyn felt?

'She did a fabulous job and, despite all the rush, when we look back on it now we laugh and realize what an exciting, exhilarating time it was. It's not every day you sign a pro contract, play for your country and get married in such a short time. Raewyn has always been supportive of my football career, attending every match she could when I was playing.'

Ricki and his new wife then left New Zealand for England the day after the wedding. 'I think we both adjusted to married life well. I suppose moving to England so soon after the wedding was a blessing in disguise in some ways, as we were able to spend a lot of time together. Initially Raewyn didn't work, which allowed her to settle in and make friends. There were a lot of other young married couples at the club who in time became good friends, and there were also the friends we made in our neighbourhood which helped to make being away from home a little easier.'

For the first month or so they lived in a hotel near the ground, then moved into a one-bedroom flat above a block of shops in Wombourne village. They arrived in November, when there was plenty of snow on the ground and not a lot of heating in the flat. It was what you might call an interesting introduction to the English winter.

'I had never seen it snowing before going to England, so it was something of a love-hate relationship. On the one hand it was a novelty and I loved looking out of the window at the snow falling, while on the other hand when you had to train in the damn stuff it took on a different perspective altogether. Sometimes your feet felt like they were totally frozen. I'd thought Auckland winters could be cold, but they were nothing to what I found in England. The fog, the dampness, and the feeling in winter of always being wet will remain with me for the rest of my life.

'What a relief it was when we got our own house on a little housing estate in Wombourne. Oh the joy of not only having a warm house to come home to, but having our own home in which to hang out — it made us feel we had finally arrived. We felt like locals. It was interesting, because when you know nothing about an area you have no preconceived ideas about it — whether it's good, bad or indifferent.

'Some people might turn their noses up about living in the *Black Country*, as that area was known, but we took things as we found them. I thought Wombourne was a neat little village. It had a cricket oval at its centre, and to me it epitomized what I had always imagined an English village to be. We enjoyed living there and met some really nice people. I think being a footballer helped in that regard. While footballers didn't have the profile they do now in England — or the money — Wolverhampton players were always recognized around town because the football club was part of people's lives. It was bred in people, and that was different for me because back home it was always mainly about rugby and rugby players.

'The Midlands was a hot-bed of football. The fans were so passionate about their football and Wolves in particular. They ate, drank and slept football. They were true supporters. If Wolves won, they would feel great all week. A loss and they would be miserable until the next game, and the chance to turn things around arrived. Our neighbours were always keen to talk about the game, and we got on well because I was happy to do so. That is the way I was brought up, and I think they appreciated that I was just a guy from New Zealand who happened to be playing for their club.

'Despite all that, it wasn't all plain sailing. We were both still quite young, and going to live on the other side of the world at our age wasn't something a lot of people did at that time. We both missed our families and friends, but it was a fantastic opportunity and we wanted to make the most of it. Raewyn and I enjoyed our new sense of freedom, whilst at the same time missing the love and affection of our parents. That time was a real growth period in our lives, and one that really cemented our relationship.'

It wasn't long before the first real test of living so far from home came along. Ricki's grandmother, who had been a big football fan and very supportive of his career in the game, passed away. Her death hit him hard and, unable to be at home to grieve with the rest of his family, he had no option but to knuckle down and get on with the new life that he and Raewyn had chosen.

In some ways the demands of professional football in England, along with the pressure of performing to the optimum each weekend, helped take the focus off being homesick. He had to work at making the transformation from playing in an amateur league in New Zealand to the daily grind of a professional environment. Although he had always been very fit, Ricki soon realized that he needed to be working at a much higher level of intensity than ever before. Even harder than he had under Kevin Fallon!

'I arrived in Wolverhampton on a Tuesday and couldn't wait to start training, even though the long trip had taken a lot out of us both. That wasn't surprising, because it wasn't only the travel we had to contend with. There was all the emotion attached to the wedding, along with the trauma of leaving family and friends to travel to the other side of the world and not knowing when you would see them again.

'Being the end of November, it was bitterly cold when we arrived and my first training session was indoors, something that became commonplace for a couple of months in the middle of winter. Any footballer will tell you that it can be a little nerve-wracking going into a new club. It can be even more so when it is your first "real" professional contract and the club is on the other side of the world.

'At first the other players were a bit stand-offish. I'm sure some of them were thinking, *Who the hell are you? New Zealand?* New Zealand wasn't exactly well-known for producing footballers, and here was a young Kiwi trying to take somebody's place in the team. To be fair, as is usually the case, the other lads soon came around, and it didn't take long for me to forge some great relationships with my new team-mates. Some of those friendships are still strong today. After my second day at training, I was seeing stars. I'd like to blame it on jetlag, but the session was of a much higher intensity than I was used to at home and it took me two or three weeks to adapt to what was required of me.'

While playing international football had prepared Ricki to play at the top level, those matches weren't on a weekly basis, and the preparation now required something different of him, both physically and mentally. 'Preparing yourself for a one-off international and competing for a place at training against hardened pros day after day is totally different. Mental toughness had always been one of my strengths, but the thing I had to find now was consistency. I had to be able to go into training every day and produce the goods.'

He must have done all right in those first sessions, though, because before the week was out he got the shock of his life.

'We had an 11-v-11 game between squad members, and, when it finished, Tommy Docherty took me aside and told me I would be playing on the Saturday. It took a few minutes for what he was saying to sink in, but then a feeling of exhilaration came over me. I couldn't wait to get back to the hotel and tell Raewyn what had happened. "I'm playing at the weekend!" I shouted as I walked through the door. "That's good," Raewyn said and left it at that. Nothing like a wife to bring you down to earth, is there? Here I was over the moon and she'd just burst my bubble.

'I said, "Raewyn, do you realize how important this is? I'm playing at the weekend and I've been here less than a week." Her response: "Yes, honey, but wasn't that what you came here for?" I supposed it was, but I was still hoping for a little more enthusiasm.'

Wolverhampton Wanderers were playing Brighton and Hove Albion in a second-division match that Saturday and, as Ricki thought back to that red-letter day in his life, the emotion of it was obvious as his eyes moistened.

'In the hours leading up to the game I had tried to cover every eventuality in my mind. My preparation was the best it had ever been. I was desperate to perform to the best of my ability and show the crowd that this young Kiwi was worth a spot in the team and that I would be an asset to the club in the future. Then, of course, there was the gaffer. He had shown such faith in me: there was no way I was going to allow myself to let him down.

'Then, all of a sudden, the preparation was over. I was standing in the tunnel wearing the gold and black of Wolverhampton Wanderers, an English club with a proud history. The club that led the way in Europe by becoming the first English team to take on great sides like Honved of Hungary and Moscow Dynamo — under floodlights on the very ground I was about to play on.

'There were around 20,000 fans on the terraces waiting for the teams to emerge, and here I was, 20,000 kilometres from home, about to live my dream. So many times I'd dreamt this scene, but you don't have to contend with nerves when you're dreaming. Now it was the real thing and there were a thousand butterflies fluttering in my stomach.

'The game was fast and furious; nothing like I had imagined. It would be nice to say we won and that I scored the winning goal.

This was real life, however, and we lost 0–1.'

Wolves were going through the worst period since they were one of the 12 founder member clubs of the English League in 1888. Three successive years — 1984, 1985 and 1986 — they suffered relegation and ended up in the fourth division. That didn't make life easy for anyone at the club, but, even though results were poor, Ricki was thriving in his new environment and loving every minute.

Despite that, and despite having Raewyn at his side, Ricki still missed his parents. The feeling was mutual, with his father, Clive, following his career from afar. His parents had always played an enormous role in Ricki's life, and he was longing for them to come across and watch him play.

'I had hinted several times during our weekly telephone conversations that they might like to come over. Flights in those days weren't cheap, though, and it wasn't easy for Dad to drop everything and take off for England. He was training horses, which meant he wasn't able to spend long periods away from the stables — in fact, the owners of the horses he trained didn't want him away at all, if possible. Somehow he worked it out, though, and I was really excited when he told me that he and Mum would be coming to England in April, and would be able to stay for a few games.

'My parents had always been encouraging and very proud of what I achieved in football, and it was great that they could spend some time sharing what Raewyn and I were doing on the other side of the world.

'Tommy Docherty allowed Dad to travel to a match on the team bus. He had to sit at the back away from the players, but that didn't worry him — he was so excited about being a part of it. He told me that's something he will cherish for the rest of his life.'

Clive Herbert admits losing his son to the other side of the world wasn't easy and that the family didn't really take it well at first, because it all happened so quickly.

'Everything was going along nicely, then a phone call from Tommy Docherty turned it all upside down. Ricki came home from the All Whites' tour, got married, left for England next day, and whoosh — he was gone. As parents, there weren't any prouder people than Shirley and me. Sad as it was to see them go, we knew it was a once-in-a-lifetime chance.

'I can tell you, during that period we had the most expensive telephone bills of our life. It was worth it, though. I used to be so excited when I'd call before a game to wish him luck, then talk to him afterwards to find out how everything went.

'We managed to get over to see them two-and-a-half months after they left. The club looked after us while we were there. I will never forget being taken into the gold room for tea and sandwiches before a game. Looking at the photographs on the wall — including Billy Wright, who played 105 times for England and captained the side for years — it hit home to me that the ground was steeped in history. It also dawned on me that our son was following in the footsteps of some wonderful players.

'Some things stick in your mind more than others. I borrowed Rick's car to drive to a game against Blackburn. We parked it in an alley behind the ground, and we were amazed at the number of people streaming towards the ground. I said to Shirley, "Let's get out of the way and let everyone go so we can start to find our way around." Next minute a policeman on horseback came up and asked if we were strangers. I told him we were from New Zealand and that our son was playing for Wolves. Straight away he showed us where we could pick up our tickets.'

After his parents returned home, Ricki carried on playing and, even though the team was going through a lean spell, he kept his place in the starting line-up. He went on to play 55 consecutive games — impressive for any professional, but rather special for a young man arriving unheralded from the footballing backwater that was New Zealand.

Unfortunately, the season finished with Wolves being relegated and Tommy Docherty losing his job. 'That was hard for me, because Tommy had given me the opportunity to do something I had set my heart on from when I was a kid.'

When you look at what footballers in England earn today, even outside the top division, it is a far cry from when Ricki was at Molineux. 'The money was nothing special. It was enough to be able to do the things you wanted, and probably more than the average guy was earning, but to be totally honest it probably wouldn't have mattered what the wage was. I would have gone anyway. I didn't even think about trying to negotiate. I just said yes. After being there for a while, I realized I should have looked at that aspect a bit more, but I didn't have the kind of background that involved agents and the like. At the end of the day, Tommy didn't have to ring up, did he? I'm just glad he did.'

Chief scout Sammy Chapman took over as manager after Docherty's departure, and was in turn replaced by Bill McGarry, who had coached Wolves previously from 1968 to 1976 and had since been coaching in the United Arab Emirates and Zambia. In what was something of a revolving-door situation, Sammy Chapman then returned to take over from McGarry.

While this was happening, Ricki, who was fortunate to avoid many injuries during his career, sustained an Achilles injury in training that put him in plaster for a few weeks. It was the longest period of inactivity he had ever endured and it didn't help his long-term prospects with the club.

At the end of that season, Ricki's contract with Wolves ended and, with no offer on the table to renew it, he decided to leave and return to New Zealand. 'It was an unusual period for the club. I think the owners were trying to sell the club, and certainly all the good players were being sold, which didn't help the way things were going. In hindsight, it was a difficult time to go to the club, but I'll never regret it. In football, timing has a lot to do with how things turn out.

'I often ask myself whether I should have tried to find another club in England at that stage. I think now that I should have done. The funny thing is that towards the end of my second season at Wolves I began to take a real interest in coaching. I don't know why but I did, and look how things have turned out. The only regret I have from the time I spent with Wolves was the problems I experienced in getting released by the club to play for New Zealand.

'During my time with Wolves I only played in one international, which cost me at least 10 games for my country. Because of that, I can fully appreciate the problems facing players who find themselves in a club-versus-country situation. The All Whites were, and always will be, a very special part of my life — as they are to other New Zealand footballers.

'Wolverhampton Wanderers will have a place in my heart, too, and that is the first result I look for every week.'

FROM WOLVES TO HORSES

Those last few months at Wolverhampton Wanderers was one of the most frustrating periods of Ricki's sporting life. It even got to the point where he voiced his disappointment at how things were going in Wolverhampton's sports paper, *The Pink*. Anyone who knows Ricki personally will tell you that that just isn't his way. During his years in football, there have been many occasions when he must have been sorely tempted to vent his feelings through the media. Inevitably, though, he would hide his real feelings in the gentlemanly way that has been his trademark through life.

'I had been writing a column in *The Pink* for a few months, and in my last one I expressed my disappointment at the lack of opportunities I was getting. It wasn't something I enjoyed doing, but I really felt that my performances for the club before the injury deserved some recognition.

'When I was told my contract would not be extended, I was

so disappointed that I rushed into a decision to go home. That was the wrong decision to take. Like anyone I've made mistakes during my time in football, but when I look back that was the biggest. Things were so different back then to the way things are today. Most players didn't have agents and had to rely on their own judgement. In hindsight, I should have tried to use the network of people I had established in England, but I didn't even enquire about what other opportunities might be open to me. I really regret that and I think Raewyn did as well. Should a player today find himself in that situation, his agent would be doing the rounds to find him a new club well before his contract ended.'

Four years on from the World Cup finals, Ricki was once again heading back to New Zealand, unsure what the future held for him. While he still had a burning desire to remain in football, this was easier said than done in New Zealand, especially for a young married man. There was little money to be made in New Zealand football during that period. Even the top players were semi-professional at best, and Ricki knew he was no different to anyone else.

'I'm not sure people understand what it is like trying to follow your sporting dream, especially in a country the size of New Zealand. To stay in football you had to make sacrifices and do whatever you could to earn a living.

'There were few better players in New Zealand than Brian Turner, but he couldn't make a living out of football. Brian, who has been one of my closest friends for more than a quarter of a century, went on to have 25-plus years in the corporate sector, no doubt making a few investments and securing himself financially.

'I can't say the same for myself. Sure, I could probably have gone down the same path as Brian, although I'm not suggesting I would have been as successful as he was, but I still had this burning ambition to make football my career. Over the years I took jobs that paid less than I would have liked, simply because they gave me the opportunity to play or coach football. One of those jobs was training horses with my father. It is no exaggeration to say that I could have earned five times as much elsewhere, but working with Dad had its advantages despite the lack of money. Not only did it allow me to play football without time constraints, but it gave me a love of horses that will stay with me forever.

'People probably look at me and think I'm pretty well-off because of some of the jobs I've had in football, but that isn't the case and there was a long period of my life when I didn't have much financial security at all. It is only in the last two or three years that I have benefited from what has been a long football apprenticeship. Don't get me wrong. I am not complaining. That is what I wanted to do, and there have been many experiences along the way that have meant more than money.

'The realization of the dream that I had been following came when the Wellington Phoenix club was born and I was appointed coach. At that time, I had been coaching at senior level for just under 20 years, and yet some people who had been coaching for a couple of years felt they should have got the job instead of me.'

Ricki arrived back from England in March 1986. His father, Clive, was involved with the Manurewa club at that time, and obviously keen for his son to join him there. Instead Ricki opted to return to Mount Wellington, where he knew the players and felt comfortable in the surroundings. Mount Wellington had made some good signings for that season, including Ricki, and were once again favourites to lift the title, but it almost didn't turn out that way.

With two games to play, Miramar, who had led the table for 16 weeks, were two points ahead of Mount Wellington and both the Wellington clubs' final fixtures were at home. Fortunately for the Mount, Miramar were beaten 1–0 by local rivals and playing-through champions Wellington United, and then drew their final game 0–0 with Christchurch.

Even then Mount Wellington made hard work of winning the championship, having to come from behind at home to second-bottom against Manawatu, and needing an own goal with virtually the last kick of the game to give them victory and the title.

Ricki stayed with Mount Wellington until the end of the 1989 season when John Adshead was managing the club with Dave Taylor his assistant. That same pair managed the All Whites for the 1989 World Cup qualifying campaign, during which Ricki captained New Zealand.

Looking back on that situation brings a wry smile to Ricki's face. 'Years later when people were having a pop at me for coaching the Phoenix and All Whites simultaneously, I thought about the fact that the two most successful coaches in New Zealand football history — Adshead and Fallon — both coached a club while they were in charge of the national team. Fallon at Gisborne and Adshead at Mount Wellington.'

Away from football, Ricki found himself selling cars for a living, and, while he had never envisaged such a scenario, he soon settled into his new employment.

'When I came back from England, out of the blue I got a call from Daryl Sambell, who was managing top New Zealand cricketer Martin Crowe at the time. While I wasn't under the illusion that I had as high a profile as Martin Crowe, I agreed to have a coffee with Daryl in Parnell. (Incidentally, I finished up racing a horse with Martin and his brother Jeff. It was called Javed Miandad and Peter Davis trained it for us in Christchurch.) Daryl got me a job at Cawthray Motors. The way it was sold to me was that the position would involve promotional work, but at the end of the day I was selling cars. Not that I was complaining, because it worked out well and I had a great time. I really enjoyed it and met some fantastic people. Part of the package was a little Daihatsu Turbo that I came to love, a retainer plus commission for selling cars. I believe one of my strengths has always been getting on with people, and here I was out on the lot talking to the public. Many of those who came in knew my background in football, even though it had been four years since the World Cup finals, and I think that helped me sell a few cars, which was pleasing because it meant a bit more money was coming in.

'I might have played in the World Cup finals but I was just a normal guy who was living in the real world and needing to make ends meet. It was completely different to what I had become accustomed to in Wolverhampton, but it was an environment I was comfortable in. Not that I knew much about cars — virtually nothing in fact. It was often a case of: "Here, do you want to buy this car?"

'They were good people to work for and I also enjoyed mixing with them socially.'

Eventually, however, Ricki decided it was time for a change in direction employment-wise, and it wasn't long before he joined his father in the horse-training business. It was Clive, who had started out training on his own while the family were living in Papatoetoe, who first suggested that his son should consider working with him and help train the trotters and pacers he had in the stables.

'There was no pressure on me to join him at the stables. He just asked if I would like to see if I fancied working with horses. Until then, I hadn't given working in the stables a thought. I'd often gone to the trots with Dad and loved the atmosphere, but I knew absolutely nothing about horses — apart from when I backed a winner!

'Again one of the important things about working with Dad was that it would give me more flexibility when it came to making time to play and coach football. That was a massive incentive.

'I ended up working alongside Dad and the horses for almost 10 years. I can still remember those first couple of days at the stables and laugh at just how little I knew. Actually I knew nothing at all! There was no easy start because I was the boss's son. At the start I was treated just like any other stablehand and had to do anything that was required around the place. One of the first jobs was cleaning the boxes out, and believe me it took me quite a while to get used to the smell.

'Horses are fantastic animals, and I had always enjoyed looking at them and watching them in full flight on the race track. When it came to working around them, however, there was definitely a fear factor. If you had to walk behind a horse in the confines of its box, you had to be so careful. I think it helped that I was in a family environment, and Dad made sure I took every necessary precaution.

'My first two or three months were spent shovelling manure, brushing the horses, picking stuff out of their hooves, and learning how to put all the gear on them. Dad was amazingly particular when it came to how his horses were turned out. They always had to be immaculate. The hardest thing for me to master was where all the gear belonged on them. Once I got that sorted out, though, there were no problems. It is a bit like riding a bike: you never forget — and I could walk into a stable now and put the gear on almost without thinking.

'I don't know why, but I honestly think my background in sport was a help when I began working with the horses. There was a lot to learn, though, and I went to cadet school where you learnt basic things such as grooming and tacking a shoe on right, through to knowing how to drive a horse on the stopwatch so that you could measure its sectional times while driving it. It was far from easy, but I enjoyed every part of it and worked through everything to eventually earn myself a probationary driver's licence. I drove some of Dad's horses at the trials, and that, in turn, led to me getting my full licence to drive in races.

'The stable was growing all the time, and in one particular season we were very successful. Even that season it wasn't all that rewarding on the monetary front, because training racehorses is such a tough game. It is quite draining financially and wasn't a big income earner for me, because we were a small operation compared to many trotting stables.

'The main thing was that I enjoyed doing it, and it gave me flexibility when it came to making time for my first love which was still football.'

While working with his father, Ricki took on a player-coach role with Auckland first-division club Papakura. The club was a mere 10 minutes from the Herberts' horse-training complex, which fitted in just fine: being able to continue in football while working at a 'real' job to earn money. What more could he ask for?

Dave Taylor, Ricki's lifelong friend, had asked him to become an assistant coach at Mount Wellington, but Ricki had the feeling that that wasn't the right path to take at the time. Better to do his own thing; to cut his teeth at a smaller club, rather than go straight into a national-league coaching position simply because he had played 84 times for New Zealand and played at the World Cup finals.

Training racehorses while playing and coaching football made for some long days. He was at the stables soon after 5 a.m., but such an early start meant the evenings were free for football training.

As the Herberts' stable grew, they leased another property. Clive Herbert continued training at the original stables while Ricki ran the new place at Ardmore, which was right alongside where Tony Herlihy ran an operation for Mike Barry. The pair might have been close neighbours, but they were worlds apart when it came to driving horses. Herlihy went on to become one of the world's top drivers, while Ricki had 28 race-day drives, the highlights of which were a couple of minor placings.

'I enjoyed driving, but it isn't a selfish thing because you are carrying the hopes of the horses' owners and they are the ones paying the bills. They were the ones who had to be comfortable with a novice like me driving against the big guns such as Herlihy and Maurice McKendry, although I think it is fair to say I was OK as a driver.

'One night I drove a Class-3 horse that Dad and I had bought, called Redcliffe Pass, who eventually went through the grades to Class 9. That night we were up against some of the big guns of the New Zealand pacing scene, such as Christopher Vance and Chuin. Redcliffe Pass wasn't the kind of horse that would leave the mobile gate quickly, but he could come over the top of the other horses at the business end of a race if the pace was on throughout. That night we drew five on the mobile, and I told Dad that I thought I could get him out of the gate quickly and into a good spot.

'There wasn't quite as much pressure on me as a driver this time, because I had a share in him and I was quite happy to finish up sitting outside the leader in a 2200-metre race. It got even better when another horse came around and gave me the one-one sit [a good position]. Going down the straight with a lap to go, Herlihy comes around on Christopher Vance to take the lead. I immediately pulled out and followed him. There was never any chance of me catching him, but I did manage to hold on to second, with Chuin and Maurice McKendry third. Herlihy first, Herbert second, McKendry third! It was one of the highlights of my life. As we were returning to the birdcage, Tony looked across at me and with a cheeky grin on his face said, "Gee, you got second?"'

Another driving highlight for Ricki was when he took two horses by truck from Auckland to Taranaki for a Hawera meeting. 'One was called Ribbonwood Sapphire. That horse had amazing speed but was a bit of a head-case, which I suppose wasn't surprising when you consider he had a huge dent in the front of his head. That trait made him a difficult horse to drive, especially at the start of a race when he would really perform. I got him around all right, but we were nowhere near the placings.

'The other horse on the trip was a big animal called Tai Lumber.

As soon as we got to Hawera I worked him on the track because it is grass, which is totally different to the all-weather surfaces most trotting meetings are held on. He felt phenomenal, and I rang Dad to tell him I thought we had a chance. Of course with a novice like me driving him, Tai Lumber was paying big money on the tote, but I managed to get him into third place. That was a great result, because I couldn't get out from the rail going down the back straight thanks to one of the more experienced drivers making sure I stayed there. Had I got him out, then we might just have won. Anyway third wasn't bad and I think he paid around $10 for the place. The buzz of driving when the horse was charging home down the straight was amazing — just as good as scoring the winning goal against China!

'I also owned a couple of horses on my own, including a little trotter called Pride of Ashley. She won a race at Manawatu for me, but with Maurice McKendry in the sulky rather than me.

'One of Dad's main owners, Warren Outrimm, gave me a drive on one of his horses, Raja Vance, one night at Auckland's Alexandra Park. He was a horse you had to look after because he didn't have good feet, but he wasn't a bad animal. Turning for home I began to think I had a chance of winning, and as one of the other drivers came alongside me he shouted at me to go once he realized his own horse wasn't going any good. We charged into third place. Raja Vance paid $9 or $10 for a place, and the trifecta paid thousands. Warren Outrimm was delighted and told me I could drive Raja Vance any time!

'I was supposed to be on him the following week, but there was a late driving change when Raewyn was taken into hospital for the birth of our twins. Tony Herlihy drove the horse instead, and they announced the reason for the change over the course loudspeakers. I should have stayed at the track, because Herlihy could only get him into sixth or seventh place!'

To those looking in from the outside, racing — trotting or thoroughbred — can seem a glamorous business, but there is another side to it, as Ricki found when he had to have Redcliffe Pass put down. 'It was the worst moment of all the time I spent with the horses. He had broken a pastern, and the vet said there was no choice other than to have him put down. Dad was away and I vividly remember ringing to tell him the vet's verdict. I was so upset, the words would hardly come out.

'Tony Shaw, who has gone on to be one of New Zealand's top drivers, was working for us then. We buried Redcliffe Pass on Dad's property, and I had to get Tony to walk him to the hole we had excavated for the burial. I just couldn't bring myself to do it. He was such a strong-willed horse that they had to give him two injections, because he appeared to be resisting the first one. It broke my heart to see him like that, but I am only one of thousands who have gone through such an experience. Unfortunately, that sort of thing is part and parcel of the racing game, but it doesn't make it any easier to handle when it happens.

'On the up side, there was one really good year when horses such as Franco Gold, Franco Steel, Captain Ricki and Vance Lustre were winning good races for us.

'I made some great friends in racing. While there will always be rivalries because it is a competitive industry, the people involved are so genuine. That was a fantastic time in my life. It was something I had never dreamt of doing and went into it not really knowing what was involved. I loved it and went as far as I could in it. I drove a lot at the trials and won a few, but never won on race day.

'The racing industry is 24 hours a day. I've always wondered why you have to work horses so early in the morning: that's just how it is. You get up, feed them and work them. There is always something to do around the stables. You can be tidying the property; looking after a horse; the vet might be coming; the blacksmith is arriving to do their shoes; you are getting ready for a race meeting. It is very hard work and I have nothing but admiration for those who devote their lives to horses.'

Eventually the father–son training partnership came to an end and Ricki was looking for another job. He was determined it would be something that would keep him active, and he eventually settled on a NZ Post courier run along with helping Raewyn with the hairdressing products business that she had started up.

Always happy to work hard whatever the job, Ricki put everything into his latest venture, but then came the opportunity he had been longing for: the chance to get back into football on a full-time basis.

LEARNING THE COACHING ROPES

It should come as no surprise that Auckland's Mount Smart Stadium will forever hold a special place in Ricki Herbert's heart. That, after all, was the scene of so many wonderful moments during New Zealand's fairy-tale run to the 1982 World Cup finals in Spain. It was also the ground where Ricki brought down the curtain on his international career at the tender footballing age of 28, after making 84 appearances for the All Whites.

That international retirement should come at that point in his career was a surprise to many people. Surely it must have been tempting to carry on playing in the hope of achieving the magic 100 appearances. Had he been able to regularly gain a release from Wolverhampton Wanderers to play for New Zealand during his spell in English football, Ricki would have been within touching distance of that milestone, or perhaps he would already have achieved it. During his time with Wolves he appeared only once for the All Whites, despite New Zealand playing 20 internationals.

Those who know Ricki well will testify to how stubborn he can be, and once he'd made his mind up to retire from international football, no-one was going to change it.

When the end arrived, it was where it had all started almost a decade earlier: in a World Cup campaign. This time there was to be no fairy-tale ending. A campaign that began in December 1988 with two wins over Chinese Taipei (4–0 at Wellington's Newtown Park, and 4–1 at Western Springs Stadium in Auckland) petered out with a 0–1 loss to Israel in Tel Aviv, a 1–4 loss to Australia at the Sydney Football Stadium, and a 2–2 draw with Israel at Mount Smart. Sandwiched between the Sydney loss and draw with Israel was a 2–0 win over the Aussies at Mount Smart.

Ricki captained the All Whites in all six qualifying games, and had announced beforehand that the match against Israel would be his last international appearance. It is a day Ricki remembers with pride and more than a little sadness.

'To play for your country is very special. To captain a national team is an honour not many people get to experience. I had been fortunate to play so often for New Zealand. I had loved every minute of it. There had been some incredible highs and some real disappointments. On the morning of the Israel game, when I saw the newspaper headlines that it would be the last time I pulled on the All Whites shirt, the memories began flooding back. I had been determined this game would be like any other. But it wasn't. There wouldn't be any more. I began to think about some of the games I'd played for the All Whites, and about those who I'd played alongside. About the trips to far-off lands and the camaraderie in all the teams I'd been part of.

'The game itself is a bit of a blur, though I remember vividly the moment the final whistle went, mainly because of the tears welling up in my eyes. As I walked around the field I tried to compose myself, but that became almost impossible as my team-mates clapped me off the field. It was only when I got back into the dressing room that the finality of the situation kicked in as I sat with my head between my knees, physically and emotionally drained.

'I'd also just finished playing for Mount Wellington, so you can imagine the void that was going to be left in my life. For as long as I could remember football *was* my life, and now it was gone — although I didn't intend it to stay that way for long. I had set my sights on a career in coaching. It might never let me reach the heights I had as a player, but at least I would still be involved in the game I had loved since I was four years old.'

It wasn't long, however, before doubts began to creep in. Had he pulled the plug on playing too soon?

'I began to question why I had stopped. Perhaps it was because I'd reached the top level at such a young age. Maybe I thought 10 years of unwavering commitment was long enough. Was it because I trained so hard? I know that playing at such a high level made me think I had to do extra training whenever possible.

'Looking back, I do regret stopping playing when I did, even though I've been fortunate enough to remain in football ever since. What's the saying? "You are a long time retired." How apt that is.'

At the time, however, there was no opportunity for regrets. A new career in the game had to be carved out, and a decision needed to be made about which path should be taken in order to achieve that.

While playing, Ricki had always taken an interest in how training sessions were run. Others might arrive, do the work required and go home, but Ricki was keen to learn how the sessions were devised and why. It was while in England with Wolves that his interest in coaching increased. Even today he is at a loss to explain why that was.

'[Playing in England] was when I really began to think seriously about coaching. I couldn't tell you why I suddenly became more aware of it. I wasn't sure how I would do it, but I knew that's what I wanted to do.

Debbie, Rickie and Shirley, camping.
HERBERT FAMILY COLLECTION

With big sister, Debbie.
HERBERT FAMILY COLLECTION

Clive, grandmother Kit (Clive's mother), Shirley, Ricki and Debbie, before Clive left for the 1968 Mexico Olympics, where he managed the New Zealand cycling team.
HERBERT FAMILY COLLECTION

Clive helping Ricki with some football practice.
HERBERT FAMILY COLLECTION

At Middlesbrough's training ground during a three-month trial in 1980.
HERBERT FAMILY COLLECTION

Representing Franklin and Districts, Ricki (left) with Lawrence Penny and Nigel Harbrowe.
HERBERT FAMILY COLLECTION

Young Player of the Year, Ricki Herbert, with Player of the Year, Brian Turner, in 1980.
HERBERT FAMILY COLLECTION

Playing for Nelson United against North Shore. Left to right: Alan Gilchrist, Ricki Herbert, Ken Cresswell, and Neil Haines.

HERBERT FAMILY COLLECTION

Playing against Australia in the opening game of the 1982 World Cup qualifiers. The game ended 3–3.

THE NEW ZEALAND HERALD

Ricki in the 1982 World Cup qualifier against Indonesia, which New Zealand won 5–0.

The New Zealand Herald

In action against Indonesia.

The New Zealand Herald

Ricki scores the vital goal to beat China at Mount Smart.
HERBERT FAMILY COLLECTION

You beauty! Ricki celebrates scoring the winning goal against China.
P. ESTCOURT, THE NEW ZEALAND HERALD

On the way to a 3–3 draw with Australia.

ERIC JELLY

Hero's welcome at Auckland Airport during the 1982 World Cup qualifying campaign.
HERBERT FAMILY COLLECTION

Ricki, on holiday from the Wolves, wishes Franklin junior team good luck on the way to a tournament, 1985.
HERBERT FAMILY COLLECTION

Ricki photographed at Newmarket Park, where he launched his National League career, during a visit home from England in 1985.
HERBERT FAMILY COLLECTION

In action for the Wolves.
HERBERT FAMILY COLLECTION

Wolves v Bolton, 1 February 1986. Eyes right in anticipation of a Wolves corner.
DENISE PLUM

Ricki in his All Whites shirt, ready for the 1986 World Cup campaign.
HERBERT FAMILY COLLECTION

Ricki and Clive, with their stable star, Vance Lustre, 1992.
HERBERT FAMILY COLLECTION

Ricki (No. 4) challenges for the lead during a trial.
HERBERT FAMILY COLLECTION

First picture on joining Wolves.
DENISE PLUM

Relaxing by the pool with All Whites team-mates at the Don Carlos Hotel during the 1982 World Cup finals in Spain.
HERBERT FAMILY COLLECTION

Clive, Shirley and Raewyn congratulate Ricki on getting his driver's ticket, at Alexander Park.
HERBERT FAMILY COLLECTION

Taking gear off after working a horse.
FRED FREEMAN

Ricki driving Captain Riki at Alexander Park trials.
HERBERT FAMILY COLLECTION

Early morning workout.
HERBERT FAMILY COLLECTION

Raewyn with her parents, Valerie and Leo, on her wedding day, November 1984.
HERBERT FAMILY COLLECTION

Ricki and Raewyn on their wedding day, November 1984.
HERBERT FAMILY COLLECTION

With twins, Kale and Sacha.
HERBERT FAMILY COLLECTION

Part of the territory: signing autographs for the fans.
WELLINGTON PHOENIX

Training: (from left) Richard Johnson, Karl Dodd and Ricki.
WELLINGTON PHOENIX

Gear man and co-author, Russell Gray.
WELLINGTON PHOENIX

A few words with captain, Andrew Durante.
WELLINGTON PHOENIX

With Central United junior team. Son, Kale, is fourth from the left in the front row.
HERBERT FAMILY COLLECTION

A training session with Richard Johnson.
WELLINGTON PHOENIX

Shane Smeltz doing some ball work with Brazilian 'Fred'.
WELLINGTON PHOENIX

Team talk after training.
Left to right: Troy Hearfield, Ricki, David Mulligan and Greg Draper.
WELLINGTON PHOENIX

Announcing the team for the next day's game, with Brian Turner on Ricki's right.
WELLINGTON PHOENIX

Game night!
WELLINGTON PHOENIX

Hats off to All Whites Brian Turner, Duncan Cole, Adrian Elrick, Ricki Herbert, and Clint Gosling at an All Whites reunion at Auckland's Sheraton Hotel in 2002.
HERBERT FAMILY COLLECTION

Ricki's All Whites cap.
HERBERT FAMILY COLLECTION

Visiting the Wolves' Molineux stadium in 2001.
HERBERT FAMILY COLLECTION

Legendary Manchester United manager Tommy Docherty signs a copy of his latest book for Ricki, Manchester, 2009.
HERBERT FAMILY COLLECTION

Time out: a night out on Roy Keane's vist to New Zealand to video Graham Henry's All Blacks coaching for their coaching diploma. Left to right: Ricki, Phoenix CEO Tony Pignata, Roy Keane, and Phoenix owner Terry Serepisos.
WELLINGTON PHOENIX

Mission accomplished. With former Manchester United and Ireland legend Roy Keane on completing the UEFA Pro-licence Coaching Diploma.
HERBERT FAMILY COLLECTION

'At that time, football in New Zealand was very much part-time or amateur. It is still the same today, with Wellington Phoenix the country's only professional club. That didn't mean a coach didn't take it seriously or wouldn't spend a lot of time doing the job. Quite the contrary, in fact. He just wouldn't be paid much for doing so.

'One of my best friends, Dave Taylor, was coaching Mount Wellington when I stopped playing, and he suggested I could look at assisting him. It would have been an easy way to start a coaching career, and I did give it a lot of thought, but I had to find out if I wanted to do it on my own, and in turn if I really could do it on my own.

'Papakura were looking for a coach at that time, and, with me being a south Auckland boy, what better way to start a new career than with a south Auckland club. I joined the club as a player-coach, which isn't something I would recommend to any aspiring coach, and set about learning my trade.'

Papakura was an aggressive club looking for success. To help their cause, the year before Ricki joined they had imported players from outside the south Auckland area, and it hadn't worked out for them. Those players had left before Ricki joined, and, with their departure, some of the local players began to return. The profile Ricki had in the game through his All Whites and Mount Wellington deeds also helped in the recruiting drive, including some players from Rotorua, a regional-league club that had reached the Chatham Cup final the previous season. Rotorua was well beaten, 1–7, by Christchurch United in that final, but the fact they'd made it so far showed they had some reasonable players.

'We assembled a good squad; the players worked hard and got on well. I began to enjoy coaching immediately. There wasn't much money in it, but that didn't matter. It was perfect for cutting my coaching teeth, and I was earning money working with the horses at Dad's place.

'I spent a lot of time at the club, because I wanted to do things the right way and wanted people to see that I was taking the job seriously. There were plenty of challenges, believe me. Players not being able to get to training because of work commitments was commonplace. For someone who had come out of a professional environment with Wolves and a top-class semi-pro club in Mount Wellington, that was hard to adjust to. Here I was, an enthusiastic new coach who wanted to give his all, and I didn't even have a full complement of players to work with at training sessions. I soon learnt that you just had to get on with the job and work with the material you had. I wasn't the first budding coach — and definitely not the last — to find myself in such a situation.

'You can react in different ways to finding yourself in such an environment. You can let it get to you and become frustrated, or use your coaching skills to make the best out of the situation. I chose the latter, because I was determined to prove, to myself in particular, that I had what it takes to become a successful football coach.'

At Wolves and Mount Wellington, Ricki would turn up for training, put on his gear and boots, and be ready to go. Now it was a different story. He was the one who had to set the field up for the training session before his players arrived. That wasn't a chore as far as he was concerned. He was always at the ground early, because that's the way he was.

Once out on the training field, Ricki felt comfortable, knowing he was learning what he was capable of with every session. 'When you are starting out, it can be easy to just go with the things you have become used to — what you've seen other coaches do — rather than develop your own way of doing things. From the start I wanted to develop my own way. I knew it would take time, but that was definitely the way I wanted to go. You are always learning in coaching. It would be foolish not to use some of the good things you have picked up along the way, but it is important that you stamp your own mark on the way things are done.

'There are drawbacks for someone who has played at a good level and then starts out lower down. It is only natural that you set the same standards you have aimed for as a player when you turn to coaching. Unfortunately, that can be way above what it should be for the players you are working with. You want them to play a certain way when, in reality, it might not be possible for them to do so at the time. When that is the case, you have to try different things until you find what you are looking for at the level the players can perform at.'

The player-coach role lasted only the first season for Ricki, although he did make two or three appearances during his second season. By that time he had lost some of his enthusiasm for playing. Coaching, and the challenges it presented, had taken over, yet off came the coaching hat and back on went the playing boots as he headed to Papatoetoe for the remainder of the season.

The following season, Ricki took up the coaching reins at Papatoetoe, as the national-league format changed to three regional leagues with the winners playing off to find the champion. The new position wasn't without its own challenges. 'Whatever the reason, players left the club, and when I arrived for my first training session there were only three players — and they were from the previous season's reserve team! I wondered what the hell I had let myself in for.

'The biggest problem was that the club had been really aggressive in the player market and had brought in a lot of players from outside its catchment area. When things didn't go well, those players either disappeared back overseas or went to other clubs. One good thing came out of a bad situation, in that their departure opened the door for players who lived in the area to return.

'I always look back on those times as a good learning experience, because we pulled together and survived that season. It was a bit of a struggle the following season, and we finished up in a relegation play-off. I was so determined that we wouldn't be relegated, I took the drastic step of putting myself in the team, something I had always said wouldn't happen. We played Oratia home and away to decide which club would be relegated, and beat them 6–0 in the away leg and 3–1 at home. I'm not saying my presence made the difference, but it did show the players how seriously I was taking it.

'I don't look back on those days negatively. I learnt from a lot of situations I would never have faced had I taken the easy option and stayed at Mount Wellington as an assistant coach. Had I stayed to assist Dave Taylor, I would have been working with some of the best players in the country. That would have been nice, but nowhere near as challenging and satisfying as what I had to do at Papakura and Papatoetoe.

'There were good times, and times when we struggled. My expectations of players were that they would train properly during the week and dedicate their weekends to football; in many ways I was learning to coach by trial and error, because in those days there weren't many people I felt I could talk to.

'Because of the coaching experience I have accumulated, especially with the New Zealand team and Wellington Phoenix, I like to think that aspiring coaches can pick up the phone and talk to me, but back then coaches were just grafting away and doing what they thought best without worrying about anyone else.'

Even though he was enjoying coaching, Ricki found it hard to resist the challenge when Kevin Fallon asked him to play at Central United in the national league. Fallon had a young team and astutely wanted Ricki to pass on his experience sweeping behind the defence.

Ricki also kept his coaching eye in by helping out with Central United's reserve team. Two seasons later, he was offered the chance to coach Central with Paul Posa, and ended up staying at the club for five years. During that time at Central, Ricki began to compile an attractive coaching résumé. At the end of his first season, Central finished mid-table. In the next two years, 1997 and 1998, Central United won the Chatham Cup knockout competition, as well as finishing second in the national league. When New Zealand reverted to separate North Island and South Island competitions the following year, with the winner of each competition playing each other for the national title, Central United beat Dunedin Technical 3–1 in the championship final.

From the moment he made the decision to take the coaching road, Ricki was desperate to soak up information that would eventually help him reach the same heights in his new field as he had as a player. The only way to do that, and earn the qualifications necessary to work at a high level, was to attend coaching courses.

The first time Ricki went to a coaching course was during his first year with Papakura. The course, which was held over weekends in Auckland, was run by New Zealand staff coach Doug Moore, who, coincidentally, had played for Wolverhampton Wanderers 20 years before Ricki.

Thanks to his playing career, Ricki had the framework to quickly adapt to what was required of him on that course. Later, as the courses he attended developed and began to be based around strategies, tactics, man-management, finance and dealing with media, he was ready for the challenge they presented. The thing he still enjoyed most, however, was working with players, something that has never changed to this day.

A course run by All Whites coach Ken Dugdale followed, and then he began attending Oceania Football Confederation ventures that led to him acquiring an instructor's licence, which meant he was able to run qualification courses for other coaches.

It was time-consuming, with very little financial reward, but that didn't matter to Ricki. He was still involved with football. That was all that mattered.

Then, in 1999, the landscape of New Zealand football changed dramatically. The unwieldy number of associations that had made up the New Zealand Football Association for decades — 23 — was whittled down to seven federations. Each federation would require a director of football, a job that would involve developing the growth of both players and coaching.

It was just what Ricki was waiting for: a full-time position in football. His application for the position with the federation, that was to be known as Soccer 2, was successful — and football was once again his life.

For some, that might have been enough: a safe position with a national football association. It would have been easy simply to do what was required, making sure to dot the i's and cross the t's along the way — but it wasn't enough for Ricki. The new job only increased his thirst for coaching knowledge.

Trips across the Tasman brought him the top Australian coaching qualifications, but still that wasn't enough, and he began to look towards Europe where the coveted UEFA Pro Licence courses were held. If Ricki needed a coaching carrot, that was it. As a player, he had appeared on the biggest stage of all. Why not aim for the world's highest coaching qualification?

'I enjoyed the courses right from the start, even those modest ones that were run over weekends so that they wouldn't interfere with anyone's full-time employment. I found the environment stimulating, especially the overseas ones later in the piece.

'In football, as in life, a certificate or diploma is no guarantee you'll be successful. It can't be, otherwise no-one would ever fail. There used to be a mindset in New Zealand that fostered a lack of appreciation of qualifications in football. There is a lot of work involved, and there have always been those who think: *Why bother, I don't really need it.* However, the importance of going through the process of qualifying is invaluable, and the qualification itself is important.

'We've always taken an "It'll be OK" approach. That isn't being negative about what has happened in the past — it is simply fact. In the early '80s, Charlie Dempsey had a vision of New Zealand playing in the World Cup finals. He thought outside the square to make it happen. Unfortunately, nothing flourished off the back of that. We were successful, but the game in New Zealand went backwards. The necessary fundamentals weren't put in place. In fact the opposite happened in many cases. As an example, the national league — a competition that produced the players who got us to Spain — was constantly tinkered with and eventually discarded. It was that sort of thing that gave credence to those who were critical about football in New Zealand. But it is so easy for people to be critical without offering alternatives. I used to get sick of reading that football had shot itself in the foot over various things. Did football really keep shooting itself in the foot? I'm not sure that it did.

'I think those outside the game find it hard to understand just what difficulties the code has had in New Zealand. As an example, they don't realize how hard it is to get an international programme up and running, and to be able to get the players together for any time.

'Recently, especially on the women's side of the game, they have been able to bring players together for a decent period of time. The under-17 girls were together for a long time leading into the women's under-17 World Cup, which New Zealand hosted, and the players performed admirably. Many of those youngsters went on to do even better within a couple of weeks at the under-20 World Cup in Chile. That build-up couldn't have happened without the support of the girls' parents. The players were kept together in Auckland, meaning those from outside Auckland had to change schools and settle into a different kind of life.

'That isn't easy, and I think a lot of New Zealand people would have trouble coming to terms with doing it. In countries where football is the No. 1 sport — and that is most of the world — it would happen automatically. The parents wouldn't question it. Full-time football for their child? They wouldn't think twice.

'It is very hard for New Zealand football even to compete with our closest rival Australia, a country that is becoming recognized as being able to provide players capable of playing in the world's top teams. They can do so because their players are in the right environment from an early age. Australia has top-class academies and institutes. The game over there has been nurtured and has therefore progressed. The Australians realized that being part of the Oceania confederation was holding them back. They decided that, if their game was to progress, they needed to be part of Asia where they would regularly get better competition to play against. They made that happen through visionary thinking, and their teams will soon be the best in Asia.

'New Zealand can't compete with Australia when it comes to developing young players. We experienced that at the Phoenix. The young New Zealand boys I signed as our youth players hadn't come through any formal system, whereas the Australian A-League clubs can pick up players such as Evan Berger and Kaz Patafta, who have had a solid institute grounding.'

A solid grounding in coaching was what Ricki was aiming for when he applied to attend the UEFA A Licence course at Lilleshall National Sports Centre in England's Midlands. The A Licence is run in two parts, which meant two trips across the world for Ricki, while others on the course could jump in their car and head off up or down the motorway.

'A long plane journey was a small price to pay for what I found at Lilleshall. I loved every moment I was there, even though it was very hard work. You were among fresh faces, and those attending were coming out of good environments. Everything about the place and the people was positive. It all made for a great working environment.

'The first part of the course was fairly straightforward. It was all about learning how to teach, and you were assessed on how you performed as a coach.

'When I went back for the second part, it was a different story. There was tremendous pressure on everyone taking part throughout the whole two weeks. During the first week you were assessed once on your work, while in the second week you had to coach an 11-v-11 game. There were 42 people taking the course, so consequently you had 42 sessions of around 30 minutes each to get through. That took from Sunday right through to Friday and, once you had finished the topic you had been given for the 11-v-11 session, that was it.

'You got no feedback from those who assessed you. It wasn't until Saturday, when the graduation ceremony took place, that you'd find out if you had been successful. That ceremony is held in a large auditorium. When your name is called, you go up to your tutor, who starts with either "congratulations" or "unfortunately". I did my session on the Monday, then had to wait until Saturday morning to find out how I had done. At least I was the second up on the Saturday, because I had to get to Heathrow Airport to catch a flight back to New Zealand.

'It was different earlier in the course, with the tutor taking you through what you had done during the first three assessments and making any points they felt necessary. Points were awarded after each of those sessions, and it was the same with the final 11-v-11 session. That is the critical one, but you have no idea how your tutor thought you had performed. Once I'd done my session, it was a case of waking up each morning, thinking, *OK, we'll have another eight 11-v-11 games today, and I'll be another day closer to knowing my fate.* During that last week, when you weren't doing your own session, 22 of you would be making up the teams for someone else's assessment.

'Someone asked me whether it was better to get it over with early in the week, or would there be an advantage by being on later, having had the chance to see how others did things. I believe going early was better, because you'd been given your topic early and had plenty of time to prepare. If you spent three or four days watching others, it would have been easy to become confused with so much going on.

'The camaraderie was fantastic. When you are not coaching, you are out on the field as part of someone else's session, thinking: *I've got to do my best for Roy/Jack* . . . or whoever is being assessed. Everyone was willing the others to do well, and it was an atmosphere that I loved being in.

'With so much going on, and with the days being so physically demanding, there wasn't much time to socialize away from Lilleshall, but on the Friday night before learning our fate the following morning we went into the nearest town for a few quiet beers. Some more than others! It was a fantastic night, with everyone taking the opportunity to relax after being in such a pressure situation for the previous five days.

'Next morning my heart missed a beat as I approached my tutor. Thankfully, the first word I heard was "congratulations". It would have been a miserable flight home had it been "unfortunately". Luckily, I was one of the seven out of 42 who were successful. The beers on the flight home had never tasted sweeter.

'As I said, a diploma doesn't guarantee anything but I'm pleased that I dedicated myself to getting it.'

With that qualification safely in the bag, Ricki waited to see if he would be invited to attend the UEFA Pro Licence course. Unlike the courses leading up to it, the Pro Licence is by invitation only. Coaches don't go there to prove their coaching ability; that has already been done in acquiring an A Licence. The Pro Licence is more about topics such as strategies, tactics, how to manage a football club and dealing with media.

When the invitation arrived, Ricki steeled himself for another three long plane journeys to England and Lilleshall. The flights were a chore, but once there he quickly fitted into an environment that is a football coach's dream.

When the course wasn't in session at Lilleshall, those on it were involved in regular conference calls where different footballing topics were discussed among the group. Thanks to Ricki being on the other side of the world, he would have to get up at three in the morning, even when he was with the Phoenix at away games in Australia. The others taking part were probably on their mobile phones on the way home from training!

'The main practical exercise during the course was done in groups of three, and involved preparing a team for a game. It ranged from preparing training sessions, to deciding on nutrition, to what strategies you would be taking to the game. It could be a scenario such as West Ham away to Arsenal. What team would you pick for the game? What formation would you use them in? What training sessions would you put on and when? What meals would you want the players to have and what time would they eat?

'Young professionals are brought in to play as the team you have chosen. Two of your group give the presentation of the build-up you have decided on, while the other goes out on the field wearing a microphone to explain what is happening. There are 20 of your peers on the bank, and they can hear every single word that you say out on the pitch, thanks to huge speakers around the ground. They can even hear your breathing.

'I got the microphone job in our group, and you are naturally a bit nervous when the likes of former Manchester United and Ireland captain Roy Keane, who was then managing Sunderland, is listening to everything you say. Once you get going the nerves disappear, and when it is all over the adrenaline is pumping and you think, *I'd love to go through that again.*

'I loved it, and I think if you are doing OK people respect it whether you have come all the way from New Zealand or live three hours up the road; are in charge of the Wellington Phoenix or managing Sunderland.

'The final part of the Pro Licence involved visiting a sporting environment and reporting back on how the club or organization operated. While it was easy for others on the course to organize their assignment within England, I was going to be on the other side of the world. Also it wasn't feasible for me to ask an A-League club to allow me to visit and observe how they run their organization.

'Because I already had a relationship with Graham Henry, I asked if it would be possible for my assignment to be the All Blacks. Those running the course thought it was a great idea, and Roy Keane immediately said he would like to work with me on it if possible because he loved the All Blacks. It just so happened that the All Blacks would be playing Ireland at the time! Graham Henry gave Roy and me the green light and it turned out to be a fantastic experience.

'Roy and I presented our assignment when we returned for the final three-day gathering that also included graduation. It was in the form of a DVD and a colour brochure, and we must have done a good job because we were named runners-up. That was a real thrill.

'The incoming group that was just starting their Pro Licence was invited to our graduation ceremony, as we had been the previous year when we arrived. It was a terrific night; something I will never forget. They had video clips of many of the things we had done over the previous year, set to music. It was fantastic to look back on.

'While I am proud to have earned the UEFA A Licence and Pro Licence, just as important to me are the friendships I made during those five trips to England.

'Middlesbrough manager Gareth Southgate was one of those

in the incoming group at our graduation. I had met him once previously when I'd visited Middlesbrough, and it was good to renew the acquaintance. Talking to Gareth that night led to Wellington Phoenix full-back Tony Lochhead being invited to trial for Middlesbrough. It didn't turn out as Tony would have hoped, but had I not met Gareth again he wouldn't have had the opportunity.'

BACK WITH THE ALL WHITES

Ricki's job as director of football at Soccer 2 was based around developing coaches and players. Duties included running New Zealand Football courses, putting in place player-development programmes, and selecting coaches to take teams to federation age-grade tournaments. For someone who loved anything to do with football, the cross-section of duties that the position demanded was right up Ricki's alley. There was precious little time for Ricki to catch his breath. In the office planning courses and programmes during the week, as well as running those ventures and clinics at the weekend, made for a busy schedule.

While Ricki was totally immersed in his new role, others were watching with interest how he handled it. One of those was New Zealand Football chief executive Bill MacGowan, who was impressed enough to offer Ricki the high-performance manager's role in the national office. Ricki didn't have to think twice before accepting.

At the time Ricki joined New Zealand Football, Ken Dugdale was coach of the national team, with Mick Waitt as his assistant. Dugdale also ran the senior-level coaching courses for the national body, but, as he was living in Wellington, Ricki did much of the organizing in Auckland. Again, it was a busy schedule for Ricki, as he administered courses, organized venues, put in place academies for young players and brought in coaches to run them, as well as attending federation tournaments. He also played a major role in setting up a national-academy system based around King's College, Rathkeale College and Christchurch's St Bede's College.

When New Zealand Football brought in Englishman Paul Smalley as director of football, Ricki's title changed to director of technical development. Different title; similar workload and duties.

The job definitely didn't just involve coaching, but, while he was thoroughly enjoying himself, Ricki still had a hankering to be coaching a team again.

His appetite had been whetted when asked by then national coach Joe McGrath to become one of two assistant coaches — Ron Armstrong was the other — with the New Zealand Olympic team for their qualification series. Safely through the Oceania section of qualifying, New Zealand was beaten 3–2 and 1–0 by South Africa in a home-and-away tie to decide which team should go to the 2000 Olympic Games.

Having had a taste of being involved with a team again, Ricki was delighted when the opportunity to take on the New Zealand under-17 side arrived.

Dugdale and Waitt were running all of the national teams between them at that time, and had taken the under-17 side to Australia a year out from the age group's World Cup. The trip was far from a success, and New Zealand Football even considered pulling the team out of the World Cup. Instead, they offered Ricki the chance to coach it — and a record of two wins, two draws and a 1–3 loss to Australia on the Sunshine Coast was better than anticipated.

When Dugdale went overseas, it meant a reshuffle in the coaching ranks. Waitt became the All Whites' coach, with Ricki as his assistant. Ricki was also given the reins of the under-23 Olympic team, and asked 1982 team-mate Brian Turner to assist him.

The Oceania series was once more successfully negotiated, but the two-leg play-off against Australia proved a step too far, with a 0–2 loss in Sydney and a 1–1 draw at North Harbour. It was a useful under-23 team, and it is no surprise that players such as Shane Smeltz, Leo Bertos, Tony Lochhead and Tim Brown have gone on to play professionally.

Again MacGowan was keeping a close watch, and when Mick Waitt lost the All Whites job in June 2004, after a shock World Cup qualifying exit thanks to a 2–4 loss to Vanuatu, MacGowan recommended to new NZF chief executive Graham Seatter that Ricki be given the job.

'Ricki had a good track record in his high-performance role, but I always saw him as more of a team coach,' MacGowan says. 'I've always been a firm believer that team coaching is totally different to setting up high-performance programmes. As a team coach, you need to understand the technical stuff without being too technical. For instance, Paul Smalley was great at putting structures in place, but I felt Ricki was the man for the job. Having said that, I feel that Paul's mentoring of Ricki did him no harm. Ricki had done his coaching apprenticeship, and I could see he had a good relationship with most players. I had talked to Brian Turner about where he saw himself in football, and when Ricki said he was going to have Brian as his assistant, I thought it was a great idea. What more could you ask for: two Kiwis each with a great record in international football at the helm of the All Whites. It was also good that he was working for New Zealand Football, because the All Whites coaching position has never been, and never will be, a full-time position.'

On 25 February 2005, Ricki was called into Seatter's office along with MacGowan and offered the position of All Whites coach. It was a moment Ricki will never forget: 'It was an incredible feeling. I suppose I should probably have thought that it might happen, because, all through the football world, when a head coach or manager leaves, it is often the assistant who steps up. Football is a funny business, though. I can't honestly say that it was my dream to coach the All Whites. When I started out in coaching, I had ambitions; the same as I did as a player. But when you see how many disappointments there are in football, it doesn't pay to get too far ahead of yourself.

'Once it had happened, it took some time to sink in. It is hard to describe how I felt, but, when you are a born-and-bred south Auckland boy, you don't really see yourself coaching the national team. No Kiwi had done it before — they had always gone for someone from overseas. It was like the old joke about the Englishman, the Irishman and the Scotsman: we'd had them all in recent years.

'We went all those years with people from other countries running our national side, so why can't we make it an aim from now on to continue having a New Zealander in charge? I'm not saying someone should get the job just because they are a Kiwi. Obviously they have to be able to do the job, but if it comes down to two people with equal qualifications and one is a New Zealander, why not go with the home-grown person? One thing I had always felt was lacking in the game in New Zealand was the opportunity for a New Zealand coach to be involved with the All Whites. When I got the job and needed to bring in people to work with New Zealand teams below the All Whites, those I invited to be involved were Kiwis.

'Because I was director of technical development as well as the new All Whites coach, I was able to support bringing in people such as Stu Jacobs and Colin Tuaa to work with the under-20 and under-17 teams. From what I had experienced, there was no clear pathway for people to progress through the system. Here was an opportunity for me to create a stepping stone for people to move up.

'Colin was given the under-17s, Stu had the under-20s, while Brian and myself would look after the All Whites and the Olympic team. I told New Zealand Football that Stu should also be part of the Olympic set-up, as there was always the possibility of clashes between that team and the All Whites. As far as Brian was concerned, he probably wouldn't be looking to move up. His was very much a part-time involvement, because he had a full-time job outside football. It was different with Stu, and he ended up taking the Olympic team to Beijing last year.

'My broader role was taking coaches such as Stu and Colin and saying: "OK, there's the under-20s World Cup campaign. It starts there; this is your lead-in period. What can we do? How do we fund it? What are your programmes? What camps will you have? How many players do you need? What should your staff look like?"

'I would work with the coach and present the eventual programme to the organization for approval and to get the budgets done. That was the main part of my job with New Zealand Football, once I had taken over as All Whites head coach.

'People have a perception that being the national-team coach is a full-time job. It might be for Fabio Capello with England, but in New Zealand that definitely isn't the case. The national-team job has never been a full-time job. In the first place, there isn't the finance available to make it full-time, and secondly, it isn't warranted. The first year I was in the job, we only played one international — against Australia at Fulham's Craven Cottage in June. Of course I got more money when I took on the All Whites, but it was minimal.

'An example of what my position entailed is the time I flew back from an All Whites game in Europe via Argentina so I could spend four days with John Herdman and his first group of under-20 World Cup girls while they were in a training camp there.

'I was basically overseeing things and I was never threatening to any of the coaches. I had given them their jobs, and they knew I wouldn't be looking over their shoulders nit-picking, which is never a healthy situation for any coach to find himself in. I made sure the guys I had given jobs to had all the breathing space they needed to do it properly. I just wanted them to get on with the job and enjoy it. If you want a hand, I'm here; if you don't, great; let's just keep communicating.

'I appointed Paul Temple to the under-17 women's coaching position, and I was so pleased to see the way the team performed in their World Cup in New Zealand. I felt I had played a small part in what they achieved. The way that team played made people sit up and take notice, which was fantastic, because for me it is all about capturing more support for the game. It doesn't matter whether it is male or female; under-17s, under-20s or whatever. It is all about attracting a broader group of people who are going to come through the gates or perhaps want to invest in the game.

'Those I've had a hand in putting in those positions have all gone on with a lot of credibility and done very well. Unfortunately, it is beginning to break down because no-one is sitting in New Zealand Football co-ordinating it any more. Everything is now done in isolation, unlike when there was a process with discussions and consultation. If you leave someone on their own for long enough, they will continue to function on their own. It was much more productive when there was a bubbly, bright group offering support if it was needed. That was quite dynamic.'

One appointment that may have raised eyebrows in some quarters was Ricki's choice of Brian Turner to assist him with the Olympic team, and later the All Whites. Turner hadn't done a great deal of coaching, but Ricki didn't have to think twice before offering the position to his former World Cup and Mount Wellington team-mate.

'I didn't bring Brian in to coach. He was asked to join me because of other attributes he possesses, including having a great affinity with players. Brian is someone I trust implicitly, and there is a real bond between us that has strengthened over the years. We argue all the time, and he challenges me when he feels it is necessary. He was the first person I wanted to come on board when I moved to Wellington to take charge of the Phoenix, but it wasn't possible because of his employment at the time.'

When Ricki took over the New Zealand team, there wasn't a lot for him to do in that area. The squad, where he had been assistant to Mick Waitt, had performed poorly during their World Cup-qualifying campaign in Adelaide the previous year. It wasn't just that it had failed to qualify for the World Cup or Nations Cup, it also meant that New Zealand missed out on the injection of money that would have come with qualification.

Taking over the national team at that point was almost like being given responsibility for a ghost team, because there was only one game on the horizon, such was the impact of missing out.

'The only game we played that year was in June against Australia, and we went into it with around nine international players unavailable, including top-class players such as Ryan Nelsen, Chris Killen, Ivan Vicelich, Simon Elliott and Tony Lochhead. The team was: Mark Paston, Steven Old, Danny Hay, Che Bunce, Michael Wilson, Noah Hickey, Tim Brown, David Mulligan, Brent Fisher, Vaughan Coveny, Adrian Webster. Substitutes: Leo Bertos, Jeremy Christie, Shane Smeltz. Shane Smeltz was at Wimbledon at the time, and behind our dug-out, which was right up against the crowd, was a group of Wimbledon fans who kept yelling at me to get Shane on. We lost 0–1, and the only goal came in the 87th minute. It was a strong Aussie team as they were on their way to the Confederations Cup.

'For me it was the beginning of a new era. A lot of young players had come into the squad. One of the PowerPoint presentations I gave to the players before that game was about honouring the past while at the same time understanding the future. In my mind I thought there had been a drift away from what it meant to be part of the national side. Not just because I was a part of it, but the 1982 team was special and should always be remembered. It was history; the most special moment in the New Zealand football landscape.

'I wanted them to reflect on what teams before them had done, but also look to the future and create more history. When we started off on that venture in 2005, it was about three terms: short, medium and long.

'The short-term was getting the national team back playing again, because it had been in hibernation thanks to having no money and no-one that keen to play against us. The seven days we spent together in London was based around getting the All Whites back on the world stage, regaining credibility for the shirt, earning back credibility as a football nation, and beginning to introduce new players for the future.

'The medium-term was to ensure we had more games, and to do that we had to perform credibly. The long-term was about qualifying out of Oceania and getting into the position we are in now: of being two games away from qualifying for the 2010 World Cup.

'In the interim, we have had some really good results and some disappointing results. But we are back on the world stage having qualified for the Confederations Cup, and the money we receive for getting there, which is around $US1.5 million, is being injected into the game in New Zealand.

'Going into the two Oceania qualifying games against New Caledonia in late 2008, we knew we had to win one of them to progress to the next stage and make the Confederations Cup. The fact that New Zealand Football was in dire financial straits had been well documented in the media, so imagine the burden the team was carrying into those two games. All hell would have broken loose had we not qualified and the $US1.5 million had gone to New Caledonia.

'I can hear people saying, "You were only playing New Caledonia", but those games aren't easy anymore and won't be in the future. The job had to be done, and there was a lot of weight on my shoulders, especially with all the stuff that was being written about me doing the national-team job as well as being head coach at the Wellington Phoenix.

'The only solution, so far as I was concerned, was that we had to win. The only thought in my mind was that we could not lose. You can imagine what would have been said and written had we not won; had we not qualified for the Confederations Cup and the much-needed financial windfall it would bring. It didn't matter that we had beaten Fiji and Vanuatu already: we had built up momentum and now had to capitalize.'

The All Whites did what was required, beating New Caledonia 3–0 in Albany and 3–1 in Noumea. The pressure was off Ricki and his players, and it was congratulations all round with a place in the lucrative Confederations Cup in South Africa confirmed.

There had been some criticism the previous year of Ricki holding down the All Whites job as well as coaching the Wellington Phoenix, especially as he was required to take leave of absence from the Phoenix to guide New Zealand through the early stages of World Cup qualification. It didn't help that he had to take some of the Phoenix players with him, thanks to there being no international window in the Hyundai A-League, meaning the Wellington side had to field a weakened side on a couple of occasions.

There is little doubt that the criticism hurt Ricki, especially as he found himself in that position through basically agreeing to help fend off the demise of professional football in New Zealand.

The country's first and only professional football club — the New Zealand Knights, an Auckland-based club founded in 1999 as the Football Kingz — had been accepted into Australia's new professional competition, the Hyundai A-League, for its inaugural season in 2005, after previously playing in the Australian National Soccer League.

From the start the Knights struggled, and towards the end of their second season in the competition Football Federation Australia announced it had revoked the competition licence held by the Knights' owners, citing low attendances and poor on-field performances.

An arrangement with New Zealand Football saw the national body step in to manage the club for the final five weeks of the regular season, with Ricki filling the role of head coach. The fact that New Zealand managed to hold on to the coveted A-League licence through the Wellington Phoenix for the 2007–2008 season was due in no small part to the Knights winning three, drawing one, and losing to competition winners Melbourne Victory during Ricki's five games in charge.

'I wasn't coaching a professional football team when I was appointed All Whites coach in 2005, and had no intention of doing so. I was full-time with New Zealand Football when they and Football Federation Australia came together to try and get the Knights over the line at the end of the 2006–2007 Hyundai A-League season. I was asked by NZF and the FFA to help by coaching the Knights for the last five games, and part of the reason would have been because there was the accessibility for me to do it thanks to the job I was in.

'But I didn't have to do that. I could have looked at the situation and thought that it could easily tarnish my reputation. Everyone was saying, "There are only five games to go. Just let it run its course and the season will be over." I thought about that, but decided that if I was going to do it then it had to be to the best of my ability. It suddenly became a challenge.

'I didn't know the players, and the first day I went to the club I didn't even get to speak to them because of all the upheaval over their contracts.

'We got through those last five games, and when the Phoenix club was being mooted for the following season I met with owner Terry Serepisos in Auckland, and he said he wanted me to be head coach. I agreed, and both parties involved knew the situation: I was coaching the New Zealand team, and was also going to be a professional coach at a club. Both parties agreed. To this day, neither of those parties has said to me, "Ricki, I think you need to make a decision. It has to be one or the other."

'Unfortunately some people with their own agendas have tried to make it difficult for me to do both jobs, but that has never been the case with NZF or the Phoenix, and those are the only ones who matter to me. New Zealand Football and the Phoenix are the only opinions I respect when it comes to that discussion.

'It got to the point that I really believe some people were waiting for an opportunity to say, "Told you so. The All Whites couldn't qualify from Oceania." Well, we have done that. Why people should be like that is hard to understand. Whenever the "two-job" question came up, in the end I just refused to answer it. The most disappointing thing was that a lot of it was coming from people who, in my opinion, had very little respect in the game. I guess it gave them a way of getting their own little profile in the media.

'It is something I don't even think about any more. At the end of the day, I am employed by NZF and the Phoenix. If at some stage one of those organizations wanted to discuss it with me, I would respect that. But I'm not listening to some ill-informed person with their personal agenda. They are entitled to their opinion, but their views don't wash with me.

'The fact that there were no international windows in the A-League during the Phoenix's first season meant there were clashes, and that gave the negative ones some ammunition. It wasn't the club's fault, it wasn't New Zealand Football's fault, and it wasn't my fault. That was the system at the time and we had to work within it.

'The main thing is that we've got the first part of the job done on the international front, and we are within two games of qualifying for the World Cup finals. It is going to be hard and demanding, but we have the chance to do it and I'm delighted to be in that position. At the same time, the Phoenix is getting bigger and better all the time.

'If anything, the speculation about me doing the two jobs only made me more determined to do both well. When you truly believe in something, you have to go all the way with it.

'I admit I was tempted at times to say a few things back to those doing the criticizing, but football in New Zealand has it tough enough as it is. It bewilders me that we celebrate very little of our success, but some people appear to enjoy seeing others fail. I won't be the Phoenix or All Whites coach forever, but when I finish I won't be bagging the game or the people in it. I'll have my opinions, but I will keep them to myself. The last thing the game needs is another critic.'

On a more positive note, the short-, medium- and long-term targets set during those seven days in London before the game against Australia had been ticked off. More games had been secured, the All Whites had qualified out of Oceania for the Confederations Cup, and credibility had been gained while on a European tour in May–June 2006.

The All Whites played Hungary, Georgia, Estonia and Brazil. While the players would undoubtedly rate the game against a full-strength Brazilian side that was playing its only warm-up game for the World Cup finals as the highlight, the most important, results-wise, was the 3–1 victory over Georgia. It was New Zealand's first international success on European soil, and the All Whites backed that performance up with a 1–1 draw against Estonia in Tillin. In Geneva, Brazil beat New Zealand 4–0 with their final two goals coming in the last five minutes.

'Beating Georgia was a milestone and we didn't have some of our top players available. The volume of games on that trip was great. Normally, we end up playing one-off games as we did against Wales at Wrexham in May 2007.

'One person who would be more pleased than most that we managed to get that game is Shane Smeltz. Shane was in a dilemma about whether he should play or trial for a Hyundai A-League club as he had planned. I persuaded him to go to Wrexham and he scored both our goals in a 2–2 draw. There was immediately a lot of talk about different clubs wanting to sign him. As I was recruiting for the Phoenix's first season, I was keen for him to join us in Wellington. He did and was an immediate success in the A-League. Who knows what would have happened had he stayed in Australia to trial? He may have got picked up by a club, maybe not. The Wales game was definitely a defining moment in Shane's career.

'That night against Wales, Ben Sigmund also made an impression in the way he performed against Craig Bellamy and Robbie Earnshaw, two pacy strikers with loads of English Premier League experience. Siggy is now at the Phoenix and is one of our most consistent players.

'Those are the things I prefer to dwell on when I think about the All Whites, rather than listen to a lot of the negative stuff that is bandied around.'

THE DEVIL'S ADVOCATE

No account of Ricki Herbert's life would be complete without mention of his relationship with former Mount Wellington and New Zealand team-mate Brian Turner. During the 1982 World Cup campaign, the coaching duo of John Adshead and Kevin Fallon were often referred to as 'the odd couple'. Spend a few days in the company of Herbert and Turner and you could be forgiven for thinking you had gone back in time and were listening to legendary English comedy duo Morecambe and Wise.

The banter between the pair starts before training at the Wellington Phoenix's Newtown Park training ground, and is still going long after the players have showered and returned to their families. There are people who would cringe at some of the things they say to each other, but those who know them well simply smile and let them carry on.

They each obviously take it all in their stride because, according to Brian, there has only been one major falling out between the pair over the past 26 years: 'It was while we were away with the New Zealand team. I took offence at something he said and got upset. For 48 hours we didn't speak to each other, which did neither of us any good. I don't know if anyone noticed we'd had this lovers' tiff, but I know it wasn't very pleasant. The day before the game, I was on the park preparing for training and was still upset. I saw he was coming towards me and began to walk away, but he caught up with me, put his arm around my shoulders and apologized for what he had said. That was the end of it. There are times when I say something he doesn't like and he walks off in a tiff, but that was the only major thing I can remember. Once in over a quarter of a century isn't bad, is it?'

In many ways, they are as different as chalk and cheese. While Ricki will always try to present a measured argument, often couching his words so as not to offend, Brian will just say what he thinks and if you don't like it . . . well, tough. When it comes to working with players on the training pitch, Ricki is in his element, while Brian appears uncomfortable until he feels his way into a session. Ricki is a south Auckland boy, whereas Brian was born in England at Plaistow, a few hundred yards from West Ham Football Club's Upton Park ground, to a New Zealand mother, Irene, and English father, Tom.

Brian's parents had met during the war when serviceman Tom was in New Zealand, and had settled in England after marrying. However, England wasn't Irene's cup of tea, so the family set off for New Zealand on the vessel *Rangitata*.

That could easily have been the end of any lofty footballing ambitions for young Brian, had he not crossed paths with Ken Armstrong, a former Chelsea player who became a legend in New Zealand football. When Armstrong saw Brian playing for Mount Roskill Grammar School, he told Irene and Tom that their son was good enough to try his luck in English professional football. Always one to back up his words with action, Armstrong organized a trial for Brian with Chelsea, and the youngster impressed enough to earn himself a contract with the famous English club.

For four years he plied his trade in England, mainly with Brentford, the club he joined from Chelsea, and played 100 Football League games before returning home in 1972 and joining Mount Wellington.

That was where, in 1980, he first met a young, enthusiastic Ricki, keen to soak up any footballing knowledge that came his way. Brian had plenty of that to offer. Besides playing a century of league games in England, he had been playing for New Zealand since making his international debut on 5 November 1967 against Australia in the unlikely setting of Vietnam's Cong Hua Stadium in Saigon.

When Ricki made his first appearance for the All Whites against Mexico in 1980, Brian was his roommate, and a friendship was born that has stood the test of time. Let Brian take up the story:

'We have a relationship that has developed over the years. I think it is more than a friendship, and there is a lot of respect between us.

'When he asked me to join him with the Olympic team, I didn't have to think twice on the football front, but there were a few difficulties outside the game. Even so, I took the job, though it meant making sacrifices. I held a reasonably important position in a national company. They were understanding of my role and position in football, but they were never willing to allow me just to take time off whenever I wanted. Every time there was a trip away with a New Zealand team, I had to use annual leave, and you only have so much annual leave to use before it runs out. In the end, I had to miss some trips. The company was supportive but they played it down the line as well.

'There was also my family to consider. After the World Cup finals in 1982, I promised my wife, Liz, that that was it; the end of my involvement in football . . . Until Ricki came along and asked me to help with the Olympic team, it was. With me working full-time as well, it would have been understandable had Liz not been keen on me joining him, but she has never questioned me getting back into football, because she knows how much I enjoy it and what a buzz I get out of it.

'I would have also loved to say "yes" when Ricki asked me to join him at the Phoenix as he and Terry Serepisos were getting the club up and running. Had the club been based in Auckland, I would have agreed immediately and left my job. But going to Wellington meant moving my wife, kids and animals, not to mention selling the house. It really wasn't on, but it was a hard decision because I knew Ricki needed support and that was why he was asking me.

'When he asked me again to become part of his team at the Phoenix during their second season, my personal circumstances had changed. I was in the process of being made redundant and would soon be looking for something to do. It also came at a time when my sons, Steven and Daniel, were working, and my daughter, Anna, was at university. The other thing was that, in the role he was talking about, I could commute rather than move everything down to Wellington. I talked it through with Liz and she said if that was what I wanted, to go ahead and do it. Liz has been 100 per cent supportive. It isn't the easiest thing to cope with, because I'm down in Wellington four or five days a week, but I would be a liar if I said I don't enjoy the involvement.

'It is different watching the games from the bench rather than on television, and a damn sight more nerve-wracking once you are totally involved. Things are obviously totally different to when I was playing. Today's professional footballers just turn up, play football and go home. Everything possible is provided for them. From outside, you think you know what happens in a football club, but when you get involved and see the time people spend making sure everything is in place for the players to do their job, it is mind-boggling. The attention to detail someone like [technical analyst] Wayne O'Sullivan shows has blown me away. The players are so damn lucky to have someone like him around, and I know they respect what he does and respond to it.

'The environment around the dressing room at a football club is good because there is usually a lot of banter, but there is also pressure on everyone to do well, especially in a competition like the Hyundai A-League which isn't easy to play in. When I was playing for Mount Wellington in the national league, you could look at the fixture list and say, "We'll beat this team and that team; that one might be a bit tougher . . .". It isn't like that in the A-League. You have to be on your game the whole time.'

What about the chemistry between them? Do they really argue a lot?

'Ricki might say we argue all the time. I prefer to say that I am playing devil's advocate, or challenging him to think about things in a different way. He does the same to me at times, so it is a two-way thing.

'What I offer Rick is that I don't always agree with him, and I believe he appreciates that. He knows I'm not going to say "yes" just because he's the boss. If he says something about a particular player that I disagree with, I tell him what my thoughts are. It gives him something to think about, but he is the one who ultimately makes the decisions.

'A classic example of that came about while we were talking about selecting a New Zealand team to play against Wales. Shane Smeltz's name came up as an option to play up front. I suggested to Rick that as he was only playing for Conference league side, Halifax Town, surely we needed to be looking at someone who was playing at a higher level and more likely to do the business. He said he heard what I was saying, but felt that as we had invested in Shane in the past through the under-20 and under-23 New Zealand teams, he should be given the chance to show he was up to it. The rest is history. He comes in, plays really well, scores both our goals in a 2–2 draw, and has gone on to be one of the stars of the A-League.

'When we are with people, Rick will often say, "Tell them the story about Shane Smeltz." I don't mind that, because it's a good story and it has a happy ending with a New Zealand boy making good.

'The other thing with Rick is that I have no ambitions to be the national coach or coach of the Phoenix. I know my place in the chain, and I think he appreciates that.

'Rick will tell you I am on the players' side all the time, and that he has to take that into account. That isn't quite right, but I think he can be harsh on the players, and there are times I have to remind him about how it was when we were playing. Sometimes I feel he gets a little unhappy with me when I do get close to the players.

'With the national team, I always try and position myself at the interface between the players, Rick and New Zealand Football. I am there as an ear for people if they want to talk about things. If they are not happy about the game, I'll talk to them, or if they are unhappy because they aren't playing . . . It doesn't matter what, I'll have a chat with them.

'Rick doesn't need players in his office every five minutes wanting to know why they aren't in the team. He trusts me and knows me well enough to know I will never say the wrong thing. I really believe he values that. I think he recognizes that sitting down and listening to people is not one of his greatest strengths. I'm not saying he wouldn't confront it, but I don't think it is something he likes to do.

'I've watched Rick grow from a young, enthusiastic player into someone who is a national coach and an A-League coach. I think it is a really good story.'

SALVAGE JOB AT THE KNIGHTS

When Chris Turner, in 1996, first mooted the idea of a New Zealand team playing in Australia's National Soccer League, the sceptics had a field day. Nowhere else in the professional footballing world was a team from one country playing in another country's competition. Of course Welsh clubs Swansea City (formerly Swansea Town) and Cardiff City were playing in the English Football League, but that was seen in a different light, with Wales being an integral part of Great Britain.

Surely FIFA, football's conservative world body, would never sanction an Auckland team, as proposed by Turner, playing in a competition over 2000 kilometres away across the Tasman Sea? Amazingly, FIFA did eventually give their blessing, and after three years of preparatory work, with help from the national football authorities on both sides of the Tasman, the Football Kingz took their place in a 16-team Australian NSL for the 1999–2000 season.

It had been far from plain sailing for Turner and his business partners, with even the original name of Football Kings having to be changed after threats of legal action from other sporting entities using the 'Kings' brand name.

Once up and running, the problems weren't over for the Kingz. They were always struggling to make their mark in the Australian competition, although there were encouraging signs with a first-season eighth placing in the 16-team competition. It was eighth again the following year, this time in a 14-team competition, but then the rot set in. Thirteenth of 13 in 2001–02, 11th of 13 in 2002–03 and 13th of 13 in 2003–4.

The on-field slump couldn't have come at a worse time, with Australia on the verge of replacing its national soccer league with a streamlined eight-team competition called the Hyundai A-League. The on-field form of the Kingz, along with dwindling crowd numbers, must have had the Australians wondering whether it was worth having a New Zealand franchise in the revamped competition. That the FFA gave the New Zealanders one of the coveted eight spots in the Hyundai A-League was a relief to those involved with the Kingz, but it was plain that there had to be changes.

The Auckland franchise was restructured and, after market research carried out by the club, it became known as the New Zealand Knights.

John Adshead, a national hero when he guided New Zealand into the 1982 World Cup finals, was the Knights' inaugural coach, but there was to be no fairy-tale this time for Adshead, as the Knights proved to be hopelessly out of their depth in their debut season. The Knights finished bottom of the table with a meagre six points, 20 behind seventh-placed Melbourne Victory, and with a one-win, three-draw and 17-loss record from their 21 games. That record cost John Adshead his job, although he resigned before he was pushed.

Englishman Paul Nevin took over as manager for the 2006–07

season, but, after 12 matches that brought only seven points from two wins, a draw and nine losses, he was relieved of the position. Things weren't much better when another English manager, Barry Simmonds, took over for four games. Two draws and two losses left the Knights anchored at the bottom of the table with nine points from 16 games.

In late October 2006, as a result of low crowd numbers at North Harbour Stadium and continual poor on-field performances, rumours began to circulate that Football Federation Australia was considering revoking the Knights' A-League licence and granting it to a new team for the following season. With five weeks of the season remaining, the rumours became reality when the FFA announced it had revoked the competition licence held by the Knights' owners.

At the same time, the FFA entered into an arrangement with New Zealand Soccer that would see the national body step in and manage the club for the remaining weeks of the regular season, with Ricki Herbert filling the role of head coach.

Ricki had watched the New Zealand franchise from the beginning. Indeed, in the early days, he did some television commentary work for Sky. As the Kingz evolved into the New Zealand Knights, he continued to follow their progress, either at the ground or on television, but not once did he express his opinion on the Knights in public.

'Why should I? At that time it had nothing to do with me. I was just there to watch the football. It wasn't for me to express an opinion. I didn't know the environment within the club, or the majority of the players. I didn't know the coaching staff either, apart from when John Adshead was there. It has always disappointed me when I see newspapers printing ill-informed information about football. It is easy for people on the outside to be critical, but, unless you really know how the club is operating — or not, for that matter — you are only looking on the surface. I've had experience of that kind of thing over the last 18 months at the Phoenix, with people making assumptions that are way off the mark.'

One aspect of the Kingz and Knights that Ricki is happy to pass comment on is how well Chris Turner and others did in getting the project off the ground.

'I don't know exactly who was involved, but to get a professional football club up and running and playing in another country's competition at a level as high as the A-League is fantastic. Chris Turner was obviously part of that, and, at the end of the day, had he and those around him not got the Football Kingz off the ground in the first instance, it is unlikely that the Phoenix would exist today.

'I can understand how tough it was to get the Kingz going and to later restructure it into the Knights franchise. Those involved were so enthusiastic, but unfortunately enthusiasm isn't enough, because it becomes very much a business venture and there are many realities to be faced.

'Eighteen months ago, I didn't have an insight into how a professional football club was run, never mind having to deal with things such as cash expectancy and budgets. During those 18 months, I've had to learn quickly because I have been involved in every facet of the Phoenix, not just coaching the team. That is how it is when you start something new, because everyone is feeling their way.'

When New Zealand Football chief executive Graham Seatter called Ricki into his office and asked if he would manage the Knights for the last five games of the 2006–07 season, Ricki asked for time to think it over.

'I remember Graham saying it wouldn't be like a normal coaching job. It was just a case of getting the club through five games and that would be it. Perhaps he had a point, but when I sat at home that night thinking things through, I realized there was a lot more to it than that. At the end of the day, the team would be playing, with me at the helm, with people watching.

'What did influence me was that the most important thing, ultimately, was to try to keep professional football in New Zealand. The chances of that happening, given the circumstances the Knights found themselves in, seemed pretty remote, but, as the old saying goes, where there is life, there is hope — so I decided to give it a go.'

Reading the newspapers and listening to the radio, Ricki must have wondered what he had let himself in for. It was hard to know exactly what had been going on within the club over the previous two seasons. There were all sorts of stories appearing in the newspapers, such as the players not being paid. Ricki quickly discovered the magnitude of the task he had been given.

'I had been on the outside looking in, but the first day I went to the club I saw for myself what an absolute shambles it was. The FFA and their legal advisers were there, thanks to all sorts of contractual agreements needing to be sorted out. I could understand the concerns of those involved, especially the players who were essentially being told that the club was about to fold and that they would be out of a job.

'That first day, I attended one of the meetings between the FFA and the players, but I didn't open my mouth. How could I when I hadn't a clue what had been going on? I just sat and listened. While I was listening to the reasons for decisions being explained, I was also thinking that the most pressing thing so far as I was concerned had to be how to get a team on the field a few days later to play against Melbourne Victory in Australia. I spent some time with the FFA trying to patch a team together, because, thanks to the contractual problems the players were having, they weren't keen to play. They were hanging tough as a group, and the FFA began arranging for Australian players from the state leagues to come in and fill any void.

'It was a very sensitive time, and, having played professionally myself, I could really understand where the players were coming from. That was why I distanced myself from any negotiations that were going on. My job was to get a team on the park and help it play the best it could. I could do nothing about what had happened in the past. There was no doubt that the job ahead of us was difficult. None of the current Knights players were going to play, so we rung round and began getting some players from outside.

'We still needed some of the Knights lads, though. I didn't know many of the players, but I drew up a list of positions and the players who I thought could fill them. The players had organized a meeting at one of their houses, and I went there to address them in the morning. We were due to fly to Melbourne later in the day. I read out the list of players I had selected to travel, and told them I would be at the airport and hoped I would see them there.

'That done, I went home, got my gear and headed for the airport with Colin Tuaa, who was also a full-time New Zealand Football employee and was going to assist me with the coaching. The finance director, Pete Elderkin, also travelled to help manage the team. That was how quickly we had to throw things together.

'Once at the airport, I got a telephone call to say all the players were on their way to join me. It was quite a big news story, so there was plenty of media around, and when the players arrived they told the FFA they all wanted to travel. That wasn't possible, though, as all the bookings had been done and the plane was fully booked.

'In the end, most of those who took the field were Knights players, but they were supplemented by youngsters such as Steve O'Dor, who came from a state league, and young Canterbury boy Jeremy Brown, who was playing in Australia for Green Gully. They were waiting for us when we arrived at the hotel, and, not knowing them from a bar of soap, I probably walked past them a couple of times before we got together.

'We squeezed in a team meeting where I announced the lineup we had patched together, and then set off for a short training session on an AstroTurf pitch. That was our preparation for a game against Melbourne Victory, who would go on to win the regular season competition by 12 points and the grand final 6–0 against second-placed Adelaide United.

'It was hardly ideal, but you wouldn't have thought that there had been so many problems the way we began the game. For the first 30 minutes we were doing really well. Ten minutes later we were 4–0 down. Luckily there were no more goals in the second half. For me, it was a tough introduction to the A-League, and after the game I made a conscious decision about how we would approach things from that point.

'We played Melbourne on 17 December, and didn't play again until our home game against Queensland Roar on the 29th. I let it be known, through the senior Knights players who had travelled, that I didn't want to see the players again until Boxing Day. I wanted to give them time to work through what had happened, and when we did come together again it would be in a football environment.

'Come Boxing Day, everyone turned up for training. I had also invited some youngsters from Auckland City and Waitakere to help with numbers, so that I could play 11-v-11 and see for myself what the players had to offer. That was the first time we did anything from a structural point of view.

'We fitted in three training sessions before the game, and I couldn't have asked for anything more from the players as we beat Queensland 3–1. People said complimentary things about me, but it was all down to the players. They were great. Less than two weeks earlier everything had come crashing down around them, and here they were in a completely different mindset, comprehensively beating a team that went on to beat champions Melbourne and second-placed Adelaide before drawing with fourth-placed Sydney in their last three games.

'That period between the first and second games had given us time to regroup; and it showed when we went on the road for two games, beating Sydney 1–0 and drawing with Central Coast

Mariners 0–0. We finished the season by beating Perth Glory 2–0 in our last game at home. That left us one point away from the second-to-last placed team, whereas five weeks before we had been 10 points adrift.

'Things flowed nicely in those few weeks I had with the Knights, but even then it was obvious some people were going to be difficult to handle. Some of the players accepted in a more professional manner than others that there was nothing I could do so far as their contracts were concerned; so that was the group I worked with, choosing not to work with those who walked around looking like ticking time bombs.

'During those final few weeks, I believe the Knights went a little way to regaining some credibility, and that was what perhaps persuaded the FFA to consider retaining a New Zealand club in the competition.

'Looking back, I think there was always the intention to have a little bit of time to try and make it work. Why else would the FFA's Rob Abernathy be seconded to help me get through that first game against Melbourne? He was tremendous, and I have a lot to thank Rob for. He made it a smooth process in very difficult circumstances when it must have been difficult for him, too. I believe there was genuine concern about what was going to happen now that the Knights' playing licence had been revoked. The FFA undoubtedly had many things to think about, including such things as television rights that would have been covered by a contract. They had to find a way for the Knights to complete the season.

'When the season ended, I think the players in some small way were proud of what they had achieved over those last five games. They had got some credibility back, and it was nice to see smiles on faces after what I had seen when I first walked in — even though there was still uncertainty surrounding their future, with some of their contracts running longer than the season that had just finished.

'For me, though, it was a case of job done and time to go back to what I was doing at New Zealand Football. Obviously I had no inkling that things would turn out the way they did with the Phoenix. There were always going to be discussions about a potential new Kiwi franchise, and, if the right circumstances presented themselves, it seemed likely there would be a good possibility that they would retain a New Zealand presence. If those five weeks contributed to that, fantastic. If it helped my coaching career as well, I am grateful.'

THE PHOENIX RISES

There can be little doubt that the five weeks Ricki spent with the New Zealand Knights, along with the results that he and the players achieved, influenced Football Federation Australia when it came to deciding who would take over the revoked playing licence.

Given the nature of the Knights' implosion, no-one could have blamed the Australians had they decided enough was enough and handed the vacant place in the Hyundai A-League to one of the Aussie consortiums keen to take over from the Auckland franchise. The problem for the FFA was that the potential Australian franchises waiting in the wings would have found it just as difficult to get a team up and running in the necessary timeframe as appeared to be the case across the Tasman.

However, once the last rites had been performed on the Knights, it didn't take long for passionate Kiwi football people to initiate talks about forming franchises to keep the licence in

New Zealand. Bids from Palmerston North, Wellington and Auckland were quickly on the move. Each was enthusiastic and able to prepare ambitious proposals, but the one thing each was missing was the upfront cash injection the FFA was demanding. At one point, those involved with the Palmerston North and Wellington bids discussed joining together in a bid, but that didn't work out either. Auckland dropped out, citing lack of time to prepare a business plan, but when the FFA granted New Zealand Football, which was handling the Kiwi bids, an extension, it re-entered the race. The Australians were giving New Zealand every chance to stay in the high-profile A-League, with FFA chief executive Ben Buckley and A-League head of operations Matt Carroll doing everything they could to assist those making the bids.

Throughout the bidding process, the proposal put forward by Wellington football identities Ian Wells and John Dow appeared to have the best chance of success. For weeks, Wells and Dow worked tirelessly in the hope that the seven-figure sum the FFA was demanding upfront could be met. The pair was convinced they could raise the amount required, but not as the FFA wanted — in cash.

As Wells and Dow were coming to terms with the fact that they would not be able to meet the FFA conditions, Wellington property developer Terry Serepisos was heading to the barber's for a haircut. As the barber clipped away, Serepisos heard a radio announcer bemoaning the fact that professional football was about to be lost to New Zealand because no-one could come up with the $1.2 million guarantee being sought by the FFA. Before most people knew what was happening, Serepisos met with those behind Wellington's bid, went through the process of applying for the licence with New Zealand Football, came up with the cheque, and the rest, as they say, is history.

Thanks to Serepisos, Wellington now had a professional football club, at least on paper.

Through those traumatic weeks, Ricki was, along with other Kiwi football fans, little more than an interested spectator. He had been sounded out by one of the bidders to see if he was interested in coaching the team should they be successful, but, knowing how difficult it would be for anyone to meet the FFA's conditions, he didn't want to get his hopes up.

'There was uncertainty throughout that period. There would be high expectations one day, then it would drop away before being resurrected a few days later as whatever bid tried to regain its momentum. I didn't have any sort of involvement with those mentioned as potential franchise-holders, apart from one or two really brief conversations with prospective interests. Looking back, New Zealand Football and the FFA were probably working together to try and save a New Zealand franchise, and thank goodness they were.

'It is crystal-ball gazing now, but my gut feeling is that, had the licence been given to an Australian team, New Zealand would never have got a team back into the A-League. I'm sure there were people who didn't realize the risk, but it would have been devastating for New Zealand football had that happened.

'One of my main reasons for taking a chance with the Knights was to hopefully keep pro football here. It helped buy prospective Kiwi replacements some time and, thankfully, everything turned out all right in the end.

'I knew nothing about Terry's involvement until everything was agreed. As far as I was concerned, it came right out of the blue and I had never met him until Graham Seatter took me for coffee with him at Sky City. From the start I liked him, and as we have continued working together our relationship has become stronger.

'Once we got through all the legal stuff that day at Sky City, the reality of what we had taken on hit home. We had to get a professional football club up and running within four months. The club had nothing, and I mean nothing — not even footballs or goals! Now that is really starting from scratch. It was vital we got our priorities sorted out very quickly. Staff had to be employed, players recruited. We had to work with the Wellington City Council, who were fantastic, to locate facilities we could use.

'Murray Naylor, who had been aligned with Terry in business, came on board to take care of the financial side of things. He took myself and Kale out on his boat, which was moored in Gulf Harbour, so we could get away from everyone and start planning what we had to do. There was a budget of x amount of dollars, and we needed x number of players. How were we going to bring the two together? Making it even more difficult was the fact that there was no-one involved who had experience of running a football club. Not that we got away from everyone that day on Gulf Harbour. It was within cellphone range and we were taking calls from player agents in Australia and America.

'It was incredible. The dimensions of putting a squad together from scratch were huge. Of course, as All Whites coach, I knew the New Zealand boys and which ones might fit the criteria and be willing to come, but we needed a lot more than them.

'There was just over three months before the team was to play its first game, so we had to move fast. There were some good decisions made regarding players, and perhaps some not-so-good ones. Thankfully, generally speaking, I think the people who mattered understood just how hard a job we had.

'During those weeks, my life was in turmoil. It was like operating in a tornado. Facilities weren't locked in; we were trying to organize training gear which was something my Dad, who had experience as a kit man, came down from Auckland to help with. We were still trying to fill the roster, and didn't know when players we signed would arrive.

'Despite all that, I wouldn't say I didn't enjoy it. In fact, I'm pleased I went through it. Would I want to go through it again? I don't know. What I do know is that we were grateful to the FFA for loaning us Michelle Phillips as acting CEO in those early days. It was another sign of how keen they were for us to do things right.'

During that period it was fortunate that Ricki was staying in one of Terry Serepisos's apartments, a stone's throw from the club's new offices on the 14th floor of the ASB Building, which was also home to Serepisos' Century City Developments.

Home for the rest of the Herbert family — wife Raewyn, and twins, Kale and Sacha — was still in Auckland, which wasn't the ideal scenario, but one that couldn't be avoided in those first few months.

'It was difficult for Raewyn, even though she has always understood what being involved with football is like and where a job in the game could take me.

'When it came to the kids, Kale and Sacha, it was different. Looking back now, I realize it is a period of their lives I have missed out on, albeit five or six months. They would come down or I would go up to Auckland at weekends, but it wasn't the same as being with them all the time, sharing their thoughts and aspirations. At the time, they were 14. Sacha was going to Corran School in Remuera, where she felt comfortable, and Kale was attending King's College, a school he loved. When they moved down to Wellington, it would be fair to say that Kale was a little more comfortable about it than Sacha, so it wasn't easy for her. Unfortunately, that is the industry I am working in.

'I'm not sure where it came from, but there was a perception in some quarters that I was reluctant to move my home from Auckland. I am an Auckland boy who has lived there all my life, apart from the periods when I was playing in England and Australia, so of course I enjoyed living there. Would it have been different had someone rung and offered me a coaching job in Singapore? That is my life and a decision would have to have been made. Moving to Wellington was never going to be a problem. It's a lot easier to nip back to Auckland to see my family from there than from Singapore or Europe.

'I'd never spent time in Wellington before. I had always flown in with whatever team I was playing for, played the game, gone to the after-match function and flown home. Living in Auckland, you tend to think of Wellington as wet and windy, but in my first year with the Phoenix I found that definitely wasn't the case. During pre-season training in particular, the Wellington weather was sensational. I can remember people teasing Vince Lia that he was working on his tan when he was being treated for an injury alongside the training pitch at Centennial Park.'

Not that Ricki's family would have seen much of him had they been in Wellington during those hectic first few months. Most of his day, and many evenings, was spent on the telephone at the ASB Building, talking to player agents.

Curriculum vitae from those agents flowed across Ricki's desk, one of which was of Wayne O'Sullivan, known affectionately throughout football as 'Sully'. Born in Akrotiri, Cyprus, to Irish parents, Sully had just spent two seasons in the A-League with Central Coast Mariners after a solid professional career in England with league clubs Swindon Town, Cardiff City and Plymouth Argyle. The road to Australia had begun with the family being evacuated when Turkey invaded Cyprus. They'd settled in England, and football became Sully's life.

Sully had joined Swindon on schoolboy forms as a 12-year-old, and, with the type of loyalty he has shown throughout his career, stayed with the Wiltshire club despite moving to the Midlands with his parents, Victor and Eleanor. While there, he trained with other clubs and could have signed youth forms with Derby County, Stoke City or Port Vale. He stuck with Swindon, because by this time the youth team coach was John Trollope, who had been his first coach at the club. Trollope was a Swindon legend, having played 770 games for the club over a 20-year period, 368 of them consecutively. That run only ended when he broke his arm in a match against Hartlepool United.

From the time he joined Swindon as a kid, Sully saw some

well-known coaches come and go at the club, including Argentine World Cup winner Ossie Ardiles, England star Glenn Hoddle, and Liverpool legend Steve McMahon.

It was McMahon who eventually ended Sully's association with the club.

'The club changed when McMahon arrived,' Sully remembers. 'For a start it stopped being the family-type club it had always been. He brought a lot of good things on a professional level, but I had some problems with the way he managed the players. He was player-manager at Swindon and I played alongside him in the midfield, which was a great experience, but towards the end he made life difficult for me. The writing was on the wall when he stopped me training with the first team, when I had been a regular. Then I found myself training with the youth team, then on my own, and finally I was told I wasn't allowed on the training ground. That was when I decided I had to get out. There is only so much you can take.

'One good thing Steve did for me was to organize an opportunity to play for the Republic of Ireland. It was quite weird the way it happened, because Wales originally approached me. It seems I was eligible for them because I had a British passport and had been born outside Britain in a British Sovereignty. Amazing. The only country I wanted to play for was Ireland, and, when Steve heard what had happened, he got in touch with the Irish Football Association. A month later I was playing the first of three games for the Republic's under-21 side. Apparently they hadn't realized I was Irish, although I thought the name O'Sullivan might have given them a clue!'

The next two seasons were spent at Cardiff, followed by two years with Plymouth Argyle. It was during his time at Plymouth that he got a call from someone linked to Dave Mitchell, a senior player at Swindon during Sully's youth-team days. Mitchell was now coaching Parramatta Power in Australia's National Soccer League and had been talking to another former Swindon player, Martin Ling, head coach at Leyton Orient. Mitchell was lamenting the fact that he'd had a bad experience with a couple of English players he'd brought to Australia. The players had done all right financially, but hadn't delivered on the field.

'Dave didn't want to get his fingers burnt a second time, and was looking for someone reliable. Apparently my name came up as the type of player and person who may have been what he was looking for,' says Sully. 'For some reason the idea appealed to me. It was at a time in my life when I thought a different lifestyle in a different country might be what I was looking for. Plymouth had offered me a new contract, but it was nothing flash. Just another deal, nothing amazing, so I told our manager Paul Sturrock that I was going to Australia. He laughed and wished me luck.

'It was a radical decision for me, because it meant leaving the family, Mum and Dad in particular. That was tough because they had followed me everywhere throughout my career. Whether it was the youth team, reserve team or first team, they were at every game. Now here I was off to Australia and they wouldn't be seeing me play anymore.

'I soon found out that the football in the old Australian NSL wasn't up to much. In all honesty it was rubbish, but Parramatta was a nice club that was trying to do things in a positive way, and Dave Mitchell, who had Lawrie McKinna as his assistant, was a good guy.'

After two seasons with Power, Sully moved on to Northern Spirit, and for once didn't land on his feet. 'They were difficult times but, despite that, it was players from Spirit that formed the nucleus of the Central Coast Mariners when the A-League began in 2005 with Lawrie McKinna as coach. It was Lawrie who set me up with a deal at Singapore's Geylang United between the NSL folding and the A-League starting.

'I didn't have a work permit at the time so needed to go somewhere to earn money. I went there with another Spirit player, Stewart Petrie. We had a great time. An Aussie guy, Scott

O'Donell, was coaching and tried to do everything professionally. He was probably a bit ahead of his time for Singapore, because the local players weren't ready for that. Stewart and I got on brilliantly with the locals, because we learnt quickly that you had to share their culture.

'It was in Singapore that I first met Andrew Durante, who went on to lead Newcastle Jets to the A-League title before joining the Wellington Phoenix. I got a call from Darren Burgess, who is now the Socceroos head sports scientist, asking me to look out for Dura who was just coming back from a broken leg. Dura had been in Singapore for three weeks and, to use Darren's words, was "suicidal" about life in Singapore, especially as he was at a club that was poorly run.

'We were playing Dura's team and I met him on the halfway line, introduced myself, and said to give me three weeks and I would change his mind about Singapore. We got on famously from that moment and had a really enjoyable time.'

Back in Australia, Sully enjoyed the first two A-League seasons with the Mariners, who lost the first grand final to Sydney FC. A popular figure with supporters, Sully was disappointed to be released by the Mariners at the end of the second season and was determined to find another A-League club where he could continue his career.

The fact that each club was allowed only four 'foreigners', and that Sully was still in the process of applying for residency in his adopted country, didn't make the task any easier. He put out feelers, and his agent began approaching clubs with a view to them employing his client. It was from that agent, Warren Craig, that Ricki first heard about Wayne O'Sullivan.

Around the same time, Sully received a call from *Sydney Morning Herald* reporter Mike Cockerill, suggesting he ring Ricki, who seemed to be a good guy and someone Cockerill thought Sully would get on with.

'I did ring Ricki, we chatted for quite a while and it wasn't long before I got a note, while on a coaching course, saying he had agreed to a one-year contract. While I would have liked a longer deal, I was happy to take anything at that point and see how things progressed. While I had started doing my coaching badges, I had no intention of retiring from playing.

'I didn't hear anything for a few weeks, so rang Ricki and found out there was a complication. He obviously hadn't picked up on my accent during our telephone conversation because he thought I was an Australian. The complication was that he had already signed four Brazilians, so his overseas player quota — and that was what I was — had already been filled.

'I realized that this was going to be my only opportunity to convince him I should be at his football club, so asked for that chance. Basically, he gave me five minutes on a soap box to talk about myself. That's never a nice, or easy, thing to do, but I thought *Desperate times call for desperate measures*, so I went for it. Part of selling myself was that I had started my coaching courses; had done my B Licence and a degree in coach education. I told him I had gone down that path because I was determined to be successful and thought I could make a difference. It was as much about helping younger players as myself. I wanted the game to move forward in this part of the world and wanted to be part of that.'

Those five minutes must have made an impression on Ricki, because a few days later he asked if Sully would fly over to Wellington to meet him and talk further. Sully didn't need to be asked twice. Tell him when and he would be on the plane. 'Day after tomorrow OK?' Ricki asked. 'See you then,' said Sully.

'When I put the phone down and told my fiancée, Renee, that I was off to Wellington to meet Ricki, she pointed out that my visa was almost up and that if I left Australia I wouldn't get back in. While I began to stress out, Renee, typically, calmly said I should go down to the immigration office the following day and sort it out. Everything would be fine. The office is situated in one of the busiest parts of Sydney where it is almost impossible to get a car park, and I drove around for ages before spotting a space. It was in a one-way street and I couldn't go that way. I was so desperate that I reversed up the street. The immigration office can be a nightmare and, sure enough, there was a monster line for visas and a shorter one for general enquiries. I tried my luck at the short one and, from that point, everything fell into place. Within 30 minutes I had the visa.

'Chuffed to bits with my success, I rang Renee as I walked back to the car. "I told you it would work out," she said. I was still chatting to her when I turned into the street where the car was parked. "You're not going to believe this, Renee, but I've parked in Wellington Street!" If that wasn't a sign that I was doing the right thing, I don't know what would be. It was a done deal. Didn't really need to get on the plane, did I?'

When Sully arrived in Wellington, Ricki showed him around the club's offices and the stadium. The pair seemed to get on really well.

'Ricki then said it might come as a bit of a shock, but he wanted me to join the Phoenix as a coach rather than a player. He realized it was a big decision and told me to go away and think about it. I said that wouldn't be necessary. My life had been all about taking opportunities; my football career had spanned 16 years; I'd had a fantastic time, loved every minute of it; if this was to be the start of the next 16 years, it was an opportunity I couldn't turn down. All I wanted was a chance to call Renee and make sure she was happy with the move. I made the call, and it was all over in five minutes.'

Ricki remembers those telephone conversations well.

'Wayne rang me several times and he was always very professional in the way he went about things. I was sitting at home alone one night going through things in my mind, and suddenly decided that I would go left-field on this one. I thought, *I was like that once. Young and just starting out in coaching. Bloody hell, what an opportunity for someone like that.* With the club being new, I thought it needed new, vibrant, enthusiastic people like Wayne involved.

'I know he was surprised when I put it to him that I wanted him on the coaching staff, but his response was really positive. As time has progressed, it has proved to be one of my good decisions. This year, the Phoenix's second, has been an exceptional one for him. There were issues the first year, but I think there were always going to be teething problems. I didn't know the guy, and I think in coaching it is fair to say that there is strength around knowing your staff, and it took me a while to really get to know Wayne.'

That Ricki decided to go left-field is something Sully is grateful for, and realizes what a gamble it was for someone starting out in his first professional head-coach job. 'There had to be a reason I was there at this stage of my life. I just didn't know what it was,' he says. 'Ricki didn't know me; didn't really know anything about me. He thought I was Australian for a start! He took a punt on me. It is a big risk to take with your own life when you bring someone you know little about into the equation. There was no risk for me, other than convincing my wife-to-be to go to New Zealand. That wasn't hard, as Renee has jumped on board and supported me as always. It was Ricki who took the risk, and I was determined he would never regret it.'

Sully certainly hasn't regretted it.

'I've loved it. It was different. It was testing, especially the first four months. I had an idea what getting a new club up and running was like, because I had seen it up close with the Mariners. The big difference was that the Phoenix had come in behind the eight ball and only had a few months to do it, whereas the other A-League clubs had almost two years.

'I was driving around in a little hire car with balls hanging out the back. Everything we had was in the back of that little car. I would pick up Paul [Emanuel, fitness coach] early in the morning, collect the laundry, and get to the training ground where we would lay out the kit. Evenings were spent folding kit and planning training sessions with Ricki.

'At one point, Ricki had to go away with the New Zealand team, and [assistant coach] Stu Jacobs was away with the national under-20s. I was left with a bunch of players the same age as me and I had never done it before. The players were amazing. It was the kind of situation that wouldn't work in many places and with many players, but the help and support I got from senior players, like Ross Aloisi, Vaughan Coveny, Michael Ferrante, Karl Dodd and Tim Brown, helped me get through those first few months. I've never had any major issues with the players. Obviously you get challenged from time to time because you're young, but it's something I've never really had to deal with.

'I've not gone out of my way to be anything other than who I am. I did find it difficult at times, because it was so easy being a player. Then it is just about being yourself. It is easy to be popular as a player in a team, but you are not always popular as a coach, especially as a young coach. All of a sudden you can't hang out with the lads, can't hang out socially in bars; you aren't part of that. I also felt that someone in the role I was now in had a responsibility to set standards.

'The first year was very much a learning curve for all those on the management team, but it was a really good bunch and we got through it. At times it was brilliant, but also very challenging.

'After two seasons, I believe the Phoenix are ahead of where the Mariners were in most things at the same time. They were more successful on the field because there was a nucleus of a team that had come from where they had developed a culture; the personalities were there. The team was made up of people who had been successful in Australia and had all come from similar types of background.

'The difference at the Phoenix was that in that first year we had 23 different personalities from different places in the team. There was a new coaching staff; it was a strange city for most, which meant people getting into accommodation and waiting for their families to arrive. In the circumstances, I think we did really well.'

The other members of the Phoenix coaching staff for its first season in the Hyundai A-League were New Zealand under-20s coach Stu Jacobs and goalkeeping coach Chris Pile. The fact that both lived in Wellington was part of the reason Ricki took them on board. With time at a premium, it was always going to be an advantage when someone lived in Wellington, because it avoided the logistical hassles associated with relocation.

'When I first spoke to Stu, I was envisaging having him on the coaching staff full-time. At that point he had the New Zealand under-20s, was helping me with the All Whites, and was involved with the Ole Academy. He was also about to become Team Wellington coach in the New Zealand Football Championship. It was Stu who made the decision to be part-time with the Phoenix. In retrospect, it should have been full-time or nothing. It was different with Brian Turner in our second season as he was not coaching. Rather he was on board as a consultant. Stu's involvement ended for a number of reasons.

'That first year had so many complications, and the fact that so many people were new, it was always going to take time to bed things down. Players, some I knew better than others, were new to the club, and from a personal point of view it was a great learning curve. I have my own personality. I bring things to the table in my way. I don't change to meet other people's needs or views. That is the way I operate. Others operate differently and that is what it is all about.

'New relationships take time to develop. People either like and follow the direction you are taking; sometimes they don't. You don't have that situation at an established professional club. Anyone joining an established club has to fit in with what is already there.'

Chris Pile was with Liverpool from 1984 to 1987, and was

a regular in the reserve side without making any first-team appearances. At that time, English domestic football allowed no substitute goalkeepers, but it was a different story in European competition. Injuries to second- and third-choice keepers, Bob Wardle and Bob Bolder, meant 18-year-old Pile, the club's fourth-choice keeper, found himself on the bench as cover for Bruce Grobbelaar for the 1985 European Cup-final loss to Juventus. Injury ended his professional career prematurely, and he eventually settled in New Zealand after originally arriving to play for Waterside Karori in 1988.

'The goalkeeping role was always going to be on a part-time basis, with whoever filled it working with the keepers once or twice a week and doing the warm-up before home games. It isn't easy to find someone who can fit that in with their employment, but Chris was able to.'

When it came to finding someone for the sports science role, the Phoenix advertised at home and overseas. 'The CV we got from Paul Emanuel was done in a way that made me think I wouldn't mind knowing a bit more about him. We got in touch, and he showed how keen he was by offering to pay his own way from Australia to take the matter further. He made an impressive presentation at our offices and that, along with his infectious, upbeat personality, led to us taking him on.

'I was pleased to have Paul on the staff but, for several reasons, his role became complicated for him. That was caused in part because, being a new club, there wasn't a strong infrastructure. 'There were expectations on everyone within the club to go outside their boundaries of expertise, and at times that can be detrimental if someone isn't comfortable doing so. That gives others the chance to challenge them, but it isn't the individual's fault.

'To move on, I think the club needed someone who had a broader range of delivery football-wise. Paul's background was in personal training, one-on-one with people. It is different in a team environment where the dynamics are broken at times. That happens when you have 23 different opinions as opposed to spending a lot of time with one person building a relationship.

'There were also family reasons for Paul moving back to Australia at the end of our first season, but I valued Paul's support. He was a good guy to have around, and was instrumental in getting the season operational. That was important.

'It was the same with Craig Newland, our first physiotherapist. I met Craig one night in an Irish bar in Wellington. His friend came over to talk football and introduced me to Craig. You could tell straight away he was a football guy through and through. He was young and enthusiastic, but a little quiet. Once he got a bit of confidence with the players, who can be testing and trying at times, he came out of his shell. Craig did a good job but he was still learning and, for our second season, we were looking for someone with more experience for a head of medical services role.'

Craig Newland remembers the night he met Ricki. Well, he did eventually. 'To be honest, me and my mate had had quite a few beers when I noticed Ricki in the bar and pointed him out. My mate went over to chat and I joined them. I have no idea how it came up that I was a physio, but when Ricki heard that, he asked if I was looking for a job. Next morning, I found a napkin in my pocket with a mobile number and Ricki's name on it. I thought, *How the hell did I get this?* Then it all came back to me. I rang him, we set up a meeting at Terry Serepisos's office and it went from there.

'I was pretty lucky, in that I had only been qualified for 18 months. I had played football my whole life, so it was a dream job. I loved my time with the Phoenix and was disappointed I didn't get appointed for another season.'

Craig and his fiancée, Becks, are now doing their OE in England, and he would love to get a job with a professional club. 'I wouldn't mind where it was. You don't go looking for a job with a premiership club, but I would be willing to work anywhere, the Nationwide Conference or whatever. The A-League is getting more and more recognized overseas so having the Phoenix on my résumé won't do me any harm. My brother's friend was a physiotherapist with the England team and is now with Portsmouth, so maybe that will help in getting in to see how things operate in clubs over there.'

There was one spot on the backroom staff to be filled as the Phoenix prepared for their opening pre-season game against Sydney at Wellington's Westpac Stadium, that of kit man, or gear steward, as the Australians call it.

I — Russell Gray, co-author of this book and a sports journalist for over 20 years — had known Ricki since the 1981–82 World Cup campaign when I covered the finals in Spain for Wellington's *The Dominion* newspaper. Upon *The Dominion* and *Evening Post* amalgamating to form *The Dominion Post*, I had taken the redundancy package on offer and headed for the golf course.

When the possibility of a Wellington franchise being accepted in the A-League was raised, I was more than a little sceptical, especially after seeing how poorly the Knights had performed. Once it eventuated, however, I had no inkling of how the new club would change my life. The only thought I had at the time was that it would be good to catch up with Ricki again. Once he moved to Wellington, we arranged to meet up for a drink at the Leuven pub in Featherston Street, where we spent the evening reminiscing about past adventures and downing one or two Stella Artois.

A few weeks later, Ricki rang to say I owed him a meal and that we should meet up again at the same pub. I found a Stella Artois waiting. 'I've got a job for you,' Ricki said. 'Before you finish that beer I want to know if you will be the Phoenix kit man.' Not a drop passed my lips before the deal was settled with a handshake. As far as I was concerned, the details could be sorted out later. I was now part of a professional football club and could wear my heart on my sleeve, unlike 20-odd years of trying to be objective as a reporter.

The objectivity part is something Ricki will dispute, forever reminding me what a one-eyed Wellingtonian I was. 'We [Mount Wellington] would fly in, win 5–0, and read next day in *The Dominion* how unlucky Miramar or Wellington United had been,' was his usual jibe.

The rest of the night became something of a blur as we went to Paul Emanuel's apartment to meet him and his wife, Alison. Sully and Renee were also there, along with a recently signed player, Richard Johnson, and his wife, Vanessa. We finished up in Courtenay Place at around 2 a.m. I rang my wife, Barbara, who was waiting for a call to come and pick me up. 'Don't worry, I'll get a cab. And by the way I've got a job with the Phoenix.' Now she knew I'd had too much to drink!

To say the job came out of the blue is an understatement, but it turned out to be as good as anything that had happened to me during a lifetime involved in sport.

Mind you, the perception I had of the kit man's job simply being to lay out the training or playing gear and then get it washed once the session was over was well off the mark. That was just one part of a job that had wide-ranging responsibilities, but what fun it has become.

Those early days were crazy. The club provided me with a van, and for the next few months we literally lived out of the back of that Nissan Caravan as we became sporting nomads moving from one training venue to another. The people responsible for Wellington's sports grounds, and Trevor Jackson in particular, did everything they could to help us, but often had to move us to another training ground at late notice for various reasons.

We regularly moved between the Basin Reserve, Endeavour Park in Whitby, and Miramar's Centennial Park, and, because of the possibility of a late change, everything had to go in the van at the end of the day. Kelly Duxfield, the Phoenix's acting football operations manager, called the van Tardis because it was crammed with playing and training kit, balls, cones, medicine balls, poles and drink containers . . . if a football club needed it, the van had it. If anything could not be found, Kelly would ring and say it must be in the van. Invariably she was right — whatever was missing was usually found under a mountain of laundry or ball bags.

For the second season Newtown Park became our training base, where the Wellington City Council groundsmen did a marvellous job providing us with what is as good as any pitch in Wellington, Westpac Stadium excepted, of course.

Having a base made things much easier, but during those early days the players were fantastic. There were times when they could not have been blamed for having a moan. Perhaps they did mutter under their breath, or have a gripe among themselves, but the smiles and handshakes they greeted me with each morning were genuine.

There are times, as in any job, where things can go wrong, but they are soon forgotten when you are fortunate enough to be sitting on the Phoenix bench and listening to the best supporters in the league — Yellow Fever — roaring the team on.

Off the field, Football Federation Australia had provided Michelle Phillips to get the club going, but on 16 July 2007 Tony Pignata took over as the Phoenix's first chief executive officer. Pignata came to the franchise with a background of 18 years in investment banking, during which he'd held senior positions with National Australia Bank, AXA and HSBC.

Just as important as his business experience, however, was the passion he had for football. 'I played the game from a young age to my mid-30s, which is a time when your body, or the coaches, start to tell you it's time to give up,' he says. 'After so long in banking, I felt it was time to move on, and fortunately the opportunity came up to get into football administration as CEO of the Victorian federation. I enjoyed my two-and-a-bit years in that role, but when the A-League began I was very keen to get involved and the opportunity to do so came through the Phoenix.

'I only saw the ad on the website about a day before applications closed. I made a couple of calls, one of which was to Matt Carroll. I asked his thoughts on the Phoenix and whether they would stay around given the history of New Zealand teams in Australia. He was very positive about the whole set-up, so I threw my hat in the ring. I was invited for an interview and, after meeting Terry, I went home feeling very positive. I tabled a full strategic plan to Terry on how I saw the club developing and moving on. I think it helped that I was involved from a federation point of view when the Melbourne Victory was gearing up for the A-League. Without having day-to-day involvement, I got a taste of what was required.

'I perhaps surprised myself when I applied for the job, because I'm happy to put my hand up and say that, from the perspective of an Australian football person, I didn't feel a New Zealand team should be involved in the A-League. I felt what the Knights had brought to the league had detracted from the competition. Looking back, I'm pleased to be proved wrong, but a lot of people were sceptical at the time. A lot of credit has to go to Matt Carroll and John O'Neill for allowing the licence to remain in New Zealand, and that decision has given me and my family, along with a lot of players, a good opportunity. Had the Phoenix not got the licence, it would have been the end of professional football in New Zealand, because the country isn't big enough to have its own league.

'Australia has the market to sustain a competition. Even though there was a slight decrease in crowd figures in season four, attendances overall have been very good, while television, media and everything around the league has been fantastic. It has provided jobs for a lot of people who otherwise wouldn't be involved in the game. It has also provided good employment conditions for a lot of players who would otherwise have been playing in the state leagues, and having to hold down a job outside football as well. Everyone involved should thank the owners and stakeholders for putting in their money.'

The Pignata family has settled well in Wellington. At first Pignata was going to commute, returning to wife Anna and sons Jack and Max every few weeks, but it took only a week for him to realize that he wanted the family with him. 'We let them finish the school year, and they moved here in January 2008. Wellington is an easy place to settle in and they are enjoying it.'

Pignata is satisfied with the progress the Phoenix has made, despite being disappointed that they missed the play-offs in their second season. 'At the FFA's first review at the end of the 2007 season, their first comment was that it was going to be easy compared to the previous two [with the Knights] as we had ticked all the boxes. Even though we finished last equal, we had shown we were a competitive unit, and off the field we had done a lot of good things, including attracting some very good sponsors. In the second season we improved further, and in the end were a little unlucky not to make the finals. Going forward, we are going to be right up there.'

RECRUITMENT STARTS

The other seven Hyundai A-League coaches had already fine-tuned their squads for the 2007–2008 season when Ricki and Terry Serepisos began the process of recruiting the 23 players they needed to fill the Phoenix's roster. On the plus side, there were several New Zealand All Whites keen to be a part of the new Wellington franchise.

The downside was going through the CVs and DVDs that were arriving at the club day by day. While Ricki could make judgments on the Australian A-League players being offered by agents, it was a different story when it came to those from other parts of the world. No football coach or manager has ever seen a bad DVD of a player, as only the player's best attributes are on show when an agent is trying to secure his client a contract.

While wading his way through them, Ricki got things moving by concentrating on New Zealand and Australian players.

As Ricki went through available Australian players, one of

the first names he looked at seriously was Ross Aloisi, who had recently been released by Adelaide United after captaining them in a disastrous 0–6 A-League final loss to Melbourne Victory during which he had been sent off.

'Ross wasn't a guy who had been 16th in the squad and with Adelaide for years. He had played regularly and captained arguably the league's most successful club at the time. From a profile point of view, it was a signal we were serious. Ross was a no-nonsense, heart-on-the-sleeve guy. He would have loved to come here and get to a final, but unfortunately that didn't pan out for him. He wasn't everyone's favourite, and was coming off the back of a difficult couple of months at Adelaide with the grand-final loss and sending off. But those things happen in football, and we looked upon him as someone who had been a leader in a successful team.'

Aloisi's playing experience wasn't confined to Australia. The midfielder had had spells with FC Aarau in Switzerland, French club FC Lorient, and Grazer AK in Austria, before spending four years in Italy with Alzano Virescit and Pro Sesto.

While Ricki and Terry Serepisos were mulling over players to approach, Ross Aloisi was in a Professional Footballers Association meeting on the other side of the Tasman. In the same meeting was New Zealander Helen Quirke, as Aloisi remembers well.

'Helen was talking about Wellington getting the A-League licence and was really enthusiastic about Terry Serepisos being involved. She was adamant that Wellington was a good sporting city and that the Phoenix would have a good fan base, something that had been lacking with the Knights in Auckland. She also thought Ricki would be coaching the team. I was pleased about that for Wellington's sake, because Ricki had impressed me when he took over the Knights for the last few games of the season.

'Around the time we were talking, I was feeling really down after being released by Adelaide. In fact, I was devastated, because I never wanted to leave the club. It would be fair to say that I wasn't in a good state mentally at that time. Apart from all the drama of the grand-final loss, it had become obvious to me that the club wanted to get rid of coach John Kosmina. I believe that one of the reasons I wasn't popular was because I supported Kossie. As far as I was concerned, there was nothing wrong with that, because I think players should stand by their coach.

'When I got a call from my agent asking if I was keen to go to Wellington, my first reaction was, "That's a long way away, mate." Then he told me that Ricki Herbert had been confirmed as coach of the new franchise, and my exact words to him were: "Do what you can to get me there." I had seen what Ricki did in those few games with the Knights, and he was also coach of New Zealand's national team.

'It didn't take long for everything to be signed and sealed. When I got to Wellington I still wasn't in a good mental state, but Ricki was great. He got me through that bad patch and into the right frame of mind for captaining the team, which, despite what some people think, isn't an easy job. It was made harder by the fact that we had 20-odd players coming into a new club, along with a management team that had been put together in very quick time.

'I was also warned that some of the Kiwi lads could be easily offended and that I should be wary about what I said. That wasn't my way of doing things. The successful team I'd captained in Adelaide included seven players who'd played overseas and they were used to being yelled at on the field. They knew that what was said on the field stayed on the field. It isn't about a pass going astray; that happens. You get yelled at if you aren't doing your job for the team, either not closing down or not making runs you are supposed to be making.

'I was also used to the way Aussie sportspeople strive to win. They are ruthless. At times it seemed that some of the New Zealand lads in the Phoenix were happy just having got into a professional club. I did bite my tongue at the start, but then thought *Enough is enough*, and went back to my way of doing things. I think I helped change the attitude within the squad, which was necessary if the Phoenix, and the All Whites, are to keep moving forward.

'The fans aren't silly, either. They know who is running his heart out for the team and who could be putting in more. When a back problem began to slow me down later in the season, I think the Wellington fans appreciated that I was still giving everything I had.

'We played some good football at times in that first season which was down to the freedom Ricki gave to the players. Unfortunately, though, we conceded too many goals.

'I loved my time in Wellington, and one of the best moments of my career happened in the Westpac Stadium the night we played LA Galaxy. I shouldn't have played in the game, because I had a really sore calf thanks to the back injury I had been carrying. Ricki was great. He told me to toss the coin, play a couple of minutes, and then come off. That was the plan, but when I scored after about 12 minutes the adrenaline began flowing and I carried on. When I did leave the field, I got a standing ovation from the fans, and, to cap the night off, I got David Beckham's shirt.

'Had my back problem not deteriorated, I think I could have gone another season with the Phoenix, but it wasn't to be. I had talks with Ricki and Tony Pignata about staying on in a coaching capacity if the Phoenix got a youth team. Unfortunately, the FFA didn't allow that to happen.

'I was sad to leave Wellington because it was a fantastic place to be during that first season. I have so much respect for Ricki and Terry. Terry is a brilliant person, and we became good friends during my time with the club. He has done a fantastic job for Wellington and New Zealand football.

'The memories of the time I spent in Wellington will remain with me forever, especially those Yellow Fever fans. At Adelaide I was loved and hated at different times, but I believe I was loved by Yellow Fever throughout my time there. Off the field, everyone was so nice to me wherever I went. I am told that New Zealand people are loyal to people who are loyal to them, and that was what I found. I was sad to leave Wellington and to be out of football. All my life I have had a passion for football, and when you suddenly can't play any longer it leaves a massive hole.'

Aloisi is now coaching the under-17 squad at Campbelltown City in his home city of Adelaide, and is planning a return to Italy to study their coaching methods. 'I learnt a lot from the training sessions while I was playing in Italy, because they are always trying to better themselves. You are always learning in football. I know how to play 4-4-2 with my eyes closed. It is a different matter coaching it!'

Reflecting on his reasons for recruiting Aloisi, Ricki felt the former Adelaide skipper had proved him right in that having someone of his stature and pedigree coming in from Australia and running things among the players was important for the club in its debut season.

'Ross became a favourite with fans, and played a big hand in getting us to the end of the first year with some credibility as a professional club. I know Ross wasn't everyone's cup of tea, but he had the strong character to be a good leader and always led with his heart. Other clubs saw him as a threat when we played them, because of what he'd done in Australian competitions previously, and it is valuable to have someone like that in your team. I'm sure Ross would have grabbed another contract at the Phoenix with both hands because he loved it here. Unfortunately, the back injury meant that didn't happen, but getting even that one season from Ross made it worthwhile for me.'

Along with Aloisi, another Australian on Ricki's radar from day one was Richard Johnson, a seasoned professional who was part of the New Zealand Knights during Ricki's rescue mission. 'I was impressed with everything Richard did during the short time I knew him at the Knights, not only on the pitch but off it as well. I liked the way he conducted himself as the players went through some difficult times.'

Everything went smoothly with Johnson's signing until the player found himself in trouble with the law in Australia. Convicted of a drink-driving offence, Johnson was sentenced to eight months in prison soon after arranging to join the Phoenix. An appeal against the sentence was successful, and Ricki showed faith in Johnson by asking owner Terry Serepisos to continue with the signing.

'I made a strong recommendation to the club that we support Richard through what had happened, rather than just release him. His response was terrific. He made a mistake, but got through it. A lot of what he had done at the Knights spoke volumes for his character, and I knew that he wouldn't let us down if we supported him.

'It has been hard from my point of view, not being able to give him more chances during the second season, and no doubt he was disappointed by that. Unfortunately, he has had injury problems and they have now really caught up with him. Richard is a great guy who had a really top-class professional career.'

Growing up in Kurri Kurri, New South Wales, Johnson's ambition from an early age was to become a professional footballer, and he can remember his father telling him that the only way that would happen was if he went to England. With English parents, there would be no passport or work-permit problems standing in his way, so, while still at school, he began writing letters to English clubs seeking an opportunity to trial. It wasn't long before replies arrived from Liverpool and Middlesbrough, and at the tender age of 15 Johnson set out to follow his dream.

For three weeks he lived every young English boy's dream at Liverpool, sharing digs across the road from the club's famous

Anfield ground with Jamie Redknapp, who had just signed from Bournemouth. Each day he and other young hopefuls would get changed at Anfield, before boarding a bus with the rest of the playing staff — from first team to youth side — and head for the training ground.

'It was a fantastic experience. There I was, a kid from Kurri Kurri, sitting on a bus along with the likes of John Barnes, Peter Beardsley, Steve McMahon and Ian Rush. Steve Heighway was the youth-team coach and went out of his way to help and encourage me. When the three weeks were up, he told me that I had a good engine but basically wasn't good enough. It was the same story after I spent a month with Middlesbrough where Bruce Rioch was manager.

'At that time, Craig Johnston was probably Australia's best-known footballer and had made his name with Liverpool. The funny thing was that Middlesbrough thought I was Craig's brother, even though our surnames are spelt differently. I've still got the letter from them saying they would love to have a look at Craig's younger brother. Being told you are not good enough is hard to take for a 15-year-old, but I was determined not to let it affect me. I wanted to play football for a living, so I wasn't going to give up until every avenue had been exhausted.'

Returning to Australia to finish School Certificate, Johnson again began writing letters, looking for an English club that would provide him with a chance to show he was good enough to become a professional. Tottenham Hotspur, the club Johnson had supported as a boy, gave him the opportunity he was seeking, and for the next six months the now 16-year-old was in footballing heaven. Tottenham had two youth teams and 24 apprentices. Johnson played for the B side under the coaching of former West Ham winger Pat Holland. 'Pat wanted to keep me, but Keith Walden, the other youth-team coach, didn't. They said I was welcome to continue training with the club, but I was looking for a pro contract and said I would move on.

'John Moncur, who was in charge of the whole Spurs youth system, was a good friend of former Spurs player Steve Perryman, then manager at Watford. He told Steve that he had a good lad, me, who he thought could do well at Watford. Off I went to play in an under-16 trial game for Watford against West Ham, and couldn't believe my ears when their youth-team coach Kenny Jackett said he wanted to sign me straight away.

'After the six months at Spurs, I completed my apprenticeship in 18 months at Watford and was offered a two-year professional contract. What a fantastic feeling that was — a professional footballer. Dreams can come true. I was at Watford for almost 14 years. That is a long time to be at one club, but it was a great club and they really looked after me. I did have a couple of opportunities to leave, but was happy there and had some great times.

'The only down side came during the 1999–2000 season when I ruptured my cruciate during a home game against Manchester United, which dragged on for two years, and I never really got back to where I was before the injury. By the time I was right, a new manager had come in and changed the team around. He wasn't really interested in me, and it was obvious I wasn't going to get games in the first team, so I made the decision to leave, which was really heartbreaking after the time I'd spent there.'

After Watford, there was a period of flitting from club to club with no-one really wanting to take a chance on Johnson because of the knee injury he had suffered. He ended up at Stoke City for five months, before joining his old youth-team manager Kenny Jackett at Queens Park Rangers for three-quarters of the season and helping them win promotion back to the Championship.

The following season, Johnson made four appearances at the start, and then was in and out of the team. 'I wasn't enjoying it anymore, and heard that the A-League was starting up back home. I phoned a mate, Andrew Johns, who was good friends with Newcastle Jets owner Con Constantine, and he got me some numbers to ring and it went from there.

'I'd been away long enough, and through the injuries was starting to lose the enthusiasm and hunger I'd always had. I needed something new, and joining Newcastle was a great opportunity. I signed a one-year contract for basically next-to-nothing money and thought I did well for the club, but we couldn't agree on money for a contract the following season, which was disappointing. I decided to trial for a club in Norway, but the day before I was to fly out I got a phone call from an agent who was recruiting players for the New Zealand Knights. It was a lot closer to home than Norway, so I jumped at the chance.

'I don't think the right people were in charge of the club or had the right intentions. It definitely wasn't run very well at all. I had a lot of respect for coach Paul Nevin, but some of the players the club signed just weren't good enough. Everything went downhill, the results were awful, and didn't improve when Barry Simmonds came in as a stop-gap coach.

'That's when Ricki took over, and it was a difficult time for everyone concerned. The players weren't getting the money they were entitled to. The whole thing was a nightmare, including his first game in charge, when we lost 0–4. Ricki tried to lighten things up, because it wasn't a happy place to be at that time. It must have been very tough on him, coming into that environment. The good thing was he didn't try and stamp his authority on everyone. He just got across how he wanted us to play. The players really knuckled down, because we were basically playing for our careers. We got some good results and played well over the last four games.

'I got on well with Ricki, right from the off. When I left the Knights there were rumours that he would be getting the job if New Zealand kept the franchise. I said I would love to play for him if it happened. We kept in touch, and as soon as Wellington got the franchise he rang to say he wanted me. He said he would be in touch within a couple of weeks to sort out a contract.

'It was during that time that I appeared in court and was told I was going to prison for eight months. Not only was I scared to death by that prospect, I was also sure I had blown my chance of continuing my football career. Ricki was fantastic during those dark moments. He said we have all done silly things at some point in our lives and, if I could sort things out with an appeal, he would still like to have me at the club. That lifted me, because I was in the worst place I had ever been in my life. What I had put my parents and wife, Vanessa, through was awful. I can't thank Ricki enough for the way he stood by me and helped get me through a terrible situation.

'Being part of the new franchise has been fantastic. Terry, Ricki and the people of Wellington have made it work. The way the club is run is completely different to the Knights. You can't even compare it. Unfortunately, another bad knee injury means I'm going to have to retire, but, though my career is ending, there is lots to look back on. I've had the career I always dreamt about; I've experienced different cultures and travelled the world with football. I've had a ball.'

Given the short time he spent with the Knights, it wasn't possible for Ricki to get to know Johnson overly well, but he saw enough to convince him this was someone who was a professional through and through.

'I thought Johnno would be good for the club, and he proved me right. He never let me down, was always great at training, gave 100 per cent on the pitch, and you could always rely on him. Considering the outstanding career he'd had in English professional football with some top clubs, it was a credit to him that he still had the same passion and commitment for a fledgling club in New Zealand. We have all seen former top players make what they might see as a step down and think they can coast. That was never going to happen with Richard. I don't know what he has planned for the future, but, if coaching is part of it, then I wouldn't be at all surprised to see him become a success in that role.'

Just as it didn't take Ricki long to make up his mind about signing Richard Johnson, he was just as keen when an agent offered the services of Australians Michael Ferrante and Vince Lia. The fact that both had been with Melbourne Victory during the first two seasons of the Hyundai A-League made the decision to sign them easy.

'Coming from the environment of a successful A-League club, and always being in or around the first team, made them good signings. Both Michael and Vinnie have had their contracts extended, which shows they have done what we expected, and hopefully Vinnie's run of injuries is over. I was very disappointed he picked up a bad injury that saw him miss the whole second season, but he has worked hard on his rehabilitation and deserves some luck next season.'

Want a good football trivia question? Try this for size: Which current A-League player captained a team containing Manchester United's Michael Carrick and Chelsea star Joe Cole? Answer: Michael Ferrante.

The team in question was the West Ham side that beat Coventry City 9–0 on aggregate in the 1999 FA Youth Cup final, with Ferrante captaining it in one of the two legs. The fact that Ferrante was in the team to start with was surprising, in that, unlike many of his peers, he had no aspirations to travel overseas in pursuit of a football career, even though he was regarded as one of Australia's top juniors and loved playing the game.

'I did take football seriously, but I didn't think it was my life and never really thought about going overseas. I went to the Australian Institute of Sport with the intention of playing in the Australian national league and, as I was doing quite well at school, was going to continue that as well.

'Actually, my ambition was to do well at school, become a

physiotherapist and play in the national league. That was until I got a call from West Ham United asking me to go over there. Even then I didn't make up my mind straight away, but after thinking it through, debating it, even arguing at times with my brothers and father, we decided it was a good opportunity, even if it was just to see what it was like over there.'

Once the 17-year-old Ferrante walked into the car park at the London club's Upton Park, the idea of becoming a physiotherapist instead of a footballer went out the window. 'I fell in love with the professional lifestyle immediately. You only had to look round that car park to see how well-off the West Ham players were, and I began to think this could be the life for me. I soon decided that playing football for a living was what I wanted and, fortunately, it has paid dividends. It is the best career you could ask for. Doing what you love day in, day out, and getting paid for it. That can't be bad.'

That was how young Ferrante found himself in the same team as Carrick and Cole, something he points out had its downside as well as an upside. 'It was great in that I got to play with so many unbelievable players at youth level, not to mention being able to train with the first team. Michael Carrick and Joe Cole were obviously the pick of the bunch in the youth team because of what they have gone on to do in their careers. You could tell what great players they were going to be even then. The downside was how many young players were going to be able to break into the first team within a year or two. I think one or two of us who might normally have had a chance missed out because of the quality we had in that team.

'Despite that, I wouldn't turn the clock back for anything. I loved it and still keep in touch with lads from the team. It is fantastic to see guys you got to know so well playing on the big stage. You feel proud that you played alongside them and got on well with them. They are just normal guys off the field.'

When Ferrante's West Ham contract ended after four years,

it was suggested that he might be better suited to playing on the continent rather than in England. With both his parents having been born in Italy before moving to Australia at a young age, it was only natural that Ferrante's next port of call should be to that country and Serie C side Benevento. 'I had two years in Italy and it was an experience. I enjoyed it and hated it at the same time. The culture was totally different to England. Even though we didn't speak Italian at home while growing up, I did understand a little, and within five or six months I could hold a conversation. That was one of the positives: I now speak Italian. I also got to see another side of football and that helped me grow as a player, but it wasn't a successful stint and I only played 20-odd games in two years.

'There is a lot of pressure on players in Italy, even at a lower level. In England, footballers are celebrities. In Italy, people think players are working for them. Their life is going to football, and you are performing for them. When that doesn't happen, it can get a bit nasty, but that is part of the beauty of Italian football.'

Ferrante returned to Australia in March when the transfer window was closed. His only option was to play as a semi-professional for Fawkner Blues. One person delighted to see Ferrante back in Melbourne was his girlfriend, Antonia, whose parents are also Italian. The pair met as 15-year-olds, and are still together today with a baby on the way. 'Living apart has become almost normal for Antonia and me. We joke that we're worried what will happen when we are living together, but we are really excited about the baby.'

After 12 games with Fawkner Blues, Ferrante signed for Melbourne Victory for the first two seasons of the Hyundai A-League, although it didn't turn out as well as he'd hoped. After featuring in all Victory's games in the first season, he hardly got a look-in during the second year. 'That second year is a time I would like to forget. I didn't enjoy it, and towards the end didn't want to be there. I came out of contract with

Melbourne and didn't know what I was going to do. A few A-League clubs said they were interested, but there was nothing concrete. I organized through a friend to go to Scotland to trial with Dundee United.

'I was meant to leave on the Friday, and Ricki Herbert got in touch with my agent on the Wednesday. I really wanted to stay in the A-League. I had seen the results Ricki had got with the Knights, and had heard some good things about him. It was a new club and I decided it was the right move for me, and that is how it turned out. I enjoyed my first two years and have signed on for another year.'

Ferrante had come from a big, successful franchise in Melbourne where he'd played a lot of football in year one, but a lot less in year two. Ricki looked at him as someone who would grab an opportunity if it presented itself. In that he was proved right, but he also found out that here was the type of player who could at times be his own worst enemy.

'Michael is a fantastic worker who has never shirked anything since his first day at the Phoenix. Unfortunately, at times he puts so much pressure on himself that it can have a detrimental effect on his game. That is why he had some up-and-down performances, but one thing about Michael is that he is always very honest. When you sit down with him and go through that sort of thing, he is the first to acknowledge that he may not be performing at the level he has intended, which is an honesty you don't always get.

'There came a point where he wasn't playing well. He had been beaten up a little bit in the media, and had had some goal-scoring opportunities he hadn't managed to put away. I felt it was starting to affect him psychologically and that he needed to get away from the club for a few days to freshen up. When I called him in to explain what I intended doing, I could see this little glint in his eye that suggested he thought this might be a little shove sideways, and that I might be trying to tell him he wouldn't be featuring in the future. I could understand that, because, having been a player, I know how easy it is to look for the negative.

'We gave him four days back home in Melbourne to freshen up, and when he came back he thanked me and said it was what he needed. He got his position in the team back and went on from there. It came down to a manager–player relationship that he understood, at the end of the day, though he might not have at the start. It is the type of decision a manager has to make on a day-to-day basis. You don't always make the right one, but in this case, I did.

'It wasn't a hard decision to offer him another contract, because he breeds everything you want around the team. His work rate at training; his work ethic; someone other players respect and whose company they enjoy. If Michael pitches himself at the level he is capable of, he will be very good for this club.'

Having former Victory team-mate Vince Lia join the Phoenix at the same time was a bonus for Ferrante. 'I've spent every day with Vinnie for the past five years,' Ferrante says with a laugh. 'Us moving here together wasn't planned, but it has made it easier for both of us. We are comfortable with each other and get on like a house on fire. Now I've got another year with him!'

If any Phoenix player deserves some luck in the club's third A-League season, it is Vince Lia, who missed all of the club's second season through injury after making a late start to the first year for the same reason.

Born in Shepparton, a country town two hours north of Melbourne, Lia moved to Melbourne as a 16-year-old to pursue a football career with South Melbourne in the old national league, after travelling three or four times a week began to affect his schooling. Lia was with South Melbourne for the last three seasons of the NSL, and, in the 18-month break before the

A-League, began played for Fawkner in the Victorian Premier League.

Like Ferrante, Lia joined Melbourne Victory when the new competition started, and, again like his great mate, he found his second season with the club hard-going. 'In that second season they only lost four games, so kept the same team for most of the season. It is very hard for someone to break in when a team is playing that well. I was upset when I got released at the end of the season but, in retrospect, had to move away to get game time. My agent, John Grimaud, talked to Ricki, and he was good enough to give me a year's contract to show what I could do even though I had had an injury late in the season.

'I had an arthroscope before going to Wellington and should have been right for pre-season, but it took longer than expected to clear up, which didn't help. I finally got fit, only to tear my quad in training. That kept me out for seven weeks, but once fit I played in every game. It had been really frustrating. I had gone to Wellington to get fit and for the first three months I was injured.

'I was really looking forward to getting a full pre-season under my belt going into the second season. I did, and it was the fittest I've ever felt. I thought I was playing well and got into the team. Then, in the first game, right on half-time, I landed awkwardly and felt something go in my knee. Roly [physio Roland Jeffery] thought it may be a torn lateral ligament, because there was no swelling that night or next day.

'On the Tuesday, a scan showed that the ACL [anterior cruciate ligament] was torn, along with the lateral ligament plus the capsule around the knee which let the fluid seep out. That was why it wasn't swelling. Getting the results of the scan was hard to take. I went back to Melbourne for the operation before returning to Wellington for my rehabilitation. I worked hard to get back, and for the last two months of the season was able to do quite a bit in training.

'Luckily, I'd signed a new two-year contract at the end of the first year, so it gave me a chance to recover. Being part of a new club again has been good, and I think we achieved a lot in the first two seasons. I can't wait for the new season to get underway.'

Ricki echoes those sentiments, hoping that, at last, the player's luck will change and that Phoenix fans will get to see the real Vinnie Lia, the one they got a glimpse of in the first campaign.

'I had a lot of expectations for Vinnie, for the same reasons as Michael Ferrante. He had come from the same franchise, was hungry, at a good age and a good athlete. In that first year, it took a while for Vinnie to get fully fit, for a variety of reasons, but once he did you saw what he was capable of. Come the second season, he had himself physiologically where he needed to be. He looked really exciting during pre-season, and was playing in a position where he would be very beneficial for the team. Unfortunately, in the first game against Central Coast he got a serious injury that put him out for the season. My money's on Vince Lia playing a leading role for the club in season three.'

Queenslander Karl Dodd was another Aussie who met the criteria Ricki was looking for. A central defender, Dodd had played in the A-League for Queensland Roar, as well as holding down a regular first-team place during a spell with Scottish Premier-League club Falkirk. Born in Southport on Australia's Gold Coast, Dodd was always going to be involved in football, given his father Dennis's love for the game.

Dennis Dodd was born in Shap, part of northern England's Lake District, and, according to those who knew him well, could easily have carved out a professional career in football. That it didn't happen was possibly due in part to him following Susan, the girl who was to become his wife, to Australia when she emigrated there with her family. The pair had first met in a football setting with Dennis's father running the Preston North End supporters' club, and that was where he first set eyes on Susan.

As a four-year-old, Karl began tagging along with his dad, who was coaching at Palm Beach Football Club. 'Everyone who has worked under my dad says he is one of the best basics coaches you could find. Shane Smeltz will confirm that,' says Karl. 'When I was young, he trained both the youth team and first team at Palm Beach, and I loved to sit on the bench and watch him coach. I picked up a lot doing that.

'The club was just around the corner from our house, so I was always there and I trained with all the teams. Dad was football through and through. When you got home from playing a game, we would talk it through most of the night and I loved it.'

By the time Dodd was 14 he was playing senior football, but when he finished school, his father said he should have a career to fall back on, so the youngster put his thinking cap on. 'I was pretty smart at school, but didn't give it as much attention as I should have because I wanted to be a footballer. I chose to go to university, and went out to Toowoomba, which is two hours west of the Gold Coast, to study civil engineering, and was hoping to get a scholarship to America and play football over there. Unfortunately for me, the guy who had been organizing that sort of thing got dumped by the Americans because the players he was sending over there didn't last and returned home early. After studying for 18 months in Toowoomba, I decided I had better do something about it if I really wanted to play football for a living.

'There weren't many options. Queensland had only one team in the national league and they had more than enough players. Luckily the state league was really strong at that time, so I joined Gold Coast City.'

A knee reconstruction that sidelined him for six months cost him a contract with the Brisbane Strikers, but once recovered he signed with the NSL team and had a good season that culminated in him being voted Player of the Year. Another knee injury, and another knee reconstruction, meant Dodd was rehabilitating during the break between the NSL folding and the A-League starting, but by the time the new competition kicked off, Dodd, who had signed for Queensland Roar, was, in his own words, 'the fittest I've been in my life'.

There was a clause in the contract he signed with Roar that said if an overseas club came in for him, he could leave at any time. Twelve games into the inaugural A-League season, Romanian club Craiova did just that, and Dodd agreed to join them, ignoring warnings from some of his peers. 'Some of the Aussie guys warned me that some Romanian clubs were a bit dodgy. Those comments made me set my contract up so that I got money upfront when I arrived. A lot of good that did. There was no money waiting for me, and in the three weeks I was there I didn't get a cent. I talked to a lad who was playing for Falkirk in Scotland who'd had the same trouble as me in Romania. He told me his case was still before the courts after two years and that, as I had only been there a month, I should cut my losses and get out.

'At that time, Falkirk was struggling and needed defenders, so he called the manager who agreed to have a look at me. Once I got out of my contract, Falkirk flew me to Scotland and put me in a hotel for a week while they looked at me. The manager, John Hughes, liked what he saw and gave me a contract until the end of the season. I played in every game and we avoided relegation.

'Falkirk gave me another year's contract and, while the club did well, a run of injuries didn't help me. I got mumps twice, as well as a cheekbone fracture that kept me out for 13 weeks. It was all pretty rough on Nike, my girlfriend at the time. She was struggling with living in Scotland and missed her family, so I wasn't surprised when she went home. Falkirk offered me another contract, but my mind wasn't in it. I needed to sort things out with Nike, so followed her back to Australia and asked my agent if he could get me a contract with an A-League club.

'Both Wellington and Adelaide were interested, and I went

for Wellington because I always like the underdog. At the same time, I was trying to sort out my relationship with Nike. It didn't work out, but you learn from every experience. The hardest thing I have found is balancing my education with football and my personal life.'

Dodd's first season with Wellington was difficult, with him playing at the centre of defence alongside some young, inexperienced players. 'I really didn't enjoy it. It took too much out of me. I've never been so tired after a football season in my life. I was 27, which isn't young, but not old either. The second year was better because I had some more experienced players alongside.'

Ricki can understand where Dodd was coming from with his comments about the first season at the Phoenix. 'He did struggle to cope with the younger players around him. I believe that was a maturity thing, because some players take until 28 or 29 until that comes. If you look for consistency, however, it is hard to go past Karl as one of our better performers on a regular basis. We tried him in a holding midfield position at the start of season two, which didn't quite come off, but when he returned to the back four, his confidence and form came back. I found him to be an individual, a deep person, who is quite strong with his opinions, but there is no arguing he did a good job for us.'

Another Queensland product, Royce Brownlie, will surely look back at Wellington Phoenix's first A-League game and think about what might have been. With more than 14,000 fans roaring them on, Phoenix fought back from 0–2 down, to champions Melbourne Victory, to be level at 2–2 in the final minutes of a pulsating game.

With virtually the last kick of the game, Brownlie, who had taken the field as a substitute, fired in a shot that beat the goalkeeper and looked headed just inside the far post for what would have been the winning goal. At the last second, the ball spun on the damp turf, touched the outside of the post, and rolled over the dead-ball line. Had that shot gone in, Brownlie would have been an instant hero and his confidence would have gone through the roof.

That may have been just the kick-start he needed to go on one of the scoring streaks that were a feature of a career that took him to Brisbane Strikers, Brisbane Lions, Marconi Stallions, Parramatta Power, Queensland Roar and English League 2 club Swindon Town. At one point, he held the NSL scoring record by finding the net eight times in four games, and for Brisbane Lions he netted 12 times in 11 appearances.

Ricki also looks back on that opening game and wonders if things would have been different. 'We were looking for a front-runner and Royce fitted the bill, in that he had done well while playing overseas. Football is all about taking opportunities, and it could have been very different had he taken the last-minute chance against Melbourne. What a fairy-tale start that would have been for him, the club and the fans. It didn't happen, and as the season progressed Royce didn't get a lot of game time. He always worked hard and trained well, but at the end of the season we thought it was in his best interests, and ours, to move on.'

Ricki first came across Steven O'Dor during his short stint coaching the New Zealand Knights with the youngster, who was playing for South Melbourne in the Victorian Premier League, one of those drafted in for the coach's first game against Melbourne. O'Dor, who was also studying law, played in three of the five games Ricki had with the Knights and performed well enough to be offered a contract with the Phoenix.

'Steven did a really good job for us. He was a great kid. He never moaned if he was left out, was totally committed during his time with us, and tried his heart out. Unfortunately, he got to the crossroads where he had to consider his life outside football as well. He got a letter from Deakin University saying he had to resume his studies or lose his place. When he first joined us, he was able to put the studies on hold. When it came to a head, he decided to terminate his contract. I have a feeling that Steven will still finish up playing football at a good level.'

The most precarious part of recruiting players came when looking for the four overseas players that A-League rules permitted. Given the limited time available to the Phoenix it was necessary to go down the DVD route, and Ricki spent countless hours going through the amazing number of DVDs that landed in the Phoenix offices. 'There were hundreds of DVDs from all over the world, and I still have them piled up in my house. Over a few weeks I watched so many that I could probably put mine together now and make myself look good.

'At the time there was a marked Brazilian presence in the league, and we decided to go down that path because I wanted some attacking flair in the team. Daniel Cortes's DVD was very good — not that I've ever seen a bad DVD of a player — but Daniel's had a cross-section of everything we wanted to see.

'Adelaide were interested in signing him as well, but he chose to come to us and Wellington football fans have taken him into their hearts. Daniel began to understand New Zealand very quickly, and made every endeavour to become part of the landscape.

'The other Brazilians we brought in — Cleberson Gois, Felipe Campos and George Paladini — were a bit different. It is understandable that some people fit in and others don't, because of their different backgrounds and different cultures. There is always some uncertainty about what you are getting when you don't get the chance to meet a player and spend time with him. There are a multitude of reasons why things sometimes don't work out.'

That Daniel has endeared himself to Wellingtonians is because he is what he comes across as: a genuinely nice guy. Add to that the rapport he has with kids, and it is no surprise how popular he has become in New Zealand's capital city. At one point, it became almost commonplace for someone to turn up at the dressing-room door with a child in tow and explain that he had met Daniel in a restaurant, or even in the street, and been invited to bring his son along to meet the other players.

As a youngster in Niteroi, a city of beautiful beaches 21 kilometres from Rio de Janeiro, Daniel played football non-stop, be it on the beach, in the street, or at the local football club. If his mother, Alaete, or father, Ricardo, wanted to find him, they knew exactly where to look.

Growing up, Daniel played for Fluminense, Botafogo and Madureira in amateur football, before signing his first professional contract at 19 with Madureira. A year later, he set off for Holland to play for FC Twente. It wasn't an experience he enjoyed. 'I was too young, and the weather was too cold. I was living in a hotel room on my own, and it was the first time I had been away from my family. I missed them very much. My contract was for nine months, but I was back in Brazil playing for Madureira again after three months.'

The following year, at 21, he was in Europe again, with Hungarian first-division club FC Fehervar. This time it was a good experience. He was a year older, a bit wiser, the money was reasonable, and he could handle the weather. One year was enough, though. Brazil was still home, and he missed his girlfriend, Danielli, whom he'd met in a Niteroi disco when he was 17 and she 15. 'As soon as I met her, I told my friends, "This is my girl forever,"' Daniel says with a smile. 'We married in 2004 and my son Daniel was born last year.'

A three-year stint with Botafogo, during which Daniel had his best moment in football as the club won the Brazilian championship, ended with a disagreement with the coach. There were spells with first-division club Juventude, Guarani in Sao Paulo, and Madureira before he arrived in Wellington.

'An agent in Brazil sent my DVD to the Phoenix, Newcastle and Adelaide. All three clubs said they wanted to sign me. Newcastle and Adelaide offered a one-year contract; the Phoenix, two years. Knowing little about the A-League, I talked it over with the family and we thought two years was best for me. I know I made the right choice. I am so happy here. I have had my two years and signed for three more. I've got my citizenship and New Zealand passport, and hope I can play for New Zealand in the future.'

Daniel was the pick of the four Brazilian imports the club signed, both on and off the field, something that came about thanks to an early arrival. 'Coming in early was a big plus for Daniel that first year. It gave him time to settle, and we insisted on him speaking English at training, which again helped his confidence, compared to his three compatriots. He grew as an individual and had a very good season, including being voted import of the year by Australia's *FourFourTwo* magazine. His second season was clouded a little by injuries, and it can be disappointing for a player when they are not part of things as much as they would like.

'Daniel took teams by surprise first-up, but coaches get to know opposition players and how to reduce the impact they have on games. That, along with a few bumps and bruises, meant Daniel didn't figure as much as he would have liked, but in the best interests of the team we have raised the bar and everyone is having to lift. My confidence in Daniel hasn't diminished. I believe he will become dominant again in season three. If he can get through pre-season injury-free, we will get to see what he is capable of producing.'

The final Phoenix signing just prior to their debut season getting underway was Mal Impiombato, who arrived from Melbourne to take up the role of Football Operations Manager. Kelly Duxfield had been filling that position in a temporary capacity from the club's first day, doing a fine job in difficult conditions, including the fact she was commuting to Wellington from Auckland where she worked for New Zealand Football.

Impiombato was no stranger to many of the Australian-born Phoenix players, having played with and against them in the Victorian State League with various clubs, most recently the Fawkner Blues. While he loved his football, when the chance came to link up with the Phoenix, he didn't have to think twice. 'It was no contest,' he says. 'It is the type of job I had always wanted and a fantastic opportunity.'

He still gets to play some football, for Waterside Karori, when his Phoenix commitments allow, and often takes part in training when injuries reduce the number of players available.

Impiombato's job is probably the most hectic and varied in the club. While working closely with chief executive Tony Pignata and coach Ricki Herbert, he also does a lot of work for the players . . . and gets hassled by the gear steward when kit doesn't arrive on time. On away trips, his organizational abilities are invaluable, and he doubles as a media contact at the same time.

If the bus is late, or not modern enough for their liking, the players give him a hard time, telling him he is having 'another nightmare', but every one of them appreciates the efforts he puts in on their behalf.

No-one at a football club is more important than the coach and his players, but Mal Impiombato gets pretty close.

THE KIWI CONTINGENT

While going through the process of signing up Australian and Brazilian players, Ricki was at the same time steadily working towards securing the services of New Zealand players such as Glen Moss, Mark Paston, Tony Lochhead, Tim Brown, Jeremy Christie, Vaughan Coveny, Steven Old and Jacob Spoonley. Shane Smeltz was to be the final Kiwi to join the club on the back of his fine game for the All Whites against Wales.

Thanks to being All Whites coach, Ricki not only had a good insight into those players' footballing pedigree, he also knew the type of people they were and the characters they possessed. Given he knew them so well, people could be forgiven had they assumed signing them would be a formality, but it wasn't quite that simple.

'I wouldn't say they were difficult or easy signings. These days, with player agents involved, it can take a little time to reach common ground. It was also new for the club having to work within the salary cap and estimate what you can and can't do.

'There are some good agents and some excellent ones that we deal with a lot. It is important to build up relationships with such people. It isn't just about networking with coaches and managers around the world. If you get a decent agent who can understand both sides of the fence, it makes things a lot smoother. The bad agents get found out. At the end of the day, a player needs an agent who has his best interests at heart, and it is worth taking the time to find someone like that.'

Ricki was lucky enough to have two top-class All Whites goalkeepers in Glen Moss and Mark Paston. Moss, though, may never have played for New Zealand but for a chance conversation he had with *Sydney Morning Herald* journalist Michael Cockerill at Sydney Olympic training during the 2003 NSL season.

'There was a young Aussie Olympic team being picked at the time and Mike asked what I thought my chances were of making it,' Moss says. 'I replied that I didn't think my chances would be too good, considering I was a Kiwi. He thought I was kidding. Mike said he often talked to Mick Waitt, who was the New Zealand coach at that time, and asked if I thought Mick knew I was a Kiwi. I told him I didn't think so, as most of the Aussies didn't know either. A couple of weeks later, I got a call from Mick saying he had heard a rumour I was a Kiwi, and would I like to join the All Whites while they were preparing for a game against Dunfermline?

'He didn't have to ask twice, and when I got to the hotel where the team was having dinner the first person who caught my eye was Smeltzy. We both wondered what the other was doing there. I didn't know he was a Kiwi. We had gone to school together on the Gold Coast and each assumed the other was an Aussie.

'I trained with the team and Mick seemed quite happy. He told me to keep in touch with Ricki Herbert, who was going to be the Olympic coach. Ricki picked me in the Olympic side, and I've been part of his plans ever since with the All Whites.'

It wasn't surprising that people didn't realize Moss was

a New Zealander. He might have been born in Hastings, on New Zealand's East Coast, but he'd moved to Australia's Gold Coast with his family as a six-year-old. That was where he grew up, did his schooling and played all his junior football. Moss's introduction to education was at what he describes as 'an ordinary Catholic school' and he wasn't overly impressed. It was a different story, however, when he moved to Palm Beach Currumbin High School.

'That was a sports school. You arrived at 8 a.m., did an hour's session at your chosen sport, and then got into normal lessons. The school catered for all sports: league, football, cricket, golf, surfing . . . you name it, the school had it. It was a great school to be at, and heaven for someone like me. It was the only way I could get through school, to be honest.

'That was where I first met Smeltzy. Karl Dodd was a couple of years ahead of us, but we played together at Gold Coast City in the Queensland State League. Dodd's dad was our coach. It was interesting having Dennis Dodd as our gaffer, but he really knew his stuff.'

Moss was chosen for the state under-15 and under-16 teams, and, just before finishing high school, went to Sydney for trials with NSL clubs Parramatta Power and Sydney Olympic. 'I ended up signing for Sydney, mainly because Frank Arok was the coach and Jim Fraser the goalkeeping coach. They seemed to think quite highly of me, which is always nice for a 16-year-old to hear. I shipped all my stuff to Sydney so I could finish high school down there, and ended up having five seasons at the club. The first season was in the youth team, where I played alongside Andrew Durante. We both got first-grade contracts the following year under Branko Culina, and I was second-choice keeper behind Clint Bolton for couple of years as we won the NSL one year from Perth and lost it the following year to Perth.'

Moss managed three or four games in the final year of the NSL with Olympic, then had a year with Bonnyrig FC (West Sydney) in the NSW State League. That was the season all NSL players were playing in the state leagues while the FFA prepared for the start of the Hyundai A-League.

'It was a Serbian club, and I enjoyed playing for it. Our big games were against Sydney United, which was a Croatian club. They hadn't played each other for a while, as Sydney had been in the NSL while Bonnyrig was in the state league. We beat United 2–1 at the Croatian Centre, and next day the game was all over the newspapers thanks to rioting in the crowd. I had coins thrown at me, and people were spitting on me. They didn't realize I was a Kiwi rather than a Serb. We had to go straight off the field, through the tunnel and into the bus without getting changed so we could go back to our home ground to shower. That was an interesting day.'

Moss had a good season with Bonnyrig, and ended up getting picked up by the New Zealand Knights for the first season of the A-League. It was a disappointing time for everyone connected with the club, although Moss was pleased to get five games while mainly being understudy for Danny Milosevic, who had come back from Leeds United where he'd spent five years, including loan spells to Wolverhampton Wanderers, Plymouth Argyle and Crewe Alexandra.

Once the miserable season ended, Moss went with the All Whites to Europe, where they played Hungary, Georgia and Estonia before the tour culminated with a friendly against Brazil in Geneva.

'Following the Brazil game, I got a call from an agent inquiring about my club situation. I told him the Knights hadn't signed me and hadn't offered me anything at that time. He spoke to a couple of European Clubs while I was over there, and came back with an offer from Dinamo Bucharest in Romania. Dinamo was a big club that played in the UEFA Cup and was always challenging for the Romanian title. I joined them on their pre-season training camp in France and played against Olympique Marseille, which

I guess they used as a trial game for me. If that was the case, I must have done all right, because the owner said he wanted me to stay and go back to Romania with them.

'The whole set-up of the club was a big buzz for me; the team buses, the private jets; it was a real high for me to see how European football really worked. I couldn't wait to get on the phone and tell everyone back home what it was like. The football was top-class while the facilities and training camps were amazing compared to what I had been used to. The money was also good, especially when you converted the Euro back to Kiwi dollars. The whole experience was a big eye-opener for me, and I would love to go back there at some point.

'I only played in a couple of cup games because, being a top European club, they always had four or five goalkeepers on their books. Of course, I would have liked to be playing all the time, but the training I did while I was there was invaluable. If the football side was fantastic, the lifestyle was a bit tough. The culture was so different. I found the language difficult but I did try and learn it.

'It was while I was back in New Zealand for the Christmas break that Ricki rang and said he was involved in trying to get a franchise up and running and wanted to base it around Kiwi-based All Whites players. It hadn't been confirmed publicly that it was in Wellington, but he had a feeling it would be. We kept in touch, and when Terry Serepisos jumped on board everything looked good. I talked to Dinamo Bucharest and told them I wanted to go home because I needed to be playing games. They were really good about it and released me from my contract.

'I have no regrets about making that decision, because it has been an unbelievable two years with the Phoenix and something I'll never forget. I am proud that I came back and helped keep professional football in New Zealand. The improvement in the second year was marked, and I am happy with the way it's gone.

'I decided to move on to Melbourne Victory when my contract ended because I see it as another step forward in my career.

Melbourne is a slightly bigger club with a more experienced set-up, and the goalkeeper coaching at Victory will be better for me at this stage of my career.

'Hopefully I'll have a couple of good seasons there then maybe I'll be able to have another crack at Europe. I'll still only be 28, which I think would be a good age to try and establish myself as first-choice keeper at a decent level. The A-League is getting bigger and better every year, and players from it are getting chances with European clubs thanks to the media coverage it is getting.'

It hasn't been a bad career so far for a guy who, when asked why he had chosen to be a goalkeeper, replied: 'I hated running, to be honest. I guess you start as an outfield player at a young age, then you have a go in goal and you know immediately whether it is for you. Some of the boys jump in to have a go even now at training, but after two or three balls are smashed at them they don't want a bar of it. I love it but you go through some tough times, especially when you are younger and the ball is going past you and you are making silly mistakes. The other kids can tend to blame you, but when that happened Mum and Dad just told me to stick at it. It has to get past 10 others before it gets to you.

'I was lucky enough to be a decent size. When I look after myself, I stay at a decent weight. You need to have a lot of natural agility and a good frame to be a keeper.'

For the first two seasons, Glen Moss and Mark Paston were competing for the starting position between the posts and it was a close-run thing, given how evenly matched the pair are.

Paston had the inside running going into the historic first game against defending champions Melbourne Victory at Westpac Stadium when Ricki named him in the starting line-up. As the team went through their final training run on Newtown Park on Saturday morning, everything was going according to plan until literally the last kick of the session. With the players going through a shooting drill, Paston raced out of goal to close down young Greg Draper, who was about to shoot. As Paston dived at Draper's feet to block the shot, the striker's knee caught his head. The players and coaching staff looked on in disbelief as Paston lay prone on the ground, being attended to by physio Craig Newland. Eventually Paston got to his feet and was helped to the dressing room.

To everyone present it was obvious that Paston wouldn't be playing the following day, an opinion that was quickly confirmed. Moss would be in goal for the big day, with young keeper Jacob Spoonley taking his place on the bench. Paston grimaces as he recalls what little he can remember about that moment. 'I don't remember much about it: I was in cuckoo land — I didn't even know where I lived. Unfortunately, those sorts of things happen in football. You just hope it doesn't happen to you.'

Moss took over the goalkeeping role and played so well that Paston, once fit, spent much of the season watching from the substitute's bench. The first opportunity he got came when Ricki picked him for the away game with Adelaide on a road trip that also included Perth.

His cause wasn't helped by the 1–4 loss the Phoenix suffered at Hindmarsh Stadium, or by the stiff neck he woke up with the following morning. Moss was back in goal for the 1–0 win over Perth. 'As a keeper it isn't easy to come in when someone is injured or dropped. It takes a few games to get back into the swing of things. When Mossy got injured during our second season and I got a run in the team, it wasn't until I'd had around four games that I felt I had regained my rhythm. All of a sudden, my confidence was high and I felt really match-fit.

'It is a high-pressure position in which your mistakes are magnified tenfold. An outfield player can misplace a pass and most times nothing will come of it. A keeper makes a mistake and the odds are it will cost his team a goal. That is something a goalkeeper has to learn to deal with, because he will make mistakes. You just have to put them behind you. If you can't do that, then don't be a goalkeeper.'

By coincidence, Paston, like Moss, was born in Hastings. Unlike Moss, however, he spent all his childhood and teenage years in Hawke's Bay, starting out with the Esk View junior club as a central defender. It wasn't until age 14 that Paston became a goalkeeper, and even then it was only because the Hawke's Bay representative team he was playing for that year needed a reserve goalkeeper. What better way to find one than hold a penalty shootout among the squad? Paston came out best and was given the role of stand-by keeper. When the national tournament came around, however, the coach opted to play Paston in the games and, as they say, the rest is history.

As a 16-year-old sixth-former, Paston made his debut for Napier City Rovers in the super-club competition that had taken over from the national league that year. 'It was only a 20-minute appearance, but pretty special all the same. I loved playing for City Rovers under Keith Buckley and Mick Waitt. They were good coaches and had no hesitation in throwing me in the deep end. I learnt a lot at that club. It was as close to professional as you could get in New Zealand, and playing alongside and training with the likes of Paul Halford, Harry Clarke, Andy Birchenough, Perry Cotton and Andy Rennie was a real buzz for a kid like me.'

Since the introduction of the A-League Football Federation, Australia has done its best through an education system to ensure that players have something to fall back on when their playing careers are over. In Paston's case that wasn't necessary, thanks to a degree in computer science earned at Wellington's Victoria University.

Paston spent four years in Wellington, and, after a disappointing half-season with Wellington Olympic, spent three-and-a-half years commuting to Napier for City Rovers games while putting in the hours at university. 'I didn't enjoy my time with Olympic. Half the team wouldn't turn up for training on cold, windy Wellington nights, and that wasn't what I was used to at Napier where everyone attended training. As far as I was concerned, and still am, you either do it properly or not at all. That is why when I finish playing professionally, I don't think I could go back to amateur football. Commuting to Napier was tough and I wouldn't do it again, but at least Napier took football seriously.'

His degree completed, Paston took a year off and set out for London, purely for overseas experience rather than football. In fact, he didn't give the game a thought while overseas, at that time. Returning to New Zealand, he signed again with Napier and played well enough to get back into the All Whites squad.

Paul Smalley, NZF director of football, arranged a successful trial at Championship side Bradford in England that led to a two-year contract. Injuries, along with the club going into administration thanks to financial problems, meant Paston joined League One side Walsall, where he battled his way through another injury-plagued season. There was also a spell at St Johnstone in Scotland before he returned to marry his fiancée, Amy, and then went back to England, still hoping to break into the game there.

It wasn't to be, and when Paul Nevin invited him to join the New Zealand Knights that was the end of his English adventure — for now. For reasons already detailed, it wasn't a happy season at the Knights, but Paston performed well enough to ensure Ricki asked him to join the Phoenix when it rose from the ashes of the Auckland club.

'The Phoenix has been terrific for me, because I love playing for a New Zealand team in an Australian league. I enjoy the rivalry and it becomes almost personal for me, a case of us versus them. After the debacle of the Knights, we have regained some respect for New Zealand football; but respect is one thing, winning is another. That is what we have to aim for. It is important for New Zealand to have a football team that wins trophies.'

For the first season Jacob Spoonley made up the Phoenix goalkeeping complement, but was released when the management decided to have only two keepers on the roster for the second season. Spoonley, who qualified as one of the club's youth players, was one of the hardest trainers in the squad, but at the end of the season the coaching staff decided he needed to be playing.

Now playing for Auckland City after a spell with Miramar Rangers, Spoonley has played for the New Zealand under-20 side. He was in goal for all three New Zealand games at the Beijing Olympics, and made his first senior appearance for the All Whites as a substitute against Fiji in a World Cup qualifying game.

Ricki was delighted how his goalkeeping recruits performed over the first two seasons, although he never had any doubts they would. 'They are evenly matched, and going for them wasn't a difficult decision. Glen had been in Romania where he learnt a lot. I also knew him extremely well and was confident he would be a good signing for the club. When I went to the Knights I played Mark in every game, which wasn't a tough decision because he was outstanding each time. Glen and Mark were as good as any keepers in the league over the two seasons.'

One of the biggest disappointments for Ricki was Moss deciding to switch to Melbourne Victory at the end of the 2008–2009 season. 'The Phoenix provided the stable environment for him to go from an unknown in the A-League to arguably one of the best goalkeepers in the competition over the past two seasons. But pastures are often seen as greener elsewhere, and players make decisions to move on. I hope it is a good decision for him, because I believe he has a bright future in the game and hopefully he can progress. The one thing it does do is open the door for Mark.'

With the uncertainty surrounding the New Zealand bids over such a long period, Ricki almost missed out on signing Tim Brown, a player he had been determined to have. Brown had proven himself as an A-League player in the Newcastle Jets' strong run to the play-offs in the 2006–2007 season and, not surprisingly, the Australian club was keen to sign him for the following two years. With the Wellington bid on one day, off the next, and then back on again, Brown held off as long as he could before Newcastle set him a deadline of 5 p.m. on a Friday. While wanting desperately to be a part of it, should his home town have an A-League club, Brown knew he could fall between two stools if he stalled any longer.

Right on deadline time, he signed the contract Newcastle had given him and faxed it to the club from a mate's office. With the business done, Brown and his friend went for a drink at a nearby pub, and before they had finished their first drink his mobile rang. It was Ricki Herbert telling him that Terry Serepisos had stepped in to save the licence and that a Wellington franchise was confirmed.

'I couldn't believe it,' Brown says. 'I told him I'd sent the signed contract back to the club 15 minutes earlier. 'I rang Gary Van Egmond [Newcastle coach] to tell him what had happened and that I would like to reconsider. I expected him to chew my ear off, but he was great. I told him my heart was in Wellington and didn't want to be playing against a New Zealand team.

'He asked me to think about it and, when I still felt the same way, the clubs came to an agreement that allowed me to join the Phoenix. The easy option would have been to stay with

Newcastle, because I knew it would be difficult for the Phoenix coming into the competition so late in the piece. Despite that, I wanted to be part of what they were doing in Wellington.

'It turned out to be a really difficult year for me. Newcastle won the league; we finished last and I was injured most of the season. Do I regret making that decision? Not at all. Despite my injury problems, I've loved the first two years at the Phoenix among so many of my mates, and have just signed another two-year deal. It is like a dream I don't want to wake up from.'

No-one can begrudge Brown the success he is enjoying with both the Phoenix and the All Whites. There were many times during a journey that took him to America, England and Australia when he began to think a professional football career would forever remain out of his reach.

Born in Ascot, England, Brown arrived in New Zealand with his parents, Pauline and Jeff, as a four-year-old and fostered his love of football during many happy years at Wellington College, where he played alongside current All Whites and Phoenix team-mate Leo Bertos. They would train with the College First XI on Monday and Wednesday nights, then get a bus across town to train with Miramar Rangers. After training, Brown needed two buses to get home to Karori and it would be almost 11 o'clock before he got there.

Brown says Bertos always seemed to know he was going to do something in football, but he was different in that he was never quite sure how it would work out for him. One thing he was sure of was that he was going to give it one hell of a try.

It was only when two other former Wellington College students, Duncan Oughton and Simon Elliott, secured scholarships to American universities that Brown realized that that should be the path he followed.

'Duncan was a really good tennis player as well as a talented footballer, and while he got offered a number of tennis scholarships in the States he couldn't get a football one for quite a while.

When he did get one, to Cal State Fullerton, he did really well, which made the rest of us think that might be the way we should go. Suddenly there was a flurry of us following Duncan, and it seemed as if the whole New Zealand under-20 team was in America.

'I emailed lots of universities and received six or seven offers. To my parents' dismay, I chose the one, at Cincinnati, that involved them paying a bit of money. Luckily, they were fantastic about it. Cincinnati wasn't the best soccer school, but it had the best design programme, along with Jeff Cook, who I thought was the best football coach. Jeff had worked under former All Whites coach Bobby Clark, and after my first year there went on to Dartmouth, an Ivy League school where Bobby used to coach. I started out studying architecture, but soon found out I didn't have the patience for it and ended up doing design.'

Brown found that professional football in the United States was ultra-competitive, especially since there were very strict rules on foreigners playing in Major League Soccer.

'Duncan and Simon had again blazed a trail by getting into the MLS, but I found it difficult. I spent some time at LA Galaxy, but ended up at Richmond Kickers, a club that was in a different league but still hard to get into. They were good enough to let me finish my degree, which was important to me, and I stayed with them for two years, which was a period that coincided with me making my debut for New Zealand.

'My first involvement with the All Whites was at the ill-fated qualifying campaign under Mick Waitt, a coach I had a lot of time for. I can't explain how excited I was, because all I ever wanted to do was play for the All Whites. I also can't explain how deflated I was when I found out the atmosphere within the team was nothing like I expected. I couldn't believe the in-fighting that went on. I'm not going to blame one individual for that, but there were a number of factors that left me totally disillusioned.

'Then Ricki Herbert, whom I had enjoyed playing for in the

Olympic side, took over and there was a clear-out of a lot of the older established guys. That presented an opportunity for the likes of myself and other younger guys who may not have got a chance for a long time. Graham Seatter came on board with New Zealand Football, and the All Whites began to play more often. I'm really proud of what I've helped the All Whites achieve in recent times, and it is an ongoing thing. From the start, with Ricki and Brian Turner, it was about restoring pride in the shirt and the honour of playing for New Zealand. We went back to some of the traditions of 1982, which is where Ricki and Brian came from.

'While the professional career I've managed to carve out for myself has been fantastic, and getting paid to do something I love is hard to beat, all that really matters for me is playing for the All Whites and that is how it will always be. Ricki and Brian have made it what I always dreamed it would be all those years ago. Now we are two games away from qualifying for the World Cup. Maybe all the hard work and sacrifices, along with the frustrations when you are out of contract and going around trialling, are starting to pay off.'

Brown left America to try for a professional contract in England, and had a trial with Bristol Rovers while still under contract with Richmond Kickers. After two weeks in Bristol he thought he was on the cusp of getting a chance, but it didn't eventuate. He went on to Doncaster Rovers, where All White David Mulligan was playing, but couldn't play because of a problem with his international registration.

Brown ended up back in New Zealand thinking *What am I going to do now?* 'It was one of those low points in a career that people don't see. My father doesn't come in and say things too often, but when he does you listen. He said, "No-one is going to do this for you: you go and do it because you want to do it — if you don't want to do it, then don't do it. It isn't that you are a failure because this hasn't worked."'

One last chance appeared for Brown when a trial was arranged for him with A-League club Newcastle Jets, and in the beginning the exercise appeared doomed to failure before it had even begun. 'Apparently they didn't know I was coming, and already had a full roster. It was a disaster. I looked around and they had some fantastic players. I thought I couldn't have walked into a worse trial situation in the world. The difference was this time I had nothing to lose, and I began to play with no fear, which is something I hadn't often managed to do before.

'I can't explain how difficult it is to walk into a dressing room in England and know that no-one wants you there. I look back and think that if you can walk into an English changing room from New Zealand, having played only in America, it puts into perspective what Ryan Nelsen and Simon Elliott have achieved by playing in the premier league. If you can get through that experience you can get through anything, and that's the attitude I took into Newcastle. All of a sudden things began to go in my favour. It didn't immediately. I was there three weeks and, being on trial, wasn't getting paid. I told them I had to go home, even though they asked me to stay.

'I was only back in Wellington a day when I got a call asking me to go back immediately. It turned out that Craig Moore, who was playing for Newcastle United in England, had to pull out of the Socceroos camp. Jets defender Jade North was called in to replace him, and that opened up a spot on the roster for me. I was on a plane back the following day, and played against Melbourne the next night. From nowhere to the starting line-up of an A-League club! Things were starting to go my way. We lost 0–2 and I gave the ball away for one of the goals, but overall I did well. The next day the coach, Nick Theodorakopoulos, was sacked and I thought I was back to square one.

'Vaughan Coveny and Steven Old were two Kiwis at the Jets, and I was staying with Steven. It was a bit embarrassing, because it turned out that his flatmate was the guy the club was trying to get rid of to make way for me on the roster. I was on a one-week contract, then two weeks, and back to one week again. Then Jade North went on international duty again and I came off the bench to score against Sydney. It was a good goal and a good time to get it. Next day my contract ended again, and by this time I had become a bit of a story and was starting to get some media attention. Eventually the club got rid of Steven's flatmate and I was in. I had a 10-game run as the team turned it around. I was playing with Joel Griffiths, Nicky Carle, Paul Okon — the best I've ever played with — Jade North, Vaughan Coveny, Andrew Durante and Ante Covic.

'We couldn't lose, and the stadium was sold out every home game as we made a run to the play-offs. We needed to beat Melbourne to get in, and won 4–1. We lost the minor semi-final on penalties; had we won that, I believe we would have gone on to the title.

'Things were finally going my way, and that is when the decision had to be made between the Jets and the Phoenix. Ricki has been a big part of my journey. He has given me chances and believed in me. He has gone out and done things when others have thought it impossible. It was an obvious choice, wasn't it?'

It was just as obvious to Ricki that he should secure the services of Tim Brown. According to Ricki, it would be impossible to find a player more loyal to the Phoenix than Brown. 'He is a Wellington boy who was absolutely determined to be part of this franchise, even though he was just starting to establish himself at Newcastle and had literally just signed a contract with the Jets when I rang him.

'I think we are just starting to see what he is capable of as a player. He is very professional in everything he does, and is now beginning to grow in stature on the pitch. People outside the club didn't know how bad his injury was and how hard he worked to get back into contention for a place in the team. I would have loved to have him in earlier than we did, but there were sound medical reasons why he was introduced slowly. It paid off, and Tim is a good, long-term asset to the club. His heart is really in the Phoenix and he wants to make a difference.'

Whether someone carves out a professional career or falls on the footballing scrapheap, where the majority of hopefuls worldwide end up can come down as much to pure luck as to skill and determination.

Having an off-day during a trial, sustaining an injury at the wrong time, or quite simply not impressing a particular coach or manager on any given day are just some of the reasons why promising young players fall by the wayside. On the other side of the coin are those who perform to their potential when trying to impress or are simply in the right place at the right time, as eventually happened to Tim Brown at Newcastle Jets.

So far as the career of Shane Smeltz is concerned, it is not far-fetched to suggest that, but for a telephone conversation with Ricki Herbert, he could still have been battling on the periphery of a game he loves, or even out of football altogether. That may not have happened, but Smeltz is all-too-aware of how important that call in May 2007 was to his career.

'There is absolutely no doubt that it was a major moment of my career,' says Smeltz. 'I had gone to England in the gap between Australia's NSL ending and the A-League starting, after a season with Adelaide United during which I had been struggling with a groin injury.

'Thinking back, I was always going to have difficulty getting a club over there, because I didn't have any contacts and just went to stay with a mate and began knocking on the doors of clubs. You don't realize how things operate over there until you are in the middle of it. I went at the wrong time of the season, which made it even tougher, because basically clubs aren't interested in new players then. An agent got me a trial at Mansfield on non-contract terms and that didn't work out. Their manager at the time was Carlton Palmer, and even if he had been impressed he probably would have had no say in whether they took me on, as he wasn't on a contract himself.'

Smeltz moved down a level or two to Ryman Premier League club AFC Wimbledon in the hope of breaking through. It was a physical league where the standard wasn't very good. For Smeltz, that wasn't a concern. He had found a club that was willing to pay him, and, just as importantly, he was getting the games he badly needed coming off an injury-plagued season. 'The other thing I liked was that the club was in London, and I thought if I did well someone from a higher league might spot me. I was a bit surprised no-one was interested because I scored 26 goals in 50 appearances, but that is the way it goes sometimes.

'There was talk that a couple of clubs were interested but nothing came of it, so I decided to move on to Conference side Halifax Town, who had been in the play-off final the previous season. I was hoping they would get promoted to league football. Instead we struggled just above the relegation zone for the whole season. It didn't work out for me with the manager either, and any games I played were mainly off the bench. At the time my wife, Nicki, was pregnant, and with nothing happening for me in England we decided to head back to Australia.

'Once we had made that decision, we heard talk that a Wellington team had been accepted into the A-League. I was excited about that and thought there could be a chance for me to play there, especially as I knew the Kiwi boys and, of course, New Zealand coach Ricki Herbert. Every time I heard about the Phoenix signing another player, my chances began to look slimmer, especially when I realized they had only three or four spots left on their roster.

'It was pointless just sitting around, waiting and hoping. I had to look after myself, so I spoke to Frank Farina who was happy for me to trial with Queensland Roar. All this came at a time the All Whites had games in Europe. My thinking was that I shouldn't play in those games because I had my club future to look after, especially with a baby on the way. That was when I had a lengthy conversation with Rick on the phone. Luckily for me, he managed to persuade me to join the All Whites, because it turned out to be one of the best decisions in my life.

'I scored both the All Whites' goals in a 2–2 draw with Wales, which was a great result for New Zealand. Straight after the game, while I was doing an interview with Sky Sports, people were passing me notes with numbers to ring with a view to trialling at different clubs. That wasn't an option as we had made the decision to go back, but Ricki was obviously happy with what he had seen because he offered me a spot with the Phoenix. The way things went for me over the next two seasons was fantastic. I've never been one to look back and say, "What if?", but that phone call and scoring those two goals was definitely the turning point of my career.'

There would have been people questioning Smeltz's decision to move to a new, untried franchise, but he kept the momentum going from that international performance. He had a good pre-season with the Phoenix, and as the year progressed he got better and better, and it didn't take long for him to become the fans' favourite, along with goalkeeper Glen Moss.

In his first season with Wellington, Smeltz netted nine times. He surpassed that the following season, by scoring 12 times to win the Hyundai A-League's Golden Boot Award for most goals. He also took out the 'goal of the season' prize for his stunning strike in a 2–1 win over minor premier's Melbourne Victory. His biggest prize, though, was winning the Johnny Warren medal which goes to the best player in the competition. Not bad for someone who started out as a five-year-old with a team called the Oratia Smurfs in Auckland.

From the moment Smeltz joined Wellington Phoenix, it

was obvious to everyone that he was a professional through and through. At training he always made sure he warmed up correctly, and, just as importantly, warmed down thoroughly at the end of the session. Off the field, he is just as thorough. Those who have roomed with him on away trips tell of how organized he is, with a place for everything on his side of the room. After training, he is invariably the last one out of the changing room, and the only one to move the piece of matting the players use to offset the concrete floor on winter days. It is placed neatly behind where he sits ready for the following day. You could say he is a gear-steward's dream — that is, apart from the time he takes to get changed!

After two successful seasons in Wellington, Smeltz decided to move on to Gold Coast United, a club that will make its A-League debut in 2009. 'I was brought up on the Gold Coast, and it is a move I wanted to do. I've loved my time at the Phoenix, though, and the club will always have a special place in my heart.'

Losing Smeltz for season three of the Phoenix's A-League exploits is a bitter disappointment for Ricki. While he understands the family reasons the player cites as the main factor behind his decision to move to the Gold Coast, Ricki was disappointed to lose someone whom he has played a major role in helping to reach the heights he has achieved.

'Shane was a tremendous success for the club and himself. When he came to the Phoenix, his career was struggling and you could probably say he was staring down the barrel of finding alternative things to do with his life. He was one of several players who were part of an Olympic team I had in 2004 whom I helped to mature and develop. I am really disappointed that he decided to leave and have told Shane that. I feel I have had a strong input into getting him to the level I always thought he was capable of achieving, which makes it a big disappointment for me personally.'

For Vaughan Coveny, the rise of Wellington Phoenix couldn't have come at a better time. Born and bred in New Zealand's capital city, Coveny began his football career with Newlands United, Porirua Viard, Waterside Karori and Miramar Rangers, before moving across the Tasman to play professionally.

Starting his Australian career with Melbourne Knights in 1991, Coveny moved on to Wollongong Wolves two years later, but it was with South Melbourne that he found his 'second home'. Coveny played 247 times for South Melbourne, scoring 88 goals, before switching to Newcastle Jets for the first two seasons of the A-League. 'I thought my playing days were over when the A-League was formed, but the Jets offered me a lifeline and I had two very successful years there.'

That could easily have been the end of the footballing road for the then 35-year-old Coveny, but once Ricki Herbert and the Phoenix came calling there was only one place he was going to end his professional life. Ricki knew all about Coveny through his exploits for the All Whites. After making his international debut in 1992, Coveny played 75 times for New Zealand, scoring a record 30 goals.

'With Vaughan, you knew what you were getting: an honest professional who would give you his best every day, be it at training or on match days. Some people might have thought we had got it wrong, signing someone of his age, but I had no doubts. From day one, he set an example for the young members of the squad.'

Coveny couldn't believe that he was getting the chance to finish his career in the city where it all began and in front of his family and friends. 'It is the ultimate, really. When I left for Australia in 1991 I would never have imagined I'd be able to return in 2007 and be part of a professional team in Wellington. Ricki Herbert showed a lot of faith in bringing me to the club. Given my age, I'm sure people were asking, "Why sign him?" But Ricki stood by me, as did Terry Serepisos, and I won't forget that.'

As the Phoenix second season drew to a close, Coveny's teammates knew the striker was going to call it a day, but that didn't make the moment he told them officially any less emotional. Before training started on a sunny morning at Newtown Park, Coveny called the players and staff together at the side of the pitch. Coveny found it difficult to talk as his eyes moistened and his throat constricted. Looking around the assembled group, he wasn't the only one with tears in his eyes.

Football clubs can be cynical places, but on that morning there was nothing but respect shown for one of the elder statesmen of Australasian football. Afterwards, Coveny admitted he hadn't expected to be so overwhelmed by emotion. 'To be honest, it was one of the hardest things I've ever had to do. To stand in front of such a special group of players and coaches and say thanks to everyone, and to tell them I was ending my career, was very emotional. I didn't expect to get so teary-eyed, but I think it's a good thing to show your emotions, and all the guys had tears in their eyes when we got together, shook hands and they wished me the best. That was a marvellous tribute, to have my fellow players pay me such respect.'

Despite retiring from full-time professional football, Coveny still intends to play part-time for South Melbourne, and professional football may not have seen the back of him completely. He is currently doing his coaching badges, and no-one will be surprised if one day Coveny turns up coaching an A-League team.

Like Tim Brown, Coveney was another heart-on-the-sleeve Wellington boy coming home. The difference was that Coveny was at the end of his career, and Ricki wonders whether signing him on a two-year contract was perhaps a year too long. 'Perhaps it was. I don't know, but if I have learnt one thing in the last couple of years it is that you have to keep the environment challenging all the time. Look around the world and you see a lot of clubs with strong personalities being introduced at certain times. If I reflect back now, you bring someone in, move them on and bring someone else in. Some of the best managers in the world have mastered that art. They make sure the dressing room is always competitive. The difficulty with someone like Vaughan, who was in the twilight of his career, is that he wanted nothing more than to play.

'Unfortunately, there wasn't that vehicle available to him all the time. He would come off the bench at times, or might start one game, but there wasn't a sequence of opportunities for him. It was disappointing that there couldn't be more opportunities for him but that is the way football is.'

When Tony Lochhead arrived at the Phoenix, he soon acquired the nickname 'machine' from his peers. Lochhead, who has played 16 times for New Zealand since making his debut against Iran in October 2003, appeared to be able to glide through even the toughest training session.

His amazing fitness levels were confirmed as the Phoenix prepared for their second season under the guidance of sports science and fitness guru Ed Baranowski. Baranoswki arrived at Newtown Park via five English Premier League clubs — Blackburn Rovers, whom he helped to the title in 1995, Newcastle United, Leeds, Manchester City and Bolton Wanderers.

Some players found it hard in the early stages as Baranowski put them through drills, but not Lochhead, whose fitness Baranowski assessed as being at Premier-League standard. The Phoenix squad was tested in a Victoria University laboratory before training began, with Lochhead recording 65ml/kg. 'To give you a guide,' Baranowski said, 'in the premiership, the scores average 60–65 after an entire pre-season, so Tony was at that stage before we even commenced.'

Like Tim Brown, Lochhead was a product of the American university system after graduating from the University of

California Santa Barbara with a degree in business economics. Tauranga-born Lochhead trod the road to America after being noticed playing for the Junior All Whites in the 1999 Under-17 World Cup finals that were staged in New Zealand.

Drafted to MLS side New England Revolution, Lochhead took time out to trial in Belgium with Anderlecht, and Sweden with Hammarby, but it didn't work out. Back with Revolution, he helped the club reach the finals two years in a row, but was seeing little game time late in the second season when he went home to New Zealand for the Christmas break.

'That was when Ricki told me of the possibility of a Kiwi franchise with him as coach. He wanted to have a strong New Zealand presence if it did eventuate, and he sold me on that idea. I returned to the States for pre-season, but then Terry Serepisos came in and the Phoenix took off. It was nice to be back home after six years away, and it meant my mum and dad didn't have to travel so far to see me play!'

With an elder sister, Tracey, and younger brother, Jason, there was plenty of rivalry in the Lochhead household, with sport high on the agenda thanks to dad, Jim, playing rugby, tennis and volleyball while they were growing up. The rivalry between Tony and Jason was particularly strong in the early days, and has recently been revived thanks to the seriousness with which they both now approach golf. Not that they see too much of each other, with Jason spending around seven months a year travelling the world on the professional beach volleyball circuit.

As the Phoenix prepared for their second A-League campaign, Lochhead felt he was flying and couldn't wait to get into the season proper. That was when Ricki told him that Middlesbrough had expressed an interest in looking at him, and did he want to take the opportunity of a trial that had come about through Ricki knowing manager Gareth Southgate from his coaching courses?

'That chance came out of left-field, but it was something I couldn't pass up. It didn't get off to the best start with my flight delayed five hours. That meant missing connections and hours spent sitting in airports. Just to cap it off, when I arrived in England my bags were missing and didn't turn up until the day before I was returning home. It meant I turned up at Middlesbrough jetlagged and with no football boots.

'It is tough enough going on trial with players looking at you like, "Who's this guy?" At least this time I could have a conversation, which was impossible in Belgium and Sweden. The first couple of days were a bit awkward, but once they realize you can actually play, things change. I was invited home by some of the guys and that made it easier.

'I was training with the first team, but with my registration held by the Phoenix I couldn't play in their pre-season games. This meant I was just being judged on training and small-sided games, which put me at a disadvantage. I felt I got a good shot at it, but I probably wasn't up to their standard. It was worthwhile going, though, and I would like to give it another go if the chance came. When Gareth Southgate told me I wouldn't be staying, we had a good conversation. He talked to me about my game, rather than just saying they didn't want to sign me, which was good.'

That trip appeared to knock Lochhead off his game for a few weeks, and he admits he felt flat when he got back. He was soon back in the groove, however, and is set to be an integral part of the Phoenix in the foreseeable future as far as Ricki is concerned. 'I recommended Tony to an English premiership manager, and you don't do that lightly. Perhaps the fact he didn't take the opportunity at Middlesbrough was a mental setback, but it hasn't changed my mind that Tony has the capability to be the best left-back in the league.'

Steven Old had crammed a lot into his 21 years when he signed for the Phoenix. In fact, in a footballing sense he was something of a veteran who seemed to have been around for ages. In reality, he had been on the international scene for five years, already having captained the New Zealand under-17s, under-20s and under-23 Olympic squad, as well as making 17 appearances for the senior All Whites.

Another who took the American route — at St John's University in Queens, New York — Old cut short his marketing degree by two years to explore the possibility of a career in professional football. The 1.91-metre defender made nine appearances for Newcastle Jets in the 2006–07 season, but there was no place for Old the following season, with the limit of four non-Australian players working against him.

With the Phoenix, a lack of experienced defenders to play alongside in that first year worked against Old, and he was released at the end of the season.

Midfielder Jeremy Christie is what some would call a journeyman footballer, a player who goes about his business without fuss, turning in solid performances. An integral member of the 1999 New Zealand Under-17 World Cup team, Christie had a spell with English club Barnsley before joining the Auckland-based Football Kingz in the Australian NSL. The following season he played regularly for the New Zealand Knights in the A-League, before transferring to Perth Glory where he was virtually ever-present in the starting line-up.

Like his All Whites team-mates, Christie jumped at the chance when the Phoenix came calling and played a big part in the club's first campaign, but wasn't helped by being switched between midfield and full-back. Ricki is well aware of the disappointment Christie felt at having limited chances to shine in season two. 'Jeremy is a New Zealand lad who wanted to be part of something special. He got plenty of game time in season one, but hasn't featured as much in season two. I know he is very disappointed at the way things went for him and I don't blame him. I would feel the same.

'It becomes about opinions. As a player, I've left team meetings wondering if my chance would ever come. That's life. The decisions I make as manager can't be based on emotion or sentiment. I will get some things right and some things wrong, but I don't know anyone in this profession who gets it right all the time.

'I do know that it would help players such as Jeremy if we had a vehicle in the form of a reserve side or youth team where players on the periphery of the first team could play.'

Two of the youth players attached to the squad, Costa Barbarouses and Greg Draper, were in a similar situation. Over the two seasons, Barbarouses made eight appearances, mostly off the bench, while Draper managed just two, both as substitute.

'The hardest thing for Costa has been the limited playing time,' Ricki says. 'He has benefited from being in a professional environment and training every day, but he is at a critical stage now. We have contracted him for another year, and hopefully he will continue to improve. Because the club was new and there was so much to do, along with the fact there was nowhere for those outside the first team to play, someone like Costa has perhaps just chugged along.

'This year the pressure is on him. He needs to step up; we need to provide that challenge for him and we will. I want to see a lot of progress from him. Not having anywhere to play apart from the first team is difficult for players like Costa, but it doesn't just affect young players, the senior players suffer as well. Those coming back from injury need somewhere to play. You can do all the training in the world, but that doesn't give you the chance to make the decisions that need to be made during games. Game time is invaluable.

'The fact that the other seven A-League teams have a youth side, in which four over-age players can play, means the Phoenix are at a distinct disadvantage. Getting a youth or reserve team has to be a priority for the club, and we are trying to make that happen. If Australia won't let us play in their youth competition, we should look internally at our own country. The best scenario for the Phoenix is to have a team playing in the New Zealand Championship. We need a vehicle where those not in the first team at any given time can have somewhere to play.

'Besides having a youth team, the Aussie clubs have benefited from academies. Players such as Queensland's Michael Zullo and Tahj Minniecon are ready to play because they are training and playing in an environment where they are being tested and challenged, needing to make good decisions against good players.

'When we beat Sydney away, Manny Muscat and Troy Hearfield came into the side not having played for five weeks. That makes it very difficult, and it is a credit to both that they performed well. Not having a reserve team is the reason we let Jacob Spoonley go after one season and why we've released Greg Draper recently. We are targeting three players for upfront. Greg is not going to fit into that on a regular basis, so needs to go and play somewhere.

'It can be done. Someone just has to make a decision. The Phoenix would benefit, but so would New Zealand football as a whole.'

KICK-OFF

As Wellington Phoenix prepared for their debut season in the Hyundai A-League, the anticipation among football fans in New Zealand's capital city was growing day by day. It wasn't just football aficionados looking forward to the first game against defending champions Melbourne on 26 August 2007. There were hundreds of others who hadn't previously been to a live football match planning to front up at Westpac Stadium to see what all the fuss was about.

Another plus for the newly-formed club was that it had taken over the playing licence formerly held by the poorly supported Auckland-based New Zealand Knights, and Wellingtonians like nothing better than outdoing those who live north of the Bombay Hills. You could be sure they'd turn out in droves to show those flashy Aucklanders how it should be done.

Wellington has always supported its sports teams, be it rugby, basketball, netball, hockey or league. What other New Zealand city would fill a 3,500-capacity indoor stadium week after week when the home team is losing week after week? That is the type of support the Capital Shakers netball team got when it was struggling, and it was no different when the winless Pulse took over the franchise for the inaugural trans-Tasman netball league.

When football had a strong, successful national league during the 1980s and early 1990s, Newtown Park would be packed with fans watching either Wellington Diamond United or Miramar Rangers. It was only when the New Zealand Football Association, as the national body was then called, began tinkering with the successful format — which was the template upon which other sports later based their own national competitions — that crowds began to dwindle.

It got worse for football in Wellington when New Zealand rugby went professional and the Hurricanes arrived on the scene. While Westpac Stadium rocked to full houses at Hurricanes' home games, national-league football was consigned to the suburbs, with games at times played in front of crowds numbering fewer than 100 spectators. That was all about to change with the new kids on the A-League block taking on Australian teams every week in a competition that had had its profile boosted by the Socceroos qualifying for the 2006 World Cup.

At least Ricki Herbert would get the chance to see how the players he had put together in haste handled themselves against Australian opposition in the league's pre-season cup competition before the season proper began in earnest against the champions.

Wellington Phoenix kicked off their campaign against Central Coast Mariners at Gosford's Bluetongue Stadium on 14 July, and first-night nerves were obvious as they went down 0–2. In retrospect, that result didn't look too bad when the Mariners went on to win the minor premiership and lose a close A-League grand final 0–1 to Newcastle Jets.

Eight days later the Phoenix were unveiled at the Westpac

Stadium against glamour side Sydney FC, in front of over 6,000 fans, after the game was originally scheduled to be played at Newtown Park.

Chief executive Tony Pignata was on his first day in the job when he made the decision to switch the game to the stadium. Ricki had been keen to keep the game away from Westpac Stadium so the gloss wouldn't be taken off the season-proper opener against Melbourne Victory.

Pignata went to Newtown Park to meet council officials, and as soon as he saw the ground he knew they couldn't play there. 'It was just too small. There was very little car parking, and they were talking about using port-a-loos. I understood where Ricki was coming from, but it would have hurt our credibility to try and get over 5,000 people in there.' Pignata's decision proved justified when over 6,000 people turned up to see Phoenix beat Sydney FC 3–0, thanks to two goals from Shane Smeltz and an own goal. It was just the start needed to whet the appetite of those still tossing up whether to go and watch the new team play.

Five days later the Phoenix played Queensland Roar at Christchurch's QEII Stadium, going down 1–2, with the Roar's winning goal coming courtesy of a defensive error in the final minute. Despite that setback, Ricki was satisfied overall with the way his team was progressing, and he felt even better when they went to Melbourne's Olympic Park and beat a full-strength Victory 2–1. This time it was the Phoenix that struck in the closing stages, with Brazilian Daniel Cortes blasting home the winner after beating two defenders with three minutes remaining. Writing in the *Melbourne Age*, respected journalist Michael Lynch said: 'This was no smash-and-grab away win by a team that sat back and waited for opportunities on the break. Wellington, for most of the match, took the game to Victory, even after going behind in the first half, and was a deserved winner.'

It might only have been a pre-season competition, but the first small steps towards regaining credibility for New Zealand football had been taken. The competition was completed with a scoreless draw against Newcastle Jets at Westpac Stadium, only for the Phoenix to lose 2–4 on penalties.

With the dress rehearsals over, Ricki and his players began working towards opening night against Melbourne Victory. At the same time, Yellow Fever, a supporters group formed almost before the signature was dry on Terry Serepisos's cheque, was also getting ready for the big day. There are no better supporters in the A-League than the crowd that congregates around Aisle 22 at Westpac. Established clubs such as Melbourne, in particular, and Sydney might get double the number of fans through the gate — but make more noise than Yellow Fever? No way. The noise from Aisle 22 washes down on those sitting on the Phoenix bench at Westpac and, when the call goes out to 'Stand up for the Phoenix', hairs rise on the back of your neck. At away grounds, there is no more welcome sight for Phoenix players than the group of Wellington fans that are always present. Even in Perth, which is a nightmare to get to, a bunch of Phoenix fans can be found in the ground.

The big day, 26 August 2007, finally arrived and the waiting was over. The Phoenix players were unusually quiet as they arrived in the number-one dressing room in the bowels of Westpac Stadium, although the jokers in the group quickly broke the tension and it was business as usual — for the time being.

The coaches, fitness trainer and gear steward made sure the players had the space needed by using the adjoining number-three dressing room, while Craig Newland and two other physios worked on the players in the main area. During the 90 minutes prior to kick-off, the back-room staff are at times probably more nervous than the players, who are focused on the job ahead.

As gear steward, I quickly learnt to make sure there was sufficient coffee on hand to see Ricki, in particular, through the nervous moments before kick-off. In that first season he was a coffee-drinker, and it wasn't unusual for him to go through four or five cups before the team left the changing rooms for the warm-up. Back in for last-minute instructions before kick-off, he would down another. When the second season began, Ricki realized drinking so much coffee was bad for him, so he switched to tea, although there was no reduction in quantity. He must have a good bladder to get through to half-time!

Tony Pignata joined the staff for a while, and Terry Serepisos arrived to wish the players luck. Back out on the ground, Yellow Fever treated Serepisos to a chorus of: 'Oh, Terry, we love you' as he walked from the tunnel to savour the atmosphere.

Any doubts that Wellingtonians would not support the fledgling club were quickly sent packing as extra ticket booths had to be opened on the stadium concourse in an attempt to cope with the larger-than-expected crowd. Even then, many fans didn't get inside until 10 minutes after kick-off, and by the time everyone was seated an official attendance of 14,421 was confirmed.

After years of dismal attendances at Football Kingz and New Zealand Knights games in Auckland, professional football had arrived in Wellington and was welcomed with open arms. The Football Kingz had managed to attract 13,111 to an Australian NSL game against Marconi Stallions in March 2001, but ironically that was at Westpac Stadium in one of two games that the Kingz played in Wellington.

The atmosphere was electric as the teams walked out together, and for the next 90 minutes spectators were treated to as good a game of football as would grace the A-League all season.

Writing in *The Dominion Post* the following morning, Fred Woodcock began his match report with: 'The A-League's marketing catchphrase this season is "90 minutes, 90 emotions". If there are indeed 90 emotions, more than 14,000 Wellington Phoenix fans weaved their way through all of them at Westpac Stadium yesterday as the home side clawed back with two late goals to earn a 2–2 draw with champions Melbourne Victory in a pulsating A-League debut.' Woodcock had summed it up perfectly.

Phoenix captain Ross Aloisi chimed in with: 'I've played in some fairly big games with some pretty big crowds, but to play in front of a bunch of Wellingtonians singing for their side, I'll be honest with you, it sounded like we were in England. It was the same atmosphere as an English Premier League game.'

Perhaps understandably, given the occasion, the Phoenix started hesitantly, and it was no surprise when Victory opened the scoring from the penalty spot after Cleberson had handled. Gradually, Phoenix eased their way back into the game and were awarded a penalty after Danny Allsopp handled in the box. Unfortunately, Daniel, who had an outstanding game otherwise, hit the crossbar with his spot kick.

Allsopp made it 2–0 to the Australian side 15 minutes into the second half, but if he thought that would quieten the home crowd he was wrong. They kept urging their team forwards, and when Daniel redeemed himself by heading home a corner with 11 minutes left the stadium erupted.

Six minutes to go and Shane Smeltz looped the ball over Melbourne keeper Michael Theoklitos for an equalizer. With the adrenaline flowing and the crowd roaring, the Phoenix surged forwards, looking for a dream ending to their big day, and came within inches of getting it. Substitute Royce Brownlie hit the outside of the post with a shot that spun off the damp late afternoon turf, and Smeltz shaved the bar with a header.

There was no prouder person in New Zealand than Ricki as he made his way to the after-match press conference. 'I think we earned some credibility out there by showing we can compete with one of the best teams in the A-League, even though the club was only formed a few months ago,' he told the assembled media. 'I'm not sure you could have written a better script, outside of us getting three points. If you put the result to one side, we are 2–0 down, get ourselves back into the game, and at the end we probably should have won it. But I look at the response from the crowd, and that makes me satisfied. It is very early, but it shows we have the potential to be competitive. I'm just relieved to get the first match out of the way. The whole four months has been around this first game, but that is dead and buried now. We will wake up tomorrow morning and the start of a very good competition is there.'

Ricki's counterpart, Ernie Merrick, was disappointed not to have closed the match out in the first half while the Phoenix were still overcoming first-day nerves, but he also had praise for the newcomers. 'To their credit they came back well and were a bit unlucky in the end not to get more than a point. The fans were terrific, and we were a part of something big and exciting tonight.'

Melbourne captain Kevin Muscat said of the Phoenix: 'They put up an unbelievable challenge. It's certainly not going to be an easy place for teams to come.'

Unfortunately, Muscat was a little off the mark with that comment. The Phoenix won only three of their 10 home games, drew three and lost four. In fairness, that record could have been much improved but for goals being conceded in the closing minutes thanks to elementary defensive errors and a lack of concentration.

Away from Westpac their record read three wins, one draw and seven losses. A mitigating factor was a problem also faced by the Warriors rugby-league team when they first joined Australia's NRL: what is the best way to prepare for games across the Tasman?

On their first two trips the Phoenix had mixed success: beaten 3–0 by competition leaders Central Coast Mariners, followed by a 2–1 win over Sydney FC. For the Mariners game the team travelled to Gosford two days beforehand, but, after Ricki had discussed the problematic travel factor with Warriors captain Steve Price in Penrith the following day, he decided to mix things up by travelling the day of the game. 'Steve and I talked about the travel scenario, and, after talking to the players, we thought travelling a day before just means the players are a little more relaxed and the build-up is probably a little more familiar to what they would do at home. I'm not sure what the travel solution is, and I don't think any New Zealand sporting team has completely come to grips with it.'

Mid-season arrived with the Phoenix having lost four successive games, albeit three of them by a one-goal margin. As they headed to Perth from Adelaide, where they were beaten 4–1, Ricki issued a warning to his players: take responsibility and perform consistently or risk being cut at the end of the season.

There was no option to use the November transfer window, with marquee player Ahmad Elrich, signed from English Premier League club Fulham in September, having completed the 23-man roster. Despite scoring one of the goals of the season in the 1–2 loss to the Mariners in Wellington, Elrich, who had an anterior cruciate ligament injury while with Fulham, never won over the Phoenix fans.

Ricki was adamant that there was no point making knee-jerk decisions at that point in the season. 'Given that we were a new club and had only played 10 games, players needed to be given an opportunity to show what they were capable of. At the time, we threw down a challenge and waited to see what reaction we got. Some reacted well; one or two, not so well. It was always about building a foundation for year two, but we still had to perform in that first season.'

In Perth, Ricki finally got the reaction he was looking for. Phoenix beat Perth 1–0 on a hot afternoon at Members Equity Stadium with a gritty performance. It wasn't one of the free-flowing displays that the team had produced earlier in the season, but they showed real character to grind out a win that was sealed by a well-taken goal by Daniel.

With four games to play, Phoenix was still in with a slim chance of making the top four. A 3–2 away win over the Newcastle Jets kept hopes alive for another week, but three straight losses to Sydney, Melbourne and minor premier Central Coast eventually dashed them. To rub salt in the wound, Perth Glory had a 3–2 win over Adelaide United in the penultimate round and pushed the Phoenix to the bottom of the table on goal difference.

There was general agreement that Phoenix was unlucky to finish bottom, and the team received much praise for the attacking football it played. *FourFourTwo* magazine went so far as to award Phoenix its Team of the Season Award.

Editor-in-chief, Paul Hansford, said that Phoenix had captured the imagination of Wellington's sports-mad public with crowds well above expectations. Indeed, it took just three home games for the club to surpass the New Zealand Knights' aggregate crowd for the whole of the previous season. 'In just one season Wellington Phoenix has proved that A-League football has a healthy future in New Zealand.'

Ricki welcomed those comments, although he was smarting at finishing last, knowing his team deserved a better fate. There was no time to be spent licking wounds, however. Planning had to begin for season two.

Captain Ross Aloisi bid an emotional farewell when a back problem forced him into retirement, and he was followed out the door by Royce Brownlie, Steven Old, Steven O'Dor, Felipe Campos, Ahmad Elrich and Jacob Spoonley, while George Paladini and Cleberson had departed mid-season. Kristian Rees, an Australian defender who had come on board following Cleberson's exit, also missed out on a further contract. In came Andrew Durante, Jon McKain, Leo Bertos, Ben Sigmund, Adam Kwasnik, Troy Hearfield, Manny Muscat and David Mulligan.

It had been obvious throughout the first campaign that Phoenix had to shore up their defence, and Ricki went for proven performers in Durante and McKain. 'We needed to tighten up at the back, and had been monitoring Andrew Durante throughout the season. He is a quality player and I was pleased when he showed an interest in joining us. As the season progressed he looked better and better, and I wasn't surprised when he won the Joe Marston Medal in the grand final. By then he had agreed to join us, and I'm sure he had plenty of pressure on him to stay at Newcastle after that, but he stuck to his word and joined us. That shows the character of the lad.

'I knew Jon McKain through him having played against New Zealand for the Olyroos and he had made 12 appearances for the Socceroos. You don't do that unless you are a good player. Another thing was that he can play at the back or in midfield, and it is great to have those options available to you. Jon did well for us in his first season, and the opportunity is now there for him to grab the bull by the horns and take the club to another level, because he has the ability to do that.

'When I signed Ben Sigmund, I knew I was getting a player who would give everything. After some up and down times, Siggy made a conscious decision that he wanted a professional career and started to adopt the lifestyle needed to achieve that. Domestically, people kept putting his name up, and when I selected him for the All Whites game against Wales he played out of his skin. He made sure I didn't forget him by ringing me regularly at a time when I was thinking about him as defensive back-up. I knew the potential was there, but the way he worked when he joined us turned things around for him. Once Siggy got himself in good shape — through sheer hard work and commitment to the programme that Ed Baranowski put him on — there was no stopping him. He got a chance in the team and went on to have a fantastic season. The supporters loved him from the start, because of his wholehearted approach to the game and the way he wears his heart on his sleeve.'

Leo Bertos was always on Ricki Herbert's radar, and he would have liked him to join the Phoenix in their inaugural season, but unfortunately he was already contracted to Perth. 'Once out of contract his heart was set on the Phoenix, and he proved to be a key addition to the squad. When he arrived, he wasn't where he needed to be physiologically because of injury, but once fully fit Leo showed what he was capable of.

Manny Muscat's signing came out of the blue and turned out to be a real bonus for the Phoenix. With Tony Lochhead off to Middlesbrough and Vince Lia injured they needed some cover at full-back, and a player agent Ricki spoke to suggested Manny. 'He came to us on trial and was thrown into the team for a pre-season Cup game against Sydney FC in Wollongong at left-back when his normal position was on the right. He didn't put a foot wrong that night, and I remember Mark Paston, who was on the bench, saying at one point, "For a right-footed player, he hits a pretty good ball with his left." When we offered him a contract, I think it whetted his appetite and he went for it with everything he had. When I left him out of the team at one point he must have been bitterly disappointed, but instead of moaning he just got on with the job. Consequently, he has made the right-back spot his own. He has a good character, and with Manny you know that you will get 100 per cent.'

David Mulligan wasn't so fortunate. The Phoenix had looked at him in year one, and when they signed him for year two he didn't join them until late in the piece. He found it tough coming in when everyone around him was fully fit. 'I also think he was a bit surprised by the standard of the A-League, even though he had been playing in the lower divisions in England. He will start off next season on level terms with the rest of the squad, and then we should see the best of David.

'I believe we have only scratched the surface of Troy Hearfield's potential. He showed through the season that he is a good athlete who can play in different positions, and he also proved he could score goals. If he takes the bit between his teeth, there is no limit to what he can achieve in the coming season.

'We were pleased to acquire Adam Kwasnik, but unfortunately it didn't work out as either the club or Kwas would have hoped. I don't think it helped that he had been part of the furniture at the Mariners. It never really happened for him with the Phoenix. My opinion of him hasn't changed, but I couldn't guarantee him a spot and I don't blame him for going back to Central Coast where he has always felt comfortable.'

The signings of Andrew Durante and Ben Sigmund were made from opposite ends of Australasia's footballing world. Durante arrived with a fanfare after winning the Man of the Match Award in Newcastle Jets' 1–0 grand-final win over Central Coast Mariners, while Sigmund came out of the New Zealand Football Championship unfit and unheralded. Both played leading roles in Phoenix's second season, with Durante captaining the side and Sigmund winning the supporters' Player of the Year Award.

One of the most frequently asked questions among A-League followers during the off-season was whether or not Durante would leave the champions and join the club that finished bottom of the table. Durante admits he was asked that question several times before he even arrived in Wellington. 'The Phoenix had approached me midway through the year, and it was obvious they were really keen. I was always on the phone to Tony Pignata, and talked to Ricki a few times. It was nice they were so interested in me.

'During the season I was in and out of the team a bit, and at the same time I was in contract talks with the Jets. Two days before I went into a semi-final against Central Coast, which we lost 0–3, I had a meeting with the owner Con Constantine. He said: "I'll be honest with you. We didn't budget for you for next year because you were in and out of the squad at the start. But then you made the Socceroos train-on squad and started playing well. We want you to stay, but because we didn't budget for you, this is all we can offer you." That really made me feel wanted! Once I won the Joe Marston Medal for Man of the Match in the final, they pushed me to stay but the damage had been done.

'I spoke to my partner, Sarah, about moving to Wellington, and she was really supportive, saying she would do whatever was best for my career. In moving to Wellington, I took her away from her family and friends, because she's a Newcastle girl through and through. Once we arrived, though, everything fell into place. Sarah got a good job that she enjoys and loves the city, getting involved in whatever is going on.

'Once I made my mind up to leave Newcastle, I spoke to Richard Johnson and Tim Brown, who I knew well, and they said the set-up at the Phoenix was brilliant. I also looked at the players they were signing, like Leo Bertos and Jon McKain, who were proven performers. Add those to the players already at the club and there was quality all over the field.'

Durante's sporting childhood in the Sydney suburb of Roseberry was split between football, into which he followed older brother Michael as a five-year-old, and athletics. By the time he was 12, a choice had to be made between the sports, thanks to both taking place on Saturdays. In his words, Durante was decent rather than anything special at athletics, with long-distance running his forte, but, when it came to a choice, football won out. It is a decision he has never regretted.

With Sydney Olympic from the under-13 grade, Durante went through the club's youth system before making his senior NSL debut as a 19-year-old in 2001. He had signed a first-grade contract the previous season, and was training with the first team when coach Branko Culina told him he wasn't ready for that and to train with the youth side.

'That was pretty hard to take for a young guy who had been over the moon at getting a first-grade contract, but that was Branko. He was pretty tough on players. I did as I was told and spent the season playing in the youth team, but things changed the following year when Gary Phillips took over. Gary played me as sweeper in three trial games before the NSL season began, then took a gamble and played me in the first game against Sydney United. I ended up missing only one game. I owe Gary a lot. He got my career started. Who knows what would have happened had Branko stayed. I might have fallen out of football altogether.'

After two seasons with Olympic, Durante joined Parramatta, but after only six games broke his right leg and missed the rest of the season. By the time he had recovered from the injury, which necessitated a plate and pins in his leg, the break between NSL and A-League seasons was in force. With no football in Australia, his agent suggested playing in Singapore, in a league he described as average but which would earn him some money and provide valuable game time.

Just as he was about to up sticks and return to Australia after only a couple of weeks, he met Wayne O'Sullivan. Says Durante: 'I was really down, and found it tough. I knew no-one, and the club had put me in this poky little YMCA hostel. I hated it, but then Sully introduced himself on the halfway line before we played his team. He rang me a couple of days later, and we spent almost every day together from then on. We had a ball. I'll always be grateful to Sully for that. He didn't need to talk to me or help me out, but that is the way he is. We became close friends and still are.'

When Durante returned to Australia he was delighted that Newcastle Jets wanted to sign him, as he had been worried that clubs might not want to take the risk of someone who was coming back from a broken leg. 'They took a bit of a gamble on me, and I was grateful to them. I think I was one of their first four signings, along with Ante Milicic, Nick Carle and Liam Reddy.

Then Durante broke his right leg again in the first game of the pre-season cup and missed the whole season. 'That was a very tough time. I was away from my family, even though Newcastle isn't that far, and was on my own in an apartment most of the time as I had no girlfriend at that time. While the team was training, I was in the gym on my own or swimming. I had a full cast on from hip to toe for six weeks. I felt so good the day I went to get it off — until the doctor said I was getting a half-cast for another six weeks. There were times when I was in tears, thinking I couldn't get through it. Those bad times make the good times all the more enjoyable. To come back and win a championship, and to get Man of the Match, was a huge moment for me and something I am very proud of.

Ricki was satisfied with what he got from Durante, but believes there is a lot more to come. 'In making him captain, we put a lot of responsibility on Andrew, who hadn't been in that role before. What is a big job was all new to him, and hopefully his experiences in his first season as a skipper will help him grow into it. Andrew is a winner. He wants the club to be successful. It will be interesting to see how he can move his presence forward.'

Ben Sigmund's arrival at the Phoenix was low-key compared to Durante's, although the New Zealand players already at the club knew what an important acquisition the central defender could become. They had seen Sigmund make his international debut against Wales at Wrexham on the back of an exhausting 42-hour flight from Melbourne, and liked the way he handled striker Craig Bellamy, a player who continues to be a scourge on premier-league defences.

Sigmund's All Whites team-mates also knew that he is a player who wears his heart on his sleeve and is someone who will give everything he has for the cause.

The biggest problem for Sigmund on joining was that he was coming off a New Zealand Football Championship season with Auckland City and was carrying too much weight. Another was that he doesn't know how to give less than 100 per cent. From the first training session, he ran about like a man possessed. Fitness guru Ed Baranowski was horrified by what he saw, and warned that unless Sigmund toned things down he would do himself harm. Sigmund smiles when he remembers those first few days on the Newtown Park training ground, a time when he dreaded looking at the heart-rate monitor on his wrist in case he was in the red zone yet again.

'Arriving at the end of the NZFC season I was pretty worn out, but I couldn't stop pushing myself at training. I had been disappointed not to get a chance with the Phoenix in the first season, and had been pestering Ricki to give me a go second time around. I rang him so often he must have got fed up with me, but he gave me a chance and I wasn't going to let him down. Thanks to his great experience, Ed saw what I was doing to myself and explained what was happening to my body and why.

'He put me on a programme that gave me a bit of rest, before bringing me back and working with me so that I dropped the weight I was carrying and helped me get the body a professional athlete requires. It took off from there. From the first time he talked to me, I knew I had to cling to Ed and use him as a tool to get where I needed to be. I will always be thankful to him. I knew I had natural ability that had got me through to that point, but that wouldn't have been enough at the Phoenix.

'When I got a chance, I was pleased with the way I slotted into the team and got better and better as the season went on. I was seeing the ball so well. A hip injury that I'd been carrying for quite a while held me back a bit over the last two months. I kept playing even though it was hurting, until one night I got home and broke down. I couldn't take the pain I'd been mentally blocking out anymore. I had a couple of weeks off, even though I didn't want to, then came back and did well again. I've been blown away by the way it has gone for me. Now I have to make sure I keep my feet on the ground. It is so important you don't forget who you are and where you come from.'

Sigmund's mental toughness, along with his love of football, traces back to his grandfather Jerry Sigmund, who arrived in New Zealand from his native Czechoslovakia during World War II via two German concentration camps. Getting out of one camp, Jerry Sigmund arranged to meet up with the rest of his family in Argentina but ended up back in a camp and never saw them again. Escaping again, he had several close shaves before managing to board a boat that was heading for New Zealand. He landed in Timaru and spent most of his life in Dunedin, after meeting his future wife and starting the New Zealand side of the Sigmund dynasty.

One of his sons, Tony, inherited Jerry's passion for football, but that didn't stop him marrying Ngaire Washington who came from what was very much a rugby family. The couple had three children: Ben; older brother, Joshua; and younger sister, Kate. From the start it was dad's genes that took hold of young Ben, and football became his game, even though he attended Christchurch Boys' High, one of the biggest rugby schools in New Zealand.

'It wasn't easy being a soccer player in those days at such a rugby-mad school. You were almost considered gay, referred to as a "soccer fag", and I admit that from the Third or Fourth Form I was very close to going over to rugby. Dad wasn't keen on me going down that path, but I was under tremendous peer pressure.

'When we would play bullrush or rugby at school, I would pick out the biggest person or biggest bully and make him run at me so I could tackle him, doing as much damage as I could in an effort to get some respect. Once I did that, guys began to say, "He's not a pussy, it doesn't matter that he plays soccer." Once I got that respect, I really began to enjoy the school and have some great mates from those days, including [All Black] Aaron Mauger who really supported me at that time.

'I stuck with football, and at 16 made the New Zealand Under-17 World Cup squad. All of a sudden, I began to get real respect. The attitude was: if you make a national team, then you must be OK.'

A big difference between Sigmund and his rugby mates while growing up was that all the sporting role models were rugby players. In England, young lads have the David Beckhams to look up to, but this was New Zealand. It is something that has stuck with Sigmund, and he hopes that the Phoenix will give aspiring young footballers something to aim for. 'I get a kick out of the young guys looking up to you, and signing autographs isn't a chore to me. It is something I enjoy because it brings pleasure to someone.'

When Sigmund made that under-17 team, he moved to Auckland to prepare for the World Cup with the rest of the team. At 18, he went to Germany for a year with an amateur team in Hannover, and probably could have kicked on had he accepted the offer of a professional contract with another club in the area. 'The problem was, I'm a real Kiwi boy so I got homesick. Dad came over and wanted to know what was wrong with me, turning down what was a good contract. In the end he agreed that if I wasn't happy, I should go home.'

Two years in the national league with Christchurch United led to trials with English clubs Blackburn Rovers, Bolton Wanderers and Blackpool, but once again Sigmund was pleased to get home. 'It is probably hard to believe for someone who loves football so much, but my heart wasn't in it. I didn't want to be there. I wanted to be back in New Zealand with my family and friends. I was there in body, not in mind. You are not going to get picked up by a club when you have that attitude, are you? Still I had a good time and a good look around.'

It was while back in New Zealand once again with Christchurch City that Sigmund began drinking more than most sportspeople would advise. He says he didn't go off the rails or do anything silly, but admits he did enjoy a drink. 'Whether that was right or wrong I don't regret it, because it was a time in my life when I met a lot of good people and made some good friends. Sure, I enjoyed a beer after the game, but I didn't see anything wrong with that. When I was 11 or 12, I would go with Dad to the Shamrock clubrooms, which is now Avon United. I can still remember the smoke in the top of the roof, the room packed with people, kids running everywhere. We would have pies and soft drinks, while Dad would have a few beers and Mum would come and pick him up. Everyone would have a good time, but I doubt if the two teams would go in there now after a game. I find that a bit sad.'

A trial with the Football Kingz came and went, but Sigmund was back at the club the following year as an apprentice with no wages after Ken Dugdale took over as manager. The money didn't matter. He was on the books of a professional club, even if it meant working at The Consumables company from 6 a.m. until training at 9.30, then doing another couple of hours' work after lunch until the afternoon training session began. That busy regime looked to have paid off when Sigmund was chosen to play against Marconi in Australia.

'It was stinking hot, and I wasn't fit because I hadn't been playing. Despite that, I played out of my skin; it was one of those days where I couldn't have given any more. The following week I wasn't even in the squad to travel. I'd given it everything, and in the end I said I couldn't keep doing it. I felt they were taking the piss. The club's attitude was: "That's football". I said if that's football I didn't want it, and left.'

From that point, Sigmund drifted, even having a season of rugby at the Sumner club where the after-match ritual was a cold pie in a jug of beer. The beer is sculled and the pie eaten to the cheers of team-mates. That down-to-earth environment was just what Sigmund needed. He felt his confidence returning, and went back to football with Canterbury and began focusing on a career outside football with BJ Ball Papers. A promotion to the company's Auckland office led to him joining Auckland City, where his appetite for football returned.

By the time Paul Marshall took over as coach from Roger Wilkinson, Sigmund was known as a bit of a rebel who liked a drink, so when he turned up for training after Christmas having put on a few kilograms, Marshall gave him the message he needed to hear. 'He said, "Siggy, you are a bloody good player. Sort your shit out, get fit, lose a bit of weight and you will be a fantastic player." That was the night I began to turn the corner. We won the title, and out of the blue I went to Melbourne to play for the

Fawkner Blues. People told me I was stupid, that the standard of football was no better than our national league. It wasn't about the standard of football for me. It was about me breaking away and showing All Whites coach Ricki Herbert, and whoever else, that I was starting to do the right thing and that I was serious about a football career. Halfway through the season, I got called into the All Whites for the Wales game, and it has all gone on from there. Stupid decision? I don't think so.'

It is only natural for coaches in the New Zealand Football Championship to feel their best players should be given a chance to better themselves by being offered an opportunity with the country's only professional football club.

Their case appears to be strengthened by the success that Ben Sigmund had in his first season with the Phoenix, but to Ricki it isn't that simple. 'After two years' experience in the job, I know that it isn't just about players performing in the local competition. It is more about the depth of the potential in that person to be able to perform in the A-League. I believe Ben comes into that category. I had a good history on him, thanks to him being part of an Olympic squad I took to Japan. I didn't play him on that trip, because I didn't think he was physically right or mentally prepared for it. But he is a player who we always monitored. He always wanted to be a successful national-team player and a professional, and I think one day the light finally went on. When it did, he grabbed the bull by the horns and has never looked back, because he had the potential.

'Some people can perform well in the NZFC but won't be able to cut it in the A-League, but Ben is someone whose tank was deep. He is another one we got right because we truly believed he had the potential. He has worked fantastically hard to make it happen, and he had an incredibly good season. His contract has been extended, and professional football is a big part of his life now. That is something he has always wanted. If he keeps the hunger, he will be an extremely good A-League player.'

One thing Bertos has in common with Sigmund is having a European grandfather whom he credits with passing down the football genes that have helped him forge a professional career. Named after his Greek grandfather Leonidas, Bertos says it was football, football and more football in their Wellington home, which wasn't surprising in that his father, George, who had inherited Leonidas's love of the game, played 157 games for noted Greek club Wellington Olympic and its predecessor CYFC.

'You know the scenario, kicking a ball before I could walk,' Bertos says with a smile. 'It really was all football, though, and Mum [Gayle] must have got pretty sick of it, even though you would never have known if she had. Mum is Maori, so there was a strong rugby influence through that side of the family with all my cousins and uncles playing it. I know there was always a bit of a battle about what we should play in the back garden, but I usually lost because they were bigger boys than me. I suppose there was a bit of a temptation to give rugby a go, but it never came to anything. I enjoy all sports, but all I really ever wanted was to play football.'

In an effort to make that ambition come to fruition, Bertos set off for England as soon as he finished school at Wellington College, a familiar path for football-loving New Zealand boys. While he had no real idea what to do, where to go, or what to expect, Bertos was fortunate enough to be accepted for a trial with the academy at Manchester City, thanks to another young Wellingtonian, Chris Killen, who had just been taken on by the premier-league club. It also helped that the academy coach was former Miramar Rangers player John Murphy, who took him under his wing.

'It was a different world to what I had been used to, and the first time I'd been away from home by myself. Things didn't work out at City, so I went down to London to stay with family and began looking for a club that would give me a chance. I didn't have any luck, but then managed to get hold of former All White

Colin Walker, a good friend of Stu Jacobs, who was academy coach at Barnsley, and he organized a trial for me. When I got to Barnsley, I found five Kiwi lads already there. I didn't really know Alan Pearce, Jeremy Christie, David Mulligan, Rory Fallon or Darren Young, but knew of them. What a blessing it was, them being there. It helped me settle in quicker than I would have otherwise. We did everything together outside football. Being able to relax with those guys made it much easier to concentrate on the football. It went well at Barnsley. I signed for the club and ended up staying there for three years. One problem was that we had six or seven managers during that time, and I never really got a consistent shot at the first team.

'I decided to drop down one league in an effort to get first-team football, and joined Rochdale where former Barnsley boss Steve Parkin and his assistant Tony Ford were in charge. It was a tougher league to play in, but it was first-team experience, which was what I wanted. The plan was to stay there a year or two and then hopefully move up to a higher league. That is easier said than done over there, because every lad who has ever kicked a football wants to be a pro. It makes it harder still if you have come from another country, but, even though I didn't progress as well as I'd hoped, I enjoyed the experience.'

Leaving Rochdale, it was back to the grind of knocking on clubs' doors looking for a trial, a demoralizing experience when the doors that do open are quickly closed in your face. 'What makes it really hard to take is when you know you've done well and deserve to get a contract. But you get messed around because you are young, unknown and from another country. You start to think: *What more do I have to do?* Clubs would say: "You are good enough, but we don't have a place available", or "We don't have the money available to take you on." Luck and who you know also have a lot to do with how successful you are. I only got to the first two clubs I went to — Man City and Barnsley — because I knew Chris Killen, and Colin Walker knew Stu Jacobs.'

Despite feeling more and more frustrated, Bertos wasn't about to give up. He looked towards Europe, but that proved even more difficult than England. Then he heard that Australia's new competition, the Hyundai A-League, was about to be up and running and his performances with the All Whites had been noted. All White Danny Hay had been playing in Perth and spoke in glowing terms about Bertos to then coach Mich d'Avray, and a contract was offered. Bertos didn't need to be asked twice. Not only was he going to be paid to play football, he was going to be closer to home, in a warmer climate, and back to the way of life he had been used to while growing up. 'That was a great feeling, and so was the security of having a contract. It was like a breath of fresh air after what I had been going through with all that trialling.'

Impressive during his two seasons with Perth Glory, Bertos was always on Ricki's shopping list, and once out of contract there was only one place he was heading. 'Having a professional club in my home town is unreal. I never thought that would happen, and, with Ricki being the coach, it was a no-brainer for me to go home. I've been with Ricki through a number of age-grade teams as well as the All Whites and have a really good relationship with him.

'Having so many Kiwis at the club was also an attraction. They are not just guys I have played with, they are friends; and there is nothing better than playing football with your mates. Imagine if the Phoenix had been up and running when I left school for Europe in 1999, how good it would be now? I hope the club is around forever.

'Phoenix and New Zealand Football should work together to help bring young kids through an academy-type system. Kids coming through are the future of the club and New Zealand football. You can have all the money in the world and keep buying players to try and win the league, but you want local lads coming through. In the past, people have said Kiwi players aren't good enough, but we have started to prove that wrong with some of the players we've produced. If we had an academy, there would be more.

'Football has become very popular in schools now, but when school finishes there has never been anything for young players to go to apart from local competitions. Now there is the Phoenix to aim for, but there has to be something in between where they can get used to a professional environment and receive good coaching. Obviously England and Europe are miles ahead of us with their youth systems, but so is Australia with its academies. I know they get good financial backing, and that is what we have to aim for. As a local boy who had to go overseas to pursue my dream, I really want something like that to happen as soon as possible.'

Through working with Bertos in the All Whites' environment, Ricki always knew what a good player he was, but feels the best hasn't yet been seen of him. He is convinced Bertos's performances during the latter stages of the 2008–2009 competition, once injury-free, are just a taste of what is to come. 'Leo is a fantastic player — I believe he is capable of lighting up the league. The one thing missing from his game until now is scoring goals regularly. I think it is simply a confidence thing, because he gets himself into good goal-scoring positions. I'm sure he's been told that at different times in his career, but it is something we can work on. He is a great deliverer of the ball, and will always be instrumental in assisting players to score goals.'

When the players arrived at Newtown Park for the second season, they met new strength and conditioning coach Ed Baranowski, a Yorkshireman with more than 22 years' experience working with the cream of English football talent as a fitness trainer. Baranowski was part of the Blackburn Rovers staff when the club won the premiership under Kenny Dalglish in 1995, and he followed the former Liverpool legend when he moved to Newcastle United. He spent four years with Leeds United under managers George Graham and David O'Leary, helped Manchester City manager Joe Royle win the club promotion to the premier league, and did likewise with Bolton Wanderers and Sam Allardyce.

How did Baranowski, who has lectured in sports science and physiology around the world, end up in relative football obscurity at the Phoenix? After discovering the New Zealand way of life while holidaying with his wife, Baranowski decided it was time for a break from high-pressure English football, so when his wife got a job teaching in Christchurch the couple moved Down Under.

It wasn't long before the blunt-talking Baranowski began to miss being involved in football. He found out there was a professional club in New Zealand, applied for the job, and the rest is history. Lab-testing at Massey University, heart-rate monitoring, hydration testing and football-specific training — rather than plodding around a running track — were introduced, and the benefits showed when the Phoenix reached the A-League's pre-season Cup final. After drawing 0–0 with Melbourne Victory at Westpac Stadium, the Phoenix went down 8–7 in a dramatic penalty shootout.

Ricki was delighted with his team's form during pre-season, and had nothing but praise for Baranowski. 'He has an amazing wealth of knowledge, and did a great job getting the players ready for the season. There are times in your life when you meet someone it is a privilege to be involved with, and that is how I felt with Ed. He brought such a degree of professionalism to the club.'

There was also a new physiotherapist on board. Adam Crump, another football lover who was still playing at a good level, would look after the team pre-season before Roland Jeffery, for whose practice Crump worked in Auckland, moved to Wellington as head of medical services for the club. Crumpy was a popular figure with the players, and they were just as enthusiastic when Roland Jeffery — 'Roly' to everyone — arrived. Crump would continue to travel to Wellington for home games, assisting his boss pre-game and working with the substitutes during it.

Jeffery had been working with New Zealand teams and Ricki

for several years, and was vastly experienced in his chosen field. He was also invaluable when the team travelled to Australia almost every other week, thanks to the experience gained travelling with national teams. Through having his practice still to run in Auckland, and looking after 23 players in Wellington, Jeffery had little time to relax, but he took it all in his stride. At the training ground by 7 a.m., treating players before and after training, as well as attending gym sessions with them in the afternoon, was an average day for Jeffery.

That the Phoenix got through the season with few serious injuries is testament to the skill of Ed Baranowski during pre-season, and Jeffery's care and treatment in the season proper.

Despite it being only the club's second season, the successful pre-season had Phoenix fans anticipating a top-four finish before the season even began. Consequently, when the team didn't get off to a good start, there were some disappointed people. Two points from their first five games had the critics out in force and no-one was in the spotlight more than Ricki. Being head coach — or manager, as the position is called in other parts of the world — can be a lonely job when things aren't going well. It doesn't take long for people to starting looking for scapegoats, and soon there were questions being asked about Ricki's future.

In those circumstances, it isn't only the person involved who feels the pressure; it is just as tough on those he lives with. Ricki's wife, Raewyn, along with teenage twins, Sacha and Kale, were the ones charged with keeping his spirits up while at the same time understanding how he was feeling. At least Ricki now had his family to go home to. In his first few months at the club, Raewyn and the twins were still living in Auckland.

'When Ricki got the Phoenix job, everything moved so fast there was no other way we could have done it,' says Raewyn.

'Initially, I hoped the new franchise would be in Auckland, mainly because of the age the children were. They were in their second year at high school, and both were in good schools that they enjoyed. When Wellington was confirmed, I had no reservations about him taking the job, because I knew how much he wanted it. I also thought he deserved it because of what he had done at the Knights.

'At the start I thought it would be possible for me to stay in Auckland with the kids, and that he would come back every couple of weeks or we would go down to Wellington. As time went on, it became obvious that wasn't going to work. With so much to be done at the club, it was difficult for him to get to Auckland regularly, while for us to go down to every home game was a nightmare. We had to board the dog and cat, and I had my own hairdressing business to look after. It also meant that the kids would miss out on their weekend sport while we were away, not to mention the mad rush it was to get back to Auckland if the game was on Sunday. We missed our flight a few times.

'It was also difficult for me with two 14-year-olds wanting to go here, there and everywhere. It was different when he was away earlier in our marriage. When the kids were small, they didn't want to go out at night! Ricki had moved to Wellington in April and we joined him in September. The kids still miss their friends, but overall I think they have settled pretty well.'

Once settled in Wellington, it didn't take Raewyn long to notice the difference between Ricki the player and Ricki the coach. 'As a player, he didn't dwell on results. If his team lost, they lost. I can't ever remember him coming home grumpy, angry or moody. It is completely different now. When I'm watching an away game on television and the camera shows those on the Phoenix bench, I can see exactly how he's feeling. It doesn't help when I'm watching with Kale and he makes remarks about what Ricki should be doing. He thinks he's the coach!

'It isn't easy watching on television, but if they are going to lose

I'd rather it was in an away game so he will have time to get things out of his system before he gets home. He takes it very seriously, but at the end of the day he can only do so much. Once they are on the field it is up to the players, though having said that it will always come back on the coach.'

During the Phoenix's barren run at the start of the second season, it got to the point where Raewyn stopped reading newspapers. 'I used to buy the paper but not anymore, and things are even worse with the Internet because people can say virtually anything in that medium without any comeback.'

During the day Raewyn works in the Phoenix store, and, one day when the team was going through the bad patch, someone from the office called in and said they hoped she hadn't been looking at the Yellow Fever site on the Internet. 'I'd actually never looked at it before, but curiosity got the better of me and the following day I had a look. That was a big mistake. Some people get very personal. It is only human nature to react if they are saying things about your husband. OK, things weren't going well, but it wasn't nearly as bad as some were making out. I admit those first few weeks were a nightmare. People come into the shop not knowing who I am and make comments, but I never bite back because I didn't particularly want people to know who I was. I would say something in a different environment, such as a pub.

'I've been at after-match functions in the Four Kings when some people have been a bit cool with me. It's funny how they congratulate you after a win but ignore you after a loss. I try to be objective, but it isn't easy. It was a big relief when the team turned things around and almost made the play-offs.

'Overall though, Wellington people have been very supportive. I can see why the franchise came here. Aucklanders would never have got behind it like they have here. The other side of the coin is that we could go out in Auckland without people noticing us. Wellington is much more compact, and someone always recognizes Ricki and wants to talk to him. That's not bad, though. It means we must be doing OK!'

The Phoenix did turn things around, and with one game to play were within touching distance of the finals. The scenario was simple: they had to beat Melbourne Victory at the Telstra Dome, and Adelaide had to beat Central Coast Mariners in Gosford.

Leading into the Melbourne game, there was an upbeat feeling among the players and back-room staff. The team had been playing well, despite having won only one of the previous four games. They had gone down to a last-minute goal against Queensland Roar in Brisbane, beat Newcastle Jets 3–0 in Wellington, lost 0–1 in Sydney, again to a last-gasp goal, when down to 10 men, and drew with Adelaide 1–1 in a game they should have won given the number of goal-scoring chances they created.

Everything was going well at the Telstra Dome, with the Phoenix playing some of their best football of the season, until seven minutes from half-time when the Victory were given the softest penalty imaginable. Victory skipper Kevin Muscat wasn't going to look a gift horse in the mouth and duly made it 1–0.

Phoenix played just as well in the second half as they had in the first, without any luck in front of goal, and it was only in the dying minutes that Victory got a second as the visitors threw players forward.

It was a quiet dressing room afterwards. The players knew they had played well enough to get something from the game; to have been so close to a play-off spot, only to miss out, was heartbreaking. Still, they had shown character over those last few weeks, and those who were staying immediately vowed that close would not be good enough next time.

For Ricki there was disappointment at missing out, relief at the improvement on the debut season, and optimism about the club's future. Whatever the future holds, when Ricki looks back on that chapter of his life he will do so with a feeling of satisfaction that he was in at the beginning of something special in the annals of

New Zealand football. From the day Ricki and Terry Serepisos shook hands on the deal that took him to the fledgling Wellington franchise, it has been one hell of a ride. Of course there have been mistakes, but there have also been wonderful moments.

'Being head coach at the Wellington Phoenix is different to other coaching jobs, in that I was a foundation member. It is an opportunity that will rarely come along again for any coach. I was there for the first meeting, the first handshake with the new owner. That will stay with me for the rest of my life.

'The Phoenix, and the people within the organization, have become a massive part of my life and, whatever anyone else thinks, I am proud of what I have done. Yes, I've had my knockers, especially in the second season, but that is something that comes with the job of managing a football club. You do take it to heart, and I've often woken in the morning full of frustrations. I firmly believe this club will get stronger and stronger and make its mark on Australasian football.

'Whether I'm coaching it, on the board, or sitting in the middle of Yellow Fever, it will always be part of me. It has to be, doesn't it? Being a football coach is different to most jobs. You never know what your final destination will be, but you can be sure there will be plenty of ups and downs along the way.'

LOOKING AHEAD

Few people are more qualified than Ricki Herbert when it comes to expressing an opinion on where football in New Zealand is heading. As a player, he was part of the history-making All Whites that made the World Cup finals 27 years ago, before going on to become director of football for the Soccer 2 Federation when he turned his hand to coaching.

From Soccer 2, Ricki moved into New Zealand Football's head office as high-performance manager, eventually taking over the reins of the All Whites. Add to that his position as head coach at New Zealand's only professional football club, and he has seen how the game operates from inside and outside the national body at the highest levels. When New Zealand Football made a radical move in 2000 — doing away with the 23 district associations that administered the game and replacing them with seven federations that covered the country — it meant the end of an unwieldy system where too many personal agendas, not to mention individual egos, often blocked proposals that may have benefited the game.

Unfortunately, some of those stumbling blocks still exist and will do until, according to Ricki, there is stability within the game. 'How can there be long-term stability in the direction of the game when there is a continual turnover of board members, chief executives and directors of football? We seem to be inventing new ideas every three or four years.'

A prime example of that came with the demise of the national league, thanks to constant tinkering. It went from an eight-team competition to 10, to 12, 14, back to 10; from club teams to regions, back to club teams and then to franchises. 'In 2009, we have ended up with a watered-down version with eight teams playing a meagre 14 games before going into play-offs. Is it any wonder the supply of talented young players coming through is in danger of drying up?'

'During the 1970s and 1980s, the majority of the national team were playing their football within New Zealand because we had a strong domestic competition that made sure those playing in it were constantly challenged. I got my first game with the All Whites at 18. I was seen as good enough to include because I was playing every week in a strong competition. You don't get that now because the national competition is not challenging enough. At the time I made my debut, I think there were two or three of the squad playing in Australia. Now it is the opposite way around, with only two or three coming from within and the rest playing overseas. There's nothing wrong with having so many players plying their trade overseas. In fact it's a good thing, because they're playing at a decent level and earning a good wage. Forget the Kiwi guys playing for Wellington Phoenix: they are registered in Australia, and so are in essence overseas players. What is of concern is that tomorrow's potential New Zealand internationals have nowhere challenging to play.

'I'm not sure that the New Zealand Football Championship has a purpose any more. One outcome is that the winner qualifies for the World Club championship and a good payday. That's fine, but the jigsaw puzzle has a multitude of pieces and only a few are being worked on. For instance, the under-20s twice haven't made it to the World Cup finals, so it seems obvious there must be a void between the ages of 17 and 20, a critical stage in a player's development, and you have to ask what those players who go to an under-17 World Cup are coming back to. Having invested in them, it is vital to ensure that when they return there is somewhere for them to play where they can be challenged and need to make on-field decisions. Put 17- and 18-year-olds into the NZFC and let them survive for a two- or three-year-period; see what they are like at the end of that, along with training on a regular basis.

'If these talented young players aren't going to play in a national-league competition, they will inevitably drift away. Some will go to American universities, where there have already been some great success through that avenue, with the likes of Ryan Nelsen, Simon Elliott, Duncan Oughton and Tim Brown. Others, however, will just give football away, so why not tap into the fantastic universities we have in New Zealand? You can come out of varsities such as Auckland, Otago, Victoria and Massey with a degree that stands up against anything in the rest of the world. You aren't talking about thousands of kids. You are talking about a selected group of players who you want to move forwards so they can be successful at the highest level. Get them into an environment where they are surrounded with all the other necessary ingredients, apart from being good at the game. Their lifestyle is important and needs to be balanced with the physiological side, nutritional side, along with health and welfare.

'What sort of athletes would we have in the game if we started that at a young age? It would mean that young players would be measured physiologically throughout the year. We have seen at the Phoenix what an amazing difference that can make. At present there is no regular measurement. Because the camps they attend with national teams are intermittent, a player comes in knowing the coach will want him at x degree of fitness. After the camp he will go away and soon be back to y. He will spend time in a non-challenging environment and then go back into camp and be expected to be back up at x again.

'There is currently no consistency in how they are measured, so how can you tell if a player is moving forwards or not? Nothing in football is more important than the players. They are the ones who make you successful or unsuccessful as a nation. When New Zealand hosted the 1999 under-17 World Cup, players from outside Auckland were moved to that city so they could be with their team-mates, attending either Auckland Grammar or Westlake Boys' High. It is no surprise that they had a good tournament. It is also no coincidence that some were picked up by American universities while others got professional contracts in England.

'Having somewhere to play and be cared for is a priority, and it wouldn't just be the young players who benefited. It would also be fantastic for coaches. It is vital that coaches spend as much time as possible working with players. You can have all the theory in the world, but there is no substitute for the practical side of coaching on a regular basis.

'People talk about me wearing two hats through coaching the All Whites and Phoenix. Well, I think I'm a better coach working day in, day out, with players rather than just having the All Whites for seven games a year, which would involve around 28 days' coaching. Why not have the national under-17 coach working with the next group from 15 years of age, basing them in one centre so that they can play in a challenging competition on a regular basis?

'When an under-17 squad returned from a World Cup, they would join the under-20 coach working towards their next campaign. Wouldn't the coaches improve as much as the players?

It isn't just about these players having somewhere challenging to play. There needs to be some rational discussion about where the game is going to be in 10 years' time.

'Somewhere along the line you have to have something in place that will run that course, because we haven't had it in the past. People come in and force you to play a certain way. That lasts two years, then goes out the window when someone replaces them. There is no direction. Youth coaches just do what they want and how they want to do it. You can't have a go at them, because they don't get direction as to what is required. We are not big enough or powerful enough to have a multitude of opinions. It doesn't matter what the outcome is, let's just agree on something and get on with it.

'I accept the fact that finance is an issue, but, from a football point of view, we have to have a systematic way of taking a player from A to Z. You don't want them spending a bit of time here, a bit of time there, a private academy here, a club there, a school here, a federation there, an international team there . . . what chance have they got with that regime? It is all too bitsy. It should be about providing a platform, along with some clarity around what a player needs at a certain age. There has to be a pathway that will run more smoothly than it currently does. If a young player signs up in England — and I use that comparison simply because football people relate to it — there is a system they go through that gives them every opportunity to become a successful professional or international player. We don't have anything like that. Instead, there are a lot of separate organizations that all want a piece of the pie. It is about bringing them together to provide one smooth path.

'If I was a parent with a promising young lad, I would be totally confused as to where I should go and what I should do to help him realize his goals. I get several phone calls from parents seeking advice. It is difficult to give them advice, though, because frankly as things are, I'm not sure what they should do.

'Someone has to care about where the game will be in 10 years' time. We can all be selfish and say, "I've got a coaching job, so that's all I care about." I could say, "I'm doing the All Whites, so I don't give a toss about the rest of the game." But I do care about it. At the end of the day I won't always be the All Whites coach, but I want whoever is to be successful. I want the stream of players coming through for that coach to be plentiful.

'Statistics will tell you that the majority of kids fall out of football between the ages of 15 and 17. That is in part because decisions are being made on the basis of "you're good" and "you're not good". I'm not sure that is the time to make those decisions, but, besides that, the infrastructure isn't there for a young aspiring player to say, "Wow, look at the pathway; look at the opportunities. I'll stay in the game." A few will always come through, but we need more than a few. Our base must be broader. I don't pretend to have all the answers, but there has to be a starting point. We need to sit down over a reasonable period of time and come up with a plan. When that is done, stick with what is decided. Whatever the plan looks like, people need to buy into it and follow it.

'You would always encourage players to take up good opportunities elsewhere, such as American universities, but it is internally we need to improve. Of course you will need reviews along the way to measure how things are progressing. It needs a group of people to sit around and brainstorm. Who takes part would be important. How far do you open it up? Opening up too much can sometimes create confusion.

'There are enough people around football with the necessary experience. They would need to come to the table with an open mind and I'm not sure everyone would, but that would be vital.'

17

THE MAN WHO GAVE THE PHOENIX WINGS

Once Terry Serepisos gets an idea, it is full speed ahead until it comes to fruition. There are no half-measures with the 45-year-old Greek-born property developer, whether it involves his 'outside-the-envelope' building designs dotted around Wellington, or the little matter of buying a football club.

It is fair to say that never in the 124-year history of professional football has a club been established in such dramatic circumstances as those surrounding the birth of Wellington Phoenix. The scenario had all the ingredients of a movie as Wellingtonians tried desperately to take over the licence stripped from the New Zealand Knights a few weeks earlier, but were unable to find anyone who could front up with the required $1.2 million cash Football Federation Australia was demanding.

The architects behind the Wellington bid — businessmen, Ian Wells and John Dow — had given it their best shot. They had come up with a credible business plan, but the final piece of the jigsaw they were trying to put together — over a million dollars in hard cash — was proving to be a bridge too far. Then, at the 11th hour, with the FFA's final deadline looming large, out of nowhere came a knight in shining armour in the form of Serepisos, straight from a barber's chair.

Buying a football club could never have entered Serepisos's mind when he left his office in the ASB Tower to nip out for a haircut. As the barber clipped away, Serepisos listened to a radio announcer lamenting that the Wellington bid was about to fail because those behind it couldn't come up with the required money. On the spur of the moment, he decided to do something about it, even though his connection with football had been severed years before when the busy world of property development took him away from playing for Wellington Olympic's division-seven team.

In fact, so out of touch was he with the football scene that he needed to telephone his cousin John Serepisos to get a rundown on what had been happening and find out who was involved in the Wellington consortium.

'John told me that Ian Wells and John Dow were behind the Wellington bid so I invited them to my office. I asked what we had to do to get the licence, and was told it would cost $1.2 million. When I inquired how much they already had, they began talking about different people promising this sum and that sum. It was obvious that they didn't have the money, so I said I would put it all up but I wanted 100 per cent of the shares.'

Once that was sorted out, New Zealand Football chief executive Graham Seatter flew down to Wellington to meet Serepisos. New Zealand Football had been working with the FFA to try to keep the franchise on this side of the Tasman, and finally there was something to build on.

A meeting with FFA representatives followed; they were happy that Serepisos was good for the money. It was almost a done deal with one more thing to be agreed upon. 'One of the conditions the FFA put on it was that Ricki Herbert should be the coach. I went to Auckland and, along with Graham Seatter, met him for coffee at Sky City. We got on well straight away, and I had no problem with Ricki coaching the team. I could see where the FFA was coming from, in that he had done such a good job when he took over the Knights for those last few games. Since then I have built up a good relationship with Ricki.'

Looking back at how those events unfolded, Serepisos believes the catalyst were the deaths of his father, Jimmy, in 2005, and his brother, Kosta, from leukemia the following year. 'They were big blows to myself and my older brother, Lambros, because we were a very close-knit family. When I got into property, Kosta was my right-hand man, and it was devastating to see him shrivel away. I think it was a reaction to those losses that made me do something spontaneous like that, although had Kosta still been around he might have talked me out of it!'

Once the franchise was secured, the next challenge was to decide on a name for the new club. Serepisos approached *The Dominion Post* newspaper to canvass its readers for suggestions, and from the 300-odd replies he chose the apt Phoenix.

Owning the Phoenix cost Serepisos around $6 million in the first year, plus $1 million a year to keep it going, but there has been the odd benefit, with his company's profile skyrocketing. Despite him being so successful, with Century City Developments being responsible for much of the rejuvenation of Courtenay Place, those outside the business community knew little about Serepisos.

Terry Serepisos's business success began when he opened Trillini, a men's fashion store specializing in importing Italian designs, after visiting Rome and Milan during a six-month campervan tour of Europe and developing a passion for fashion that has never abated. Before long, he had six stores around Wellington, which were eventually sold to raise capital to invest in Courtenay Place's Ecstasy Plus bar.

Opposite the bar was a run-down building that had been empty for seven years. The more Serepisos looked at that shell, the more active his mind became. Why not convert it into apartments and shops? As with the Phoenix, once he had the idea it was full steam ahead. He bought the building for $950,000, and up went the apartments and retail businesses. Century City Developments was born.

To promote the Century City brand, Serepisos became a major sponsor of the Wellington Racing Club, with the jewel in that particular crown being the Wellington Cup, as well as backing the Wellington Saints basketball team. It was Wellington Phoenix that really put Serepisos on the map, however, and just when all the fuss over that purchase was dying down, he pulled off another marketing masterstroke by bringing the biggest name in world football to Wellington.

At a September press conference in his ASB Tower offices, Serepisos confirmed David Beckham and the LA Galaxy would play Wellington Phoenix on 1 December 2007, and promised an entertainment extravaganza over that weekend. Asked by the media why he had been so determined (to the tune of almost $2 million) to get Beckham to Wellington, Serepisos said he was driven by the desire to put football in New Zealand on the map. 'He [Beckham] is trying to make a difference in the sport in America and I am trying to make a difference for football in New Zealand. I am looking forward to having someone here who can encourage people from all over the country to come to Wellington and be part of reigniting something in football that hasn't been there for a long time.'

He certainly did that with Beckham-mania hitting the rest of New Zealand as well as Wellington from the moment the American team was greeted by 1,000 fans and a Maori welcome on landing at the airport.

Next morning, television cameras from the show *Breakfast* were trained on the Copthorne Hotel in Oriental Bay in the vain hope that Beckham would step out on a bedroom balcony. Who could have imagined that happening in rugby-mad New Zealand before an entrepreneur like Serepisos got involved in the round-ball game? Come to that, who could have predicted 15,000 school children would turn up at Westpac Stadium for a Galaxy training session? The kids cheered, clapped and shouted at the superstar's every move, reaching a crescendo when he spoke to them at the end of the session.

Reading the newspapers and watching television news, it seemed everyone was out 'Beckham-spotting' during his time in the capital, with the man himself at times apparently in two places at once. It wasn't only the public that was excited by his presence. The Phoenix players were just as keen to meet Beckham, arriving at Westpac Stadium for the game with souvenirs in their bags just needing a certain signature.

The previous night's A-League game against Adelaide United had attracted 18,345 spectators, a record for a club game in New Zealand, but unfortunately the fans didn't get the result they wanted, with Adelaide snatching a 2–1 win despite being outplayed for much of the game.

For the Galaxy match, 31,853 turned up and made it a festive occasion, even though the visitors won 4–1, with Beckham scoring the fourth goal from the penalty spot. Never has a goal against a home side been so warmly welcomed. Throughout his visit, Beckham was friendly and accommodating, and the Phoenix players were delighted to see him when he visited their changing room after the game, happily signing souvenirs and having his photograph taken with them. The after-match party turned out to be everything Serepisos had promised, with everyone, Beckham included, having a ball.

The Phoenix's first two seasons have been something of a roller-coaster ride for Serepisos, the team winning games with flowing football, throwing points away with defensive aberrations and below-par finishing in front of goal.

Has it been worth the investment? 'I didn't go into it to make money, but I obviously want it to become a self-sustaining and viable club. I wanted to put something back into the community and the Phoenix was a good opportunity. I love the club and so does my son, Julian, who works in the club shop in school holidays. It takes up a lot of my time, and watching a game is bloody stressful. But yes, it has been worth it. This club has changed a lot of people's lives and I am proud of that.'

Serepisos has reason to be proud of what he has done, and Wellington, not just its football fans, will be forever grateful for his contribution to the city on the day he gave the Phoenix wings.

A TRUE FOOTBALL MAN

In the weeks that followed the birth of the Wellington Phoenix, Ricki Herbert was in his element as he went about finding and blending together the ingredients that make up a professional football club. The task that faced him and owner Terry Serepisos was daunting. They had little more than three months to recruit not only 20-odd players, but to also put together a back-room staff that would help mould those players into a team.

There were times when all that kept Ricki going was the adrenaline coursing through his body as he launched himself into the task with an enthusiasm that could only be found in a true football man. Watching him one night in a pub on Wellington's Featherston Street during that period, as he took call after call from agents based all over the world, you were left in no doubt how excited he was about the challenge he was facing.

Not only was he involved from the beginning in getting the Phoenix up and running, had he said 'no' when New Zealand

Football and Football Federation Australia asked him to take charge of the Auckland-based Knights for the final five games of their disastrous 2006–2007, the Wellington Phoenix might never have been formed.

It meant a hectic, and at times traumatic, period in Ricki's life, and, while he enjoyed the challenge, he still isn't sure if he would like to go through it again. While all this was happening, he was going home each night to an empty apartment on Wellington's Lambton Quay while his wife Raewyn and their children were settling into bed 500 kilometres away in Auckland. That Ricki had their support was never in question, because those close to him knew that, apart from his family, football was the love of his life.

Managing the Phoenix was a dream come true for Ricki, but you get the impression he had been just as happy when taking his first tentative steps into coaching at Papatoetoe.

It was the same when he was a player. Whether playing for a Papatoetoe junior team, Mount Wellington, Wolverhampton Wanderers, or his beloved New Zealand All Whites, Ricki knew only one way, and that was to give 100 per cent, be it in training or a competitive game.

The highlight of his playing career was undoubtedly appearing on football's biggest stage, the World Cup finals, but he is also justifiably proud of being a trailblazer for young New Zealand footballers by getting a professional contract with famous English club Wolverhampton Wanderers.

When Ricki turned to coaching and took charge of the All Whites, his first priority was to restore the pride in the New Zealand shirt that he and his fellow internationals had when they qualified for the 1982 World Cup finals. Some of the younger players who were in the New Zealand team just prior to Ricki being appointed coach had been surprised, and disappointed, by what they found on joining the All Whites, and so they were delighted when he arrived and stamped his mark on the squad.

Born and bred in working-class south Auckland, Ricki is proud of his roots — a mural of himself, cricketer Gary Troup, and athlete Heather Thompson at the entrance to the old Papatoetoe velodrome, where his father Clive used to coach cyclists, means almost as much to him as the All Whites shirt.

What does the future hold for this football fanatic who has done pretty much everything in the game in New Zealand?

'The thing about coaching football is that you never know where it will take you,' Ricki says. 'Whatever happens I want to remain involved with the game. I am in the last year of a three-year contract with the Wellington Phoenix, and am also contracted to New Zealand Football until the end of the All Whites' involvement in the World Cup, which hopefully will be after the 2010 finals in South Africa. That is all I am planning for at the moment.

'The uncertainty of our industry can be concerning, and whether a contract is renewed isn't always up to the individual. It is a two-way thing with both parties needing to be happy with the way things are going. All managers and coaches go through periods of uncertainty. Look at Sir Alex Ferguson. Apparently Manchester United were within a game of sacking him back in 1990, but they won that match — a third-round FA Cup tie — and went on to win the trophy. United were eventually rewarded for their patience during five years without a trophy, and look at what he has achieved since.

'Coaching is never easy, and it is not supposed to be. Many of the challenges you face are good for you, although that might not seem to be the case at the time.'

By the time this book is launched Ricki is hoping to have his immediate future in football confirmed, but he is well aware that anyone starting out on the coaching trip knows their final destination is unknown.